Richard Nixon

Biography

The Rise, Fall, and Redemption of a Political Maverick

Gabriel Howell

Table of Content

Chapter 1: The Dragon Slayer
Chapter 2: "I Had to Win"
Chapter 3: Death, God, Love, and War
Chapter 4: A Kind of Man the Country Needs
Chapter 5: A Tragedy of History
Chapter 6: The Great Train Robbery
Chapter 7: A Candidate for the Little Man
Chapter 8: The New Nixon
Chapter 9: The Desolate Night of Man's Inhumanity
Chapter 10: The Field of Pending Battle
Chapter 11: Nixon vs. Kennedy
Chapter 12: The Greatest Comeback
Chapter 13: Nixon's War
Chapter 14: Not Fish nor Fowl
Chapter 15: The Week That Changed the World
Chapter 16: Cancer on the Presidency
Chapter 17: The Final Days

Chapter 1: The Dragon Slayer

THE UNITED STATES had crushed its enemies with steel. Now it was time to stop and go home. In the summer of 1945, Navy Lieutenant John Renneburg was stationed at the Glenn L. Martin Company's aeronautics complex outside Baltimore. It was a huge complex where the firm's large flying boats were produced and tested on the peaceful waters of the Chesapeake. At the height of the war, American industries produced 96,000 warplanes in a single year, nearly as many as Nazi Germany produced in seven years. The Martin plant was emblematic: one of the world's largest aviation facilities, with 50,000 personnel constructing seaplanes, bombers, and other aircraft.

For the few who knew him well, the concept of "Congressman Nixon" was not particularly unusual. He had a lifelong interest in history and politics. He was disciplined, hardworking, clever, and earnest, with a rudimentary aptitude for winning Whittier school and club elections. However, those whipstitch contests were held years ago. Representative Jerry Voorhis, who represented the Twelfth Congressional District, was a seasoned member of the House Democratic majority, propelled to prominence by Franklin D. Roosevelt's powerful New Deal alliance. In surveys of the capital's press corps and his fellow congressmen, the beautiful, pipe-smoking Voorhis received top-ten honors for thoroughness and integrity. He was the son of a former auto executive whose fortune might help fund his campaigns. His constituent devotion earned him the trust of the district's farmers and citrus growers, for whom he excelled on the House Agriculture Committee, a highly wanted position. In the three most recent elections, Republicans attempted to replace him with a popular coach, a celebrity preacher, and a well-known businessman. He'd whipped them all.

Richard Nixon—Dick to his friends and family; Nick in the navy; Nixie in college; and Gus in law school—was thirty-two years old in 1945, and he didn't look terrible in his dress blues. "He looked so different: younger, real tanned, thinner, and of course very handsome in his blue uniform with all the braids and the white cap," Pat told his parents.

Age would highlight his flaws—jowls, a spatulate nose, and a receding hairline—but not for decades. His hair was thick, dark, and wavy. His deep-set eyes were the darkest brown, and his face was beautifully symmetrical, especially when he relaxed and smiled. Glee clubs and choruses valued his voice, and he was an excellent pianist. He enjoyed Chopin and Brahms. "He's a romantic at heart, but he doesn't let it show," a music teacher recalls.

Nixon had played football in college, but simply to fill out the roster, as he was not athletic. His feet were large, his chest thin, his shoulders sloping. The navy had trained him to stand up straight, but his natural posture was to slump with hands drooping.

His thinking was his distinctive characteristic. It was keen and analytical, and his memory was exceptional. He adored nothing more than sprawling in an armchair with a yellow legal pad, chin on chest, legs on a footrest, and thoughts racing through his mind. He liked it there, in his restless head. It was where he had retreated throughout his miserable boyhood. As a child, he was a daydreamer, cloudbug, and bookworm. He would lie in bed at night, listening to train whistles and fantasizing about the wonderful places he would see. He could be with you without actually being there, appearing to listen while his thoughts were elsewhere. He passed people on the street and didn't notice them. He ran into them in the hallways, gave them a distracted nod and half a wave, and continued on. Some people believed he was arrogant, unpleasant, or dour.

He was difficult to like. He knew, and it stung. "All over town people talk about what a good natured fellow Don is and wonder how he could have such a sour puss brother," he wrote from the South Pacific in 1943, describing himself in a wartime "V mail" to his niece Laurene, his brother Donald's newborn baby daughter. He welcomed her into the world, gave her "the scuttlebutt about your new relations," and, as a Quaker, touched on war's injustice: "My hope for you is that when you are 17 your boyfriend will not have to use V mail to write."

It was a lovely letter, and many who saw that side of him found his awkwardness, that ungainly shyness, endearing. A buddy used to tell him a tale about Dick helping with the dishes after dinner, then leaving the kitchen and wandering through the house with a single glass, wiping it over and again until it was completely dry, entranced by a speech he was preparing for an impending high school debate. It was a distinct personality, bordering on weird. Some welcomed his obsession, while others saw calculating and denied him credit for his dreams.

He was known for doing modest acts of kindness, such as presenting red roses to shut-ins or sending small financial donations to individuals in need. At law school, he met a crippled young man, put him on his student election ticket, and carried him up the granite steps to class. He was a striver, a self-improver, and thus—given his flaws—an actor. If he was utterly awkward in small talk, he was onstage in school plays, collegiate debates, and public speaking competitions throughout high and college. His teachers recalled that he excelled as a performer. His self-control was renowned, and his preparation meticulous. Others might show up to rehearsal without knowing their lines; not Dick Nixon. He could bury himself in his trade, absorb emotions, and move and thrill an audience. He aspired above all to be a great man. He possessed a sense of drama.

In the South Pacific, Nixon served on a series of island outposts where he supervised the work of a combat air transport team, moving ammunition, reinforcements, and food and medicine to the front, and the wounded to the rear. He wrote to Pat, telling her not to worry about the recurrent Japanese shelling and bombing, for only the morons who refused to take shelter got killed, and his bunker on Bougainville was roomy and protective—with a roof of logs and sandbags. There was plenty of downtime, much of which he whiled away in the discordant style of a fighting Quaker—reading his Bible or playing poker. He sent aching letters to her and read voraciously, copying down odd lines of speech and poetry, tearing out articles from magazines and newspapers and jotting his thoughts in the margins, or in journals he kept, about such disparate subjects as the female enigma, the ability of civilian populations to endure strategic bombing, the role of China in world affairs, and the dark sides of human nature.

In a moment of self-recognition, perhaps, he jotted down a line, attributed to Tennyson, from a pulpy short story in Collier's magazine: The most virtuous hearts have a touch of hell's own fire in them.

"He was struck by what he was learning about men," said Albert Upton, a favorite college instructor with whom Dick corresponded. "It was the first opportunity that he had ever had, I think, to see how much evil there is in the world around you, not just how much evil there is in Shanghai or Timbuktu, but how much evil there may even be in Whittier, California, where supposedly everybody goes to church." Nixon came to loathe the disorder and waste of war. Writing to Upton, he spoke of the need for moral rearmament, a Christian movement that taught brotherhood, peace, and spiritual purity. His heroes were Abraham Lincoln and Theodore Roosevelt, and Woodrow Wilson, who had tried to build a structure for peace and convey America's democratic values to the world. "Men's hearts wait upon us," Wilson had said in his first inaugural—words that Nixon would one day cite in speeches. "Who dares fail to try?"

There is cool and there is square, and Richard Milhous Nixon was nothing if not square. Duty called. Work got done. Yet he was no martinet, and something of a happy finagler, treating his enlisted men to a ham dinner after helping to "liberate" the meat from a passing plane and finding beer for the Seabees, who in turn built a comfortable hut—complete with shower—for Nick and his fellow officers. He was generous with the loot. Pilots relished the offerings at "Nick's Snack Shop," the hut at the airfield where they could wind down over hamburgers, coffee, or cold pineapple juice between missions. He learned how to cuss. And for a good Quaker boy, raised in a pious community, he proved a shark at cards. The amount of his winnings would be exaggerated over the years, but by the time the war was over, lumped in with what he and Pat saved from their paychecks, they had put aside some $10,000.

After fourteen months his tour was over. He flew out, with a refueling stop at a Pacific island. "It was one of those rare nights…a soft full moon, not as warm as usual, just the whisper of a breeze in the air," he would remember, and he strolled to stretch his legs. He came upon the "lonesome beauty" of a military cemetery—"no lawn, no monuments, the simplicity of white crosses in the white sand"—and pondered the loss. He yearned "for the building of a new world, which would not know the horror of war." And then he was home and caressing Pat at an airport gate.

They were in New York when, on August 14, the Japanese surrender was announced. With two million other revelers, Pat and Dick headed to Times Square. They walked around the city, through downtown's ethnic neighborhoods and up Fifth Avenue. "It was the largest, happiest mob I ever saw. Service men were kissing all the unescorted girls and the girls didn't mind a bit ... .Chinatown looked like Christmas Eve with the Fourth of July thrown in ... .Flags, banners and decorations of all description covered the buildings," he wrote his parents. He and Pat stopped at St. Patrick's Cathedral, crowded with the faithful offering prayers of thanks. "I only hope we can keep this peace," he wrote.

Years later, remembering, Nixon saw the war as "the catalyst" that had transformed his interest in politics into a sense of mission. He was a realist about human behavior, but his generation had an obligation, he believed, to find a better way. "He seemed to be dreaming about some new order which would make wars impossible," said Gretchen King, who had befriended Pat while her husband was at war and spent time with the couple after he returned. "He impressed us in those days as an idealistic dreamer."

The war "turned a great many of them with a very high idealistic feeling into politics," said Adela Rogers St. Johns, a California journalist and Whittier neighbor who came to know Dick well. "He came back with that very strong feeling, that we fought a war, a good many men had died to save this country, and now, let us make it what those boys had died for."

AND YET...Congress. No matter how he'd grown, he was still Dick from Whittier, that "eddy on the stream of life," as a college classmate called it. People there were isolated and parochial: by choice they kept the highways outside town. Sure, the Quakers saw him as a fair-haired boy—he had been elected to student office in college, chosen to lead the junior Kiwanis club, and appointed to serve as an assistant city attorney. But he had never campaigned for public office and was thoroughly unknown in the rest of the vast Twelfth District. The lives of American presidents are often cast as Horatio Alger tales, and the stories of their rise barnacled with myths. Yet few came so far, so fast, so alone, as Nixon. Not the governor of California or his aides, nor any member of the state's delegation to Congress knew Richard Nixon's name. He was, he would remember, "somebody who was nothing."

And charm, for Nixon, was an act of will. He had endured a dismal childhood, awash in gloom and grief. Two of his brothers died of gruesome illnesses. His father, Frank Nixon, was his in-laws staked a cranky blowhard—a grade-school dropout who had come west from Ohio, married into local Quaker gentility, to a farm in nearby Yorba Linda, and managed to fail at growing lemons in one of the planet's most bountiful citrus belts. Frank moved from farming to pumping gas and then opened a grocery store. They lived not in the tree-lined neighborhoods of town, but out on the highway, where Frank peddled groceries from an abandoned church. He conferred resentment to his son.

In the South Pacific, Dick had joined camaraderie and learned to lead. But the notion that he could return to California after four years away, engage the voters of the sprawling Twelfth District, and defeat a veteran congressman seemed inconceivable. He had no name, no fortune, no political machine.

WHAT HE HAD was Herman Perry.

It was Perry, the vice president and branch manager of the Bank of America in Whittier, who had sent the letter inviting Nixon to challenge Voorhis. It arrived by airmail. "Dear Dick," Perry wrote September 29, 1945. "I am writing you this short note to ask you if you would like to be a candidate for Congress on the Republican ticket." The banker didn't offer much information. The incumbent was a Democrat, he noted, and the voters in the district were split almost evenly between Democrats and Republicans. In a postscript he remembered to ask Nixon: "Are you a registered voter in California?"

Among those who had turned to Perry for loans was Frank Nixon, who arrived in Whittier from Ohio in 1907. Perry had been a guest at Frank's wedding to Hannah, a classmate of Herman's and the daughter of fellow Hoosiers. The bank's credit helped the Nixon store survive the Depression, and Perry's son Hubert attended high school and college with Dick. When Dick returned to Whittier from law school at Duke, his office was in the Bank of America building, the Beaux Arts landmark on Philadelphia Street that towered above the groves of citrus like a Crusader castle on the Levantine plain.

Herman Perry had two great unmet goals in life: to be a lawyer and serve in Congress. And he found in Dick "a kind of fulfillment of his own ambitions," said Hubert, who had tried and failed at law school himself. "I...might even say that I thought my dad was disappointed in me and looked upon Nixon as his favorite son....He saw in Dick Nixon his own dreams that he couldn't make happen."

IN 1944, DON LYCAN, a vice president for Signal Oil & Gas, the largest independent oil company on the West Coast, had called on his friend Herman. Lycan was leading a drive to dump Voorhis, but since the oil industry was a scandalous font of corruption at the time, he had come in need of a front man. Perry was willing to play the role, but it was a fool's errand, he told the oilman: the congressman was too popular. Not so, Lycan argued. "If we really get serious we could beat him." The country was heading hell-bent to socialism and Voorhis had to be stopped. Lycan promised Perry that California's oil and business interests would supply the necessary funds.

Voorhis, a graduate of Hotchkiss and Yale, held views that decidedly tilted left. In his youth, during the Depression, he had been a member of the Socialist Party, and in Congress he had angered more than oil executives. His proposals to increase the authority of the Federal Reserve Board vexed banks. He infuriated manufacturers and big agricultural interests with his support of labor unions. He sought to subject insurance companies to tougher antitrust rules. And when voting for the New Deal's expansive structure of price controls, rationing, and commercial regulations, Voorhis irked many of the conservative small-town businessmen who, with the farmers and citrus ranchers, were core voters in his district. They had kept an aggrieved silence during the crises of war and depression. But now we're finding their voice. Roosevelt's programs sapped individual initiative, these self-made men believed; made people soft, serf-like, and dependent on government.

It wasn't that simple, Herman Perry warned him when they spoke on the telephone in the first week of October. Nixon would have to audition before a group of Republican activists and survive a primary. There were names floating in the press—men like General George Patton, the war hero, and Walter Dexter, the state superintendent of education—who could have the nomination if they wanted it. But Pat and Dick were all in. "After having been away for such a long time...it was certainly a wonderful surprise to learn that I was even being considered," he wrote Perry in a follow-up letter on October 6. "I feel very strongly that Jerry Voorhis can be beaten and I'd welcome the opportunity to take a crack at him." He promised to wage "an aggressive, vigorous campaign of practical liberalism" to replace "Voorhis's particular brand of New Deal." The congressman's "lack of a military record won't help him, particularly since most of the boys will be home and voting," Nixon noted. He had just been promoted to Lieutenant Commander and with his savings would be able "to stand the financial expense" of a yearlong campaign. He promised "to tear Voorhis to pieces."

Roy Day, a gruff forty-four-year-old advertising salesman from Pomona, was the organizer. He ran the commercial printing business of a local newspaper and was one of those indispensable men who answered a community's call when its service groups—the Lions Club, the Chamber of Commerce, the Campfire Girls—needed an indefatigable wheel horse. He was an adman, a booster. Bullheaded, he had been drawn into politics in 1944 when a Republican state legislator died in mid-election, and Day organized a friend's victorious write-in campaign. The experience had exposed him to his party's complacency. "I got disgusted," he recalled. "We were blowing our own ball game."

Day volunteered to serve and, with the blessings of the Los Angeles county chairman, recruited the rump "fact-finding" team. He picked the number—one hundred—out of the air and roamed the district, talking to Republican club women, local committeemen, and business leaders like Perry; Roy Crocker, fifty-two, a savings and loan executive from tony San Marino; and J. Arthur Kruse, forty-seven, the chairman of a thrift from the district's biggest community, Alhambra.

"We younger men didn't realize that it was impossible. We were ignorant," recalled insurance man Frank Jorgensen, forty-three, a self-described "irascible son of a bitch" from San Marino. "We young bucks came in and got busy ... .We didn't know top to bottom how to run a campaign. Except we were businessmen and we knew how to sell. We took the position that a political campaign was nothing more than selling a product." The initial gathering was at Eaton's, a sprawling hotel and restaurant on Route 66, near the Santa Anita racetrack. Over coffee or lunch, in hotel meeting rooms and at neighborhood cocktail parties, they refined their vision of a winning candidate: Young. Educated. Married. A veteran. Above all, an active campaigner.

The Twelfth District was the largest and most rural in Los Angeles County, a polyhedron with clusters of towns at its vertices and several hundred square miles of citrus, walnut, and avocado groves and dust-brown hills and ridges in between.

Patton was never a serious option, and by Christmas he was dead, killed in a car crash in Europe. Herman Perry's arm-twisting removed Dexter, a former president of Whittier College, whose career the banker had long promoted.

On October 16 Perry informed Nixon that Dexter was out of the race, and that Dick should make plans to come west to make a presentation to the Committee of 100 and have lunch with the area's top Republicans so that they could "look you over."

At the William Penn Hotel in Whittier that night, Nixon made his formal pitch to the Committee of 100. He spoke on the virtues of free enterprise and again of the need for "practical" liberalism. He was not a hard-line conservative, for he had witnessed, in war and depression, how Americans could employ an active, muscular government and achieve great things. Dick's father, who had shaped his son's political leanings, was a latitudinarian populist, while Hannah and her family were progressive Republicans. A New Deal program had helped Dick pay for law school. But Nixon shared his audience's decided belief that now—the crises abated—a continuing drift toward a planned economy was perilous. "I made a ten-minute speech," he would recall. "I did rather well, apparently." Indeed. In all three appearances, he dazzled. "He was excellent. He was just an unbelievable choice. It was like finding a diamond," Lutz marveled. "It was like saying goodbye at the gate to the race horse."

Dick took a red-eye back to Maryland. His hopes were dashed days later when he received the reviews of his visit from Bewley. "The entire district is thrilled," the lawyer wrote. "I think you will get the nomination by a landslide ... .The thing took hold and is going over big." In his own letter to Nixon, Day promised "off the record" that the Amateurs would fix the vote to make sure Nixon was selected. "Frankly Dick, we feel we have SOMETHING AND SOMEBODY to sell to this district now, and are going to do our very best to close the deal," he wrote.

Not everyone in Whittier cheered. To his friend Osmyn Stout, who had served on their college debating team with Nixon, the Amateurs represented "the most conservative, reactionary people" in the district. Stout, a pacifist, had thought of Dick as a forward-thinking, kind, and "exemplary" idealist. But now Nixon was aligned with the narrow-minded forces of conformity, Stout concluded: "He had sold his soul."

As Day promised, the first ballot was sixty-three for Nixon and fourteen for two also-rans. Pat and Dick had stayed up late in Maryland, awaiting word. It came two hours after midnight. "Dick, the nomination is yours!" Day shouted. When Perry called a few moments later, Nixon recalled a lesson that his mother had taught him—a gentleman has never heard the punch line—and acted as if he was just getting the news. The navy wanted him in New York that morning, but he and Pat, chattering, never got to bed.

Nixon was exhilarated. He was soon on the train to Washington to confer with Republican Party officials, GOP congressional leaders, and members of the California delegation. "The main emphasis should be on the constructive program we have to offer," he wrote Perry. He suggested that they seek the backing of the local college faculties and told of a speech he was writing, to be given in the churches, urging racial tolerance. "I'm sure we can win," Nixon said. "And that we can retain our integrity as well because we shall only say what we believe and do."

THERE WAS THIS, too. While visiting Washington, Nixon had hit a line of attack. The capital's left-wingers—the "fellow travelers"—were "wild about" Voorhis, Nixon reported. The Republican Party researchers had quite a file on the congressman and his voting record. It would be guilt by association, for everyone knew that Voorhis was no Communist, but if they could portray him as a Red dupe, "I believe we can make Mr. Voorhis sweat."

This was his hour; his chance to be someone. To excise the hurt. To stake his claim. He needed to win, and his plans revealed his hunger, and an incipient susceptibility to intrigue.

Set up...spies in V. camp, he wrote.

Chapter 2: "I Had to Win"

So Pat and Dick headed west, back to the nowhere they had hoped to escape. Pat took it hard; she was in her third trimester and learning about the life of a candidate's wife. The Quaker ladies had never felt she was good enough for Dick, and the matrons of San Marino mocked her fashion sense. "We were the rawest of amateurs," Pat recalls. "Our friends were sympathetic but dubious, and the real politicians were scornful." Initially, the couple lived with Dick's parents, Frank and Hannah. They were given his brother Eddie's bedroom in the back of the property. "Richard is studying." "Don't bother him," Hannah instructed her youngest. "He's...reading up a storm and making notes."

Nixon's aversion to women proved to be an unforeseen impediment. Coffees, teas, and home parties were necessary components of campaigning, but he couldn't bring himself to look female voters in the eyes. It was a serious issue in a state where Republican ladies' groups were cherished assets for the party. California females working on assembly lines in aerospace and other defense plants had made a significant contribution to winning the war. Many people, including Pat, we're going home with a greater sense of freedom. A candidate had to solicit their votes. However, Nixon "was very timid around women," Day observed. "He's not a coward; he just felt that women bothered him..."He was not that way with men at all."

Day had to coach him, advising the candidate that if he didn't look all of the voters in the eye, ladies would perceive him as shifty. Nixon worked at it, relying on his acting abilities. To put him to the test, Day invited female Scripps College students to coffee. They sat in a circle on the floor, grilling Nixon, who, much to Day's relief, answered each pointed question by complimenting the questioner and nudging the women toward his side without being combative. The glad-handing was never simple, but once Nixon was convinced that it was necessary, he hunkered down and got the job done.

Happily for Nixon, the majority of his audiences were men. In the pre-television era, American males were joiners. Organizations such as the Elks, Masons, and Lions provided opportunities for camaraderie, networking, and community involvement. Dick had only recently returned to Whittier when he went out speaking at the Optimist Club on January 14, the Rotary luncheon three days later, a Kiwanis event in adjacent Norwalk on January 28, and the Lions Club "den" on January 31. He moved on to the Pomona Valley realtors, Rotary Club, and Lions. To the South Pasadena Rotary Club, Masons, and Chamber of Commerce. To the St. James Episcopal Men's Club, the San Marino and Alhambra Kiwanians, and the El Monte Lions. By the end of March, he had given 36 speeches, addressing almost 3,700 individuals.

Dick pulled over in Whittier and rolled down the window to ask Waymeth Garrett, a childhood buddy, whether he knew of any apartments for rent. Garrett confirmed he had a leasehold property on Walnut Street. It came with a Servel refrigerator and a Wedgewood stove, and Dick performed a rapid U-turn to finalize the transaction, paying $35 per month. The Nixons quickly discovered the reason for the vacancy: Garrett kept hundreds of minks in cages on the land next door, which shrieked and stank. "They're kind of noisy, aren't they?" Nixon asked his landlady after several sleepless nights.

The duplex had minimal furnishings—the living room contained a crib and a sofa, and stacks of newspapers and Congressional Record issues. Day and the others were forced to squat on the floor during strategy meetings. Their campaign headquarters was no palace. They relocated an old leather couch to an office in downtown Whittier and borrowed a typewriter for Pat to use when answering correspondence. Eddie, a pleased new driver, drove the Nixon delivery truck throughout town and in local parades, adorned with campaign signs. Frank was his usual self, "overly enthusiastic" and bent ears, his youngest son recalls.

For some groups, Nixon went deeper. As winter gave way to spring, the news focused on the terrible Communists. On March 5, Winston Churchill appeared at a small Missouri college alongside Harry Truman.

Roosevelt believed that with charm and patience, he could handle Stalin. Churchill was equally certain that the Soviet autocrat was impervious to all persuasions, except military force.

Nixon delivered his own Iron Curtain address that spring. He labeled it "The Challenge to Democracy" and revised it throughout the campaign. It began with a tour of Russian history—"a tragic story of war, starvation, torture, rape, murder, and slavery"—of which the

Soviet rule was only the most recent chapter. The Republican Party was dominated by isolationist views, while other, more aggressive sections called for a preemptive attack on the Soviet Union or a war to liberate Eastern European states. Nixon struck a moderate ground. He had been informed on the Red threat during his travels to party leaders in Washington, but his address also reflected the lengthy hours of study and thought he put into world politics. It was enlightened for a rural politician, advocating not for war but for active containment of Soviet adventurism—for American deployment of economic, political, and military force to "hold the line for the growth of democratic ideals" that would eventually collapse the totalitarian state. He also realized the enticing danger of using the enemy's techniques. "We must use means that conform to the highest moral standards," added the minister.

Nixon's promise of economic liberty was a panacea for conservatives in southern California. Many had read Friedrich Hayek's alarum, The Road to Serfdom (if not the book, then the abridged version in Reader's Digest), a surprise bestseller that linked modern liberalism to tyranny. A flood was rising, there and elsewhere, among those who felt unheard in Washington, who saw the East as a distant realm where Ivy Leaguers relied on formulae rather than faith, where right and wrong were relative, and modernists and Manhattanites poked fun at their simple ways. Not Richard Nixon. He knew them, understood their dreams and fears, and shared their values and resentments.

The TWELFTH DISTRICT, a patchwork of small towns, had dozens of daily and weekly newspapers. The publishers and editors were conservative—Rex Kennedy, the editor of the Whittier daily, was a local Republican Party official—and were usually Lions or Rotary Club members who attended Nixon's speeches. If not, Dick made a point of swinging by on his way through town, handing them a press kit and promising to buy ads. In many of those newspapers, the warmth of the news coverage was proportional to the amount of advertising space a candidate acquired. "These publications are frequently sponsored, practically, by back page [ads] that would be accepted by a large market. If someone contacted the market owner..."If we paid $300 or so for an ad, we could often get an editorial," one Amateur recalled. "People would read the editorial and then they'd say, 'Well, this little newspaper has no axe to grind....It is our paper.'" Roy Day's employer, the Pomona daily, supported Nixon; the Whittier paper supported him; and in Alhambra, a young journalist named Herb Klein was enamored; his newspaper would criticize Voorhis throughout the campaign, and he would advocate Nixon intermittently for years.

But establishing a grassroots movement took time. Some nights, two dozen people turned up in a hall with hundreds of vacant seats. And money was scarce. Day and Jorgensen experienced the same experience in very different communities: seeing people cross the street to avoid their $20 campaign appeal. Garland reached into his pocket for the first batch of campaign materials—NIXON FOR CONGRESS bumper stickers, which were delivered to the Committee of 100. "All of them were very pleased to have something tangible for the first time," Nixon told him. It was late March, and he had been campaigning for three months.

Accounting was, by necessity, inventive. "I can remember time and time again of Frank Jorgensen calling...asking me to come down to his place...[as] it was a Friday, and we had these bills to meet," Adams told me. "We...issued checks and then beat the rushes over the weekend to get the money." Jorgensen and others sat down with their Christmas card lists, sent out letters requesting donations, and hosted $25 meals in their homes. They used the received funds to send mailings. There was no money to rent billboard space, and newspaper advertisements were modest and infrequent. "The money is not coming in," Day said. On certain occasions, "I have had to dig down in my pocket for $200."

Nixon had no significant Republican competitors to worry about in the June 4 primary election. However, the results revealed worrisome news. In California's cross-filing system, which allowed Republican candidates to run in the Democratic primary and vice versa, Voorhis received 7,000 more votes than Nixon. Had it been a genuine election, Dick would have lost by a landslide.

"Many people were disappointed," Nixon said in a letter to Day. To stop the "sniping" and "keep the wolves away," he saw the necessity to make reforms and strengthen the troops. "I think you could point out that here I was, a candidate unknown in the district in January, against a man 10 years in Congress; that we used none of our big guns, purposely (suggesting we really are holding back some stuff—as we are); that Voorhis polled 60 percent of the total on both tickets cast in the primary in 1944 and only 53.5 percent in 1946, which is really something," Dick said. "I really believe that."

However, a melancholy Nixon joined Pat and another couple on a road trip to British Columbia following the primary. The vacation was supposed to revitalize the candidate, but for most of the drive north, he remained mute and withdrawn, pondering about the contest. When they landed at Port Angeles, near Olympic National Park in Washington, Dick remained in the hotel room, brooding, while Pat and their companions explored the area.

When analyzing his campaign's performance, Nixon discovered two lacking requirements. The first significant need was money. Dick would consult Herman Perry about this. Perry would also tap oil. Many elements contributed to a successful crusade, and Nixon would later deny that energy companies played a significant role in his 1946 campaign; yet, evidence buried in Perry's archives demonstrates how the oilmen intervened, reviving Nixon's career.

At the turn of the century, the California oil industry had grown as a giant, producing more than any other state or country. When the Teapot Dome scandal erupted in the 1920s, Americans discovered how its expansion was facilitated. One of California's pioneering drillers, Edward Doheny, a generous contributor to political parties and organizations, had been given one of the sweetheart agreements revealed in the incident to explore the US Navy's oil reserves in Elk Hills, California. Following the bruising the industry received in Teapot Dome, it was assumed that the oilmen would behave more appropriately. Not so. On May 21, 1943, Voorhis spoke on the House floor and revealed a federal contract that granted Standard Oil preferential and exclusive rights to the oil at Elk Hills, the most vital wartime reserve. The contract was later declared invalid, and the terms of the agreement were revised. Voorhis had also ruffled Oil with his opposing views on the "tidelands" debate. When states like Texas and California joined the Union, the question of who owned the coastal bottom was unimportant and left unanswered. It became a major source of concern, however, as America transitioned to a carbon-based economy and massive oil and gas supplies were discovered offshore.

California was one of several states that leased its "tidelands" to oil firms in the years leading up to the conflict. However, on September 28, 1945, Truman declared that the federal government held the rights to the submerged lands and resources.

It was probably a coincidence that Perry sat down the next day and wrote Dick, suggesting he run for Congress. But Voorhis was one of only three California representatives—and the only one from a contestable district—who supported Truman and federal authority over offshore oil. Returning the tidelands to state authority, where officials could be more readily suborned, was a holy cause for the oilmen of the major producing states.

It was clearly in Oil's interest to replace Voorhis. And Don Lycan, who had joined Perry in the cause in 1944, was only one of the banker's industrial contacts. Major oil discoveries in neighboring Santa Fe Springs drew energy corporations to Whittier. Perry conducted business with them at the Bank of America. Nixon's law practice, Wingert & Bewley, relied heavily on its oil clients. Lycan's associates included his Signal Oil co-directors, Harry March, and Samuel Mosher, another Perry friend. Signal, in turn, maintained a close relationship with Standard Oil, which advertised its products.

The oilmen didn't spend any time approaching Nixon. In February 1946, he received a letter from J. Paull Marshall, a Republican lawyer who had worked with Nixon at OPA and was now advising him on his campaign for Congress. "I have had a good talk with Harry March about you," wrote Marshall, who was set to quit the navy to serve as an industrial lobbyist. Signal was "vitally interested in the tidelands oil question" and wanted to meet Nixon to discuss his opinions on the subject.

"I certainly appreciate your speaking to [March] about me because from what you say, he can be of a great deal of assistance in the campaign," Nixon informed Marshall. "I am interested in the Tidelands Oil question and I believe that my attitude on that question is somewhat similar to his."

With the results of the primary election in hand, Nixon explained his financial problems to Perry. The lender requested a thorough budget outlining how much it would cost to defeat Voorhis. Dick gave him full accounting in a letter dated August 16.

They didn't have any money for radio, Nixon informed Perry. The campaign wanted to deploy "a significant amount of outdoor advertising," but that was contingent on "the amount of our budget," he wrote. "During the primaries we had no billboards whatsoever." The number and quality of mailings would be determined by the magnitude of the campaign's budget. They intended to place advertisements in the district's thirty newspapers, but they couldn't afford to do so until October. He intended to flood the local media with images and press releases, but "here, again," the PR effort was "limited by the fact that our budget will not allow any significant expenditures." Republican volunteers could canvass friendly precincts, but he needed funds to pay workers in Democratic wards and hire young veterans to labor in VFW rooms.

On August 22, after a meeting in Los Angeles, Perry delivered Nixon's list to Standard Oil executives Stanley Natcher and Floyd Bryant in San Francisco. "For the reasons we have already discussed," Perry stated, the funds should be routed through a back channel rather than the official Nixon campaign. He requested $6,945 for mailings, canvassers, marketing, and secretarial support. Within weeks, Nixon had a professional advertising agency under contract, and eighteen enormous billboards carrying his name and likeness were being constructed across the district. Overall, Perry believed he raised $7,300 for Nixon that year.

Herman Perry "could get money from Standard on a personal basis," as his son Hubert recalls. "This was all kept very quiet by my dad so that no one, including Nixon, knew where the funds came from." The secrecy was necessary because the corrosive consequences of Oil's campaign tactics were once again dominating the nation's front pages. California oilman Edwin Pauley, a well-known Democratic fund-raiser (and future employer of Nixon's friend, lawyer Paull Marshall), had been grilled by Congress—and his nomination as undersecretary of the Navy scuttled—over allegations that he had offered $300,000 to the Democratic Party if Truman dropped the federal claim to the tidelands. When the president ordered Interior Secretary Harold Ickes to vouch for Pauley, Ickes quit, convened a press conference, and told three hundred reporters, "I don't care to stay in an administration where I am expected to commit perjury."

The other missing element in Nixon's campaign presentation was a punchy message. His conversations about the veteran during peacetime were stale. In April, Nixon received a note from an aspiring political consultant whom Day had employed part-time. "I hope you will forgive the frankness of this letter," the man wrote. However, it was necessary due to the urgency. "Meat," he said, was required for the campaign. "Sending out laudatory statements about you from people in the district will not do the trick."

Murray Chotiner was a 36-year-old Los Angeles attorney. He was a slick operator with a clientele that included gamblers and bookies, and a political bent—a moon-faced man who preferred showy suits, flamboyant ties, and gorgeous women. (He and his friend Kyle Palmer went through spouses like other men replace lawn mowers.) Chotiner was a political genius. He attended UCLA, graduated from law school at the age of twenty, founded an eponymous consulting firm, and headed Earl Warren's Southern California campaign in 1942. He offended the governor by requesting that he intercede on behalf of an unscrupulous client—"Chotiner was nothing but a two-bit crook," Warren adviser Warren Olney would insist—but when the Amateurs launched their drive in the fall of 1945, the Republican hierarchy assigned Chotiner to watch. Day hired him for a $500 retainer.

If Nixon wanted meat, Murray was the butcher. Above all, Chotiner emphasized aggression.

There was never any uncertainty surrounding what Nixon would throw at Voorhis in the fall. Since his initial travels to Washington in 1945, Nixon had been told by GOP officials that Voorhis was popular with the "pinko" crowd and voted with "the most radical element" in Congress. But constructing the argument was another matter. Nixon and Chotiner reviewed Voorhis's voting record, looking for votes to use as evidence that the congressman was a wild-eyed radical. "I sent you Jerry Voorhis' voting record on key measures for the 76th, 77th, and 78th Congresses..."On August 14, Chotiner wrote to Nixon, "Please find enclosed Voorhis' voting record for the 75th Congress." "For your purposes...rely on the complete record for the 79th Congress, which we have compiled, as well as the record of important measures for the previous sessions as supplied by the Republican National Committee." Nixon later praised Chotiner's assistance for its "tremendous value".

Nixon attributed his 1946 success to his temperance. Throughout the campaign, he focused on lunch-bucket issues and the Truman administration's mismanagement of the economy. He took various opportunities to advocate for civil rights. He criticized Southern racists like Gerald L. K. Smith and Mississippi senator Theodore Bilbo, calling them "just as dangerous on the right as the Communists...on the left." And he accepted honorary membership in a local NAACP chapter—a significant gesture in an election with incendiary fair employment legislation on the ballot and the Ku Klux Klan burning crosses in Los Angeles.

Nonetheless, Nixon spent the fall aggressively pursuing the attack. "Whatever people said...I was not dull," he remembered. Chotiner, the campaign manager for Senator Bill Knowland, had been misrepresenting the Democratic candidate, renowned war veteran Will Rogers Jr., as a Communist dupe. He now taught the Amateurs how to perfect the Nixon campaign's assaults. "I don't completely respect a lot of the ways he operated," Day told me. besides "I learned a lot about politics from Murray." Chotiner was "a shrewd little man," said Merrell Small, another Warren adviser. "Very seductive, slick, and flattering—but watch him. "Watch him."

VOORHIS WAS NOT a particularly good politician, but he was also not completely stupid. He foresaw the negative impact that Democratic economic mismanagement and militant labor tactics would have on the party's candidates. America's unions, freed from their wartime obligation to maintain peace with management, reverted to prewar militancy, and millions of striking steel, coal, railway, auto, manufacturing, and meat workers walked off the job in one of the country's most contentious labor relations years. As Truman and the Democrats in Congress debated wage and price controls, veterans and their families slept in tents or vehicles, meat and other basics disappeared from store shelves, and the cost of life skyrocketed.

The congressman despised political conflict, treated every vote as if it were the most important of the century, and believed it was critical to run a "dignified" campaign. He elected to stay in Washington for the first eight months of 1946, debating critical topics on the House floor. He was present when a bill to overturn Truman's claim to the tidelands passed the chamber. Voorhis voted to support the president, infuriating California chauvinists and oil interests. He stated, "From a purely political standpoint, I may be foolish to take the position that I do, but I cannot conscientiously vote for this bill. I can point to case after case after case in various states where the oil has been wasted and exploited without anything like adequate returns to the people."

"He was a devoted representative of the people. Now, a politician? Jerry was not an effective politician. Stanley Long, a campaign aide, stated, "I don't mean that unkindly; he just wasn't."

The strong men in Washington didn't hide their feelings about this former Mr. Smith. "Voorhis is an earnest, if ineffectual little man, a do-gooder who stumbles and bumbles...getting nowhere with all his puny might," was Secretary Ickes' private appraisal.

"I was very often extremely frustrated and downhearted," Voorhis admitted, "when I felt that you couldn't do what was really right." He worked furiously, scaring his family and friends. "If it were not for the fact that I feel you are needed badly in Washington I could almost hope that you would not have to go back again," wrote Charles Voorhis to his youngest son. There were indications that the congressman shared his father's ambivalence. Voorhis complained in a congratulatory note to Nixon following Tricia's birth, "This job is truly a man-killer." Nixon detected weakness.

Voorhis did not leave Washington for California until August. He elected to drive cross-country with his family, and the long hours behind the wheel resulted in an outbreak of hemorrhoids. He stopped in Utah for emergency surgery and developed a reaction to the spinal anesthetic. Homecoming celebrations were canceled and he suffered nausea, headaches and insomnia for several weeks. When Voorhis finally returned to the area, he was met with a thundering Nixon salvo accusing him of standing with the Communists against his voters' interests.

In the year following the war, there was a growing fear of Communism. Running for Congress in Massachusetts, a teenage John F. Kennedy told voters: "The freedom-loving countries of the world must stop Soviet Russia now, or be destroyed." J. The FBI director Edgar Hoover came before the American Legion conference in San Francisco and warned that there were 100,000 active Communists seeking to undermine democracy in America. The U.S. Chamber of Commerce, American business's lobbying voice, engaged Father John Cronin, a Roman Catholic priest, to create a leaflet titled "Communist Infiltration of the United States" and distributed 400,000 copies. "We will have to set up some firing squads in every good-sized city and town in the country," one Chamber official told a colleague, to "liquidate the Reds and Pink Benedict Arnolds."

For months, California voters had been bombarded with screaming headlines about HUAC's investigations of actors, writers, and film producers—and the often violent struggle over Red influence in the electrical workers', longshoremen's, and Hollywood studio unions, where film star Ronald Reagan was capturing attention with his battle against the Communists, and sluggers clashed at the gates of MGM.

Nixon hung the allegation on Voorhis' provisional endorsement from the Los Angeles branch of the National Citizens' Political Action Committee, a harmless group of left-wing activists, which he received in March. The NC-PAC, on the other hand, was a breakaway of the Congress of Industrial Organizations, a militant labor group with its own political action committee—the strong CIO-PAC, sometimes known as "the PAC." Additionally, Communists had infiltrated and influenced numerous of the CIO's member unions. "The CIO is drunk." They've had a nice taste of it. They like it. Charles Voorhis told his son, "And I suspect they feel strong enough to get it." No one raised the issue "but that CIO is saturated with the more radical elements of our society...including the real Communists."

The lawmaker consequently directed his campaign workers to avoid the CIO and its PAC. Voorhis wrote to a California leader of the United Auto Workers, a CIO affiliate: "I am frankly deeply concerned about the extent to which the Communists have succeeded in gaining control of some of the organizations, and I definitely do not want their support, nor would they be justified in giving it to me, from their point of view."

Nixon had little appreciation for such nuanced distinctions, and he assumed that neither would the public. "Nixon moved in and adopted an anti-Communist stance. Amateur Mac Faries noted that it was a gut-wrenching subject that aligned with his ideals. The argument was syllogistic: Voorhis was backed by NC-PAC, which was affiliated with the CIO. Therefore, Voorhis was a dupe for Communists. Fairies and a few others balked. As soon as he "objected to the strength Nixon was putting into his efforts on the Red issue," according to Fairies, "my objections were overruled."

Nixon reinforced the point at a Labor Day speech in Whittier. "It is a satisfaction and a privilege to accept the challenge of the PAC," according to him. "I will not, during the course of this campaign, remain silent concerning the radical doctrines fostered by this and other extreme left-wing elements that are seeking to eliminate representation of all people from the American form of government." The campaign began by handing out thimbles imprinted with the slogan nixon for congress—put the needle in the p.a.c. The gimmick proved to be a success.

The right time came two days later, on a beautiful, balmy California evening, when an overflow audience packed the auditorium at the South Pasadena junior high school for a meet-the-candidates event. In their notes after Tricia was born, Voorhis casually offered to join Nixon onstage in the fall to discuss the difficulties. Both campaigns were divided on the issue, and they debated it throughout the summer. There were those in the Voorhis camp who saw no benefit in giving a rival that type of exposure, and Nixon aides were wary of taking on a congressman who, after a decade on the House floor, had undoubtedly mastered the art of argument. But once the question was posed, neither candidate could back down gracefully. Each decided to attend the Pasadena rally, which was held on Republican soil but organized by local lefties.

Stand-ins for Senate candidates (Chotiner was present on Senator Knowland's behalf) energized a joyful, even raucous crowd. Then Voorhis delivered his introductory remarks, and Nixon arrived late, to whoops from his fans, as planned. Thunderbolts struck during the evening's final question-and-answer session. Both sides had sent supporters into the crowd, laden with allegations. When the PAC topic came up, Voorhis challenged Nixon, asking for "proof" of an endorsement. Nixon strode across the stage with calculated magniloquence (honed in amateur theater), pushing a piece of paper into his opponent's hands. Voorhis was surprised to see the preliminary list of favored candidates from the local NC-PAC branch.

He'd forgotten, overlooked, or ignored its significance.

The Voorhis Campaign never recovered. "It was such a demoralizing kind of an evening," Long said. As news of Nixon's march across the stage spread throughout the district, it became evident that the campaign's trajectory had shifted.

McCall dispatched telegrams to Kyle Palmer and Ray Haight, the Republican national committeeman, informing them that Nixon had fought himself into a photo finish, "through no help on your part." With eyes wide open, Republican leaders agreed to fuel an 11th-hour effort. Haight later alleged that 70 percent of Nixon's expenditures in 1946 came from opportunistic, election-eve donors. Palmer abandoned his skepticism, and the Times joined the local reporters in praising the amazing GOP tyro of the Twelfth Congressional District, who was giving Voorhis "the fight of his life." The newspaper's proprietors were pleased: the Chandlers suddenly considered Nixon a rising star.

Dick's campaign coffers, saved from a July drought by an emergency injection of oil money, overflowed with donations from commercial interests anxious to get in on the action. "It has been very discouraging to us to bet on losing horses during the past ten or twelve years," a broker said. N. Gregory wrote to his associates, asking for donations for the cause. "However, it is a long lane with no turning, and I am more confident than ever that Nixon has a good chance to win." Executives instructed employees to donate and conceal the payment on their expense accounts. Recognizing that Truman's issues had provided them with an unprecedented opportunity to seize control of Congress in this midterm election, the Republican Party targeted Voorhis. Voorhis received word that commercial interests from as far away as Wall Street were bringing out their checkbooks to oppose him.

In its official report, the Nixon campaign claimed to have spent $17,774. Years later, Day and Nixon admitted that the figure was closer to $40,000—roughly $500,000 after adjusted for inflation. But that was an approximation. No one knew because thousands of dollars were raised and spent by individual operators like Perry, came in the form of in-kind gifts, or were ultimately directed through the Republican Party.

Voorhis accepted Nixon's challenge to arrange four additional debates to regain momentum following the Pasadena incident. In the peaceful Twelfth District, people were drawn to the political bloodsport. More than a thousand individuals attended each of the final three contests in Pomona, Monrovia, and San Gabriel. "The crowd grew bigger and bigger," Holifield recalls, and Voorhis "got slaughtered every time."

Dick's former debate teammate, Osmyn Stout, described Nixon's use of half-truths and innuendos as "deplorable." He filed an objection with Nixon. "You have to do this to become a candidate," Dick said.

As Voorhis attempted to explain the complex methods of Congress to his supporters, including how members craft measures that don't often bear their names, the PAC issue resurfaced—with word that Radio Moscow had sponsored the CIO's list of candidates. And on it went. Why didn't Voorhis vote to establish the HUAC as a permanent body? Why didn't he serve in World War II? Why did he vote to provide United Nations relief monies to Soviet bloc nations? Why did he vote so many times for Congressman Vito Marcantonio of Harlem, a well-known fellow traveler?

Indeed, "every time that I would say that something wasn't true…the response was always, 'Voorhis is using unfair tactics by accusing Dick Nixon of lying.' This was used over and over," according to Voorhis. One pro-Nixon group, the "War Veterans Non-Partisan Voters League," chastised Voorhis for initiating "slanderous attacks" on the candidate. Despite reports of oil industry bagmen, there was "not a nickel of oil company money" in the Nixon campaign, the group asserted, and demanded: "What kind of a man is this Congressman Voorhis? Who is he to make baseless accusations about an honest, clean, and truthful young American who battled for his nation in the stinking muck and jungle of the Solomons? Smear accusations from a man like Voorhis, who kept safely behind the front lines in Washington, are completely unacceptable.

As Election Day approached, the drumbeats and melodies melded in one Nixon advertisement.

Voorhis was a sensitive man, both proud and conceited about his accomplishments. He yearned for polite talk. Nixon was anything but gentle. Many Democrats in the district began to perceive Dick, whom they had previously regarded as an honorable competitor, as a sneak, a trickster, and a hatchet man. An image was emerging. "He was wonderful," said Fairies, but also "much more personal...than some of us would have wished."

Whittier's Quaker elder, Herschel Folger of the First Friends Church, was disturbed. Folger expressed concern about Nixon's campaign, citing many occurrences. The strong partisanship, the win-at-all-costs mindset, and the "petty politics" of the battle against Voorhis "made me sick at heart."

However, the Voorhis campaign was a shambles: underfunded, uncertain, and unable to capitalize on any voters' reservations about Nixon's tactics. "My campaigns were never well organized," the congressman said. And the demographic tide that was then sweeping California was working against him. The postwar influx brought "a lot of new residents who didn't even know which district they were in." "They had no idea that Jerry Voorhis had been working with the old line people on agricultural assistance and numerous problems," said Stephen Zetterberg, one of the congressman's advisors. "Nixon was speaking to newer groups of people that...hadn't even heard of Jerry Voorhis." Voorhis had no strategy to approach them.

Nationwide, the New Deal coalition was dissolving. It was a momentous election day, with Republicans taking control of both houses of Congress for the first time since 1930.

In California, a Nixon campaign ploy urged supporters to answer their phones in recent days with a cherry, "Vote Nixon for Congress." If they replied correctly and it was the Nixon campaign calling, they were informed they could win a toaster. It was said that there were also unpleasant phone calls—short and from unknown sources—in which an anonymous caller asked: "Did you know Jerry Voorhis is a communist?"

The election-day decision was obvious. Zita Remley was with Voorhis that afternoon and called a friend at Alhambra City Hall to get the early results. "Nixon was far ahead," she recalled. Moments later, Voorhis saw his doom in San Gabriel's numbers. "He was very white and sort of quiet....He just sort of put his head in his hands," Remley told me.

The congressman's message to Nixon was, at best, accurate. Voorhis wished Dick luck, but avoided mentioning the current race in our district. It would only have damaged the letter."

During his march to Congress, Richard Nixon demonstrated many of the powerful attributes that would propel him to power and renown. There were attributes on display from the start that he would repeatedly demonstrate. Audacity. Resourcefulness. Resilience. Toil. He demonstrated political foresight and an almost emotional affinity with the aspirations of his constituents.

However, there are hints of tragedy in that campaign, indicating a descent into "the deepest valley" of humiliation. Some idiosyncrasies, such as awkwardness and remoteness, could be overcome with will. Others were more troubling: the decay of noble aim and its replacement by practicality. The overwhelming, nagging need and constant insecurity. Use of smears. In the furnace of the presidency, such fractures could give way, and such a man could crumble. Some months later, once Nixon had established himself in Washington, Voorhis' adviser, lobbyist Stanley Long, joined him for lunch. They revisited the campaign.

"Of course, I knew Jerry Voorhis wasn't a Communist," Nixon assured him. Of course, he understood how a congressman may contribute to the legislative process without introducing measures bearing his name. When Long objected, Nixon responded, "You're just being naïve." "I needed to win. That is something you do not understand. "The important thing was to win." He must. He'd won. Richard Nixon was heading to Congress. In four years, he would be a United States senator, and in six, he would be Vice President of the United States of America.

Chapter 3: Death, God, Love, and War

In the months following Harold's death, Dick field-tested his beliefs with the help of a controversial senior-year philosophy course. It would now be based on reasoning rather than revelation. He needed to correct the universe's brutality and indifference with the myths he had learnt as a child at Sunday school. Where was that loving Jesus, that strong and benevolent God, when Arthur, Harold, and those who loved them cried for help?

He was also looking for a moral purpose—a method to reconcile the gospel's teachings with groundbreaking advances in behavioral science, relativity, and evolution. "We are never satisfied with simply living. "We must understand why we live," he wrote. "Where my study will lead I do not know, but certainly any system of ideas would be better than this absurd collection of science, religion and philosophy that I now have."

Richard Nixon began law school in the fall of 1934, at age twenty-one. His days at Duke were much like those at Whittier College. He studied hard, stalked the stacks, and graduated near the top of his class. He made a good impression and won a few extracurricular competitions, such as the contest for president of the law school bar organization.

Nixon got by on grit. As at Whittier, he left a divided body of opinion among his classmates, many of whom hailed from affluent households. They made fun of his "iron butt," and his well-worn clothing. They praised his dedication, drive, and the hours he spent in the library—but some people considered him nasty, and even his friends dubbed him Gloomy Gus. "He never expected anything good to happen to him or anyone close to him that he didn't deserve," recalled classmate Lyman Brownfield. "Any time someone started blowing rosy bubbles, you could count on Nixon to burst them with a little sharp prick."

Dick resided in rented quarters in Durham, most notably at a cottage in the woods during his senior year, where he, Brownfield, and two other aspiring barristers shared two brass double beds. They named it Whippoorwill Manor. There was no indoor plumbing or power. They left their towels and shaving equipment on campus and took a shower at the gym. He would dress in the morning chill and jog through the woodland to the fairy-tale campus, complete with arches, stained glass, and spires. "Let me tell you about the nuttiest of the nutty Nixons," his letter to Ola read. "He remains a stolid bachelor, and I believe his hair is starting to thin out. He doesn't smoke, drinks very little, swears less, yet is still as insane as ever. "He still thinks a lot about his mother."

LIFE at Duke continued on. Dick ate Milky Ways for breakfast and lived out of a single trunk, wearing the same red sweater every day and switching between his few pieces of underwear until they were tattered and filthy. He exercised by playing handball, yelled himself hoarse for Duke's football team, and wrote an article on vehicle liability for the law magazine. During breaks, he visited Washington, Baltimore, and New York. He was captivated by the East's deciduous greenery and bustling cities filled with ethnic enclaves and tough-talking workers. In the capital, he witnessed his first major-league baseball games, witnessing Joe DiMaggio's Yankees defeat the Senators in a double header.

In North Carolina, Richard saw how the South enforced segregation. He was affected by the situation of southern blacks, who were treated horribly and unfairly. He also demonstrated empathy for Fred Cady, the polio victim he befriended and assisted in carrying up the stairs to class, Charles Rhyne, a hospitalized classmate, and Oren Mollenkopf, who never forgot how Dick made time to counsel him, offering "a kind word for a confused, homesick, and frightened young man when he needed it the most."

"Nixon disclosed himself from the beginning as what I call a true liberal," his housemate Brownfield recounted. "He was strongly sympathetic to the rights of the individual, particularly when the individual found himself opposed by the unequal and artificially created force of big government, big society, or big business." Dick's conservatism was most evident in his mistrust of New Deal solutions. The man "never felt that an individual could transfer his responsibilities to the government and at the same time keep his freedom."

Nixon's only documented law school incident occurred at the end of his second year at Duke, when he and two other students—all of whom had scholarships based on sustained academic excellence—could not wait for grades to be posted. One climbed through a transom to get access to the dean's office, where they sifted through the papers to see how they rated, relieved to find that they had all survived.

NIXON NEVER TOOK FAILURE WELL. He would brood and sulk, finding enemies to blame and despise. But then he'd rebound. He would control his resentment, take out a yellow pad, begin his lists, and summon the will to continue. No one could mistake him for Pollyanna, yet within the angry guy was a steadfast optimist.

The first traces of Duke's famous perseverance appeared in the years following his death. At age 24, he returned to Whittier, depressed and without prospects. Hannah had persuaded Tom Bewley to offer her son a position in his law business. It was a great small law partnership that was knit into the fabric of town life, handling all of the locals' everyday tasks—oil leases, marriage problems, tax concerns, and probate. But life at Wingert & Bewley was worlds apart from Wall Street or Capitol Hill. For three years of law school, he had been sparring with intelligent classmates and teachers, discussing the wisdom of Brandeis and Cardozo and analyzing Roosevelt's shortcomings. Now he'd be assisting farmers with their wills.

Dick took the California bar examination in September. With no other options, he joined the firm for $50 per month. He worked hard, stayed late, ate lunch at his desk, and completely mishandled his first large case.

Nixon considered resigning, but Bewley accepted the burden. He had given Dick a basic task to perform just days after Nixon passed the bar. Dick had asked the opposition attorney for advice and been taken advantage of. The client was upset and sued Wingert & Bewley for malpractice, accusing them of negligence, carelessness, and ineptitude. The firm resolved and paid the client $4,800.

Dick was invited to join Wingert & Bewley as a partner in 1939, and he established a branch (a handmade desk in an empty space in a local real estate office) in La Habra. By then, he had taken a second path—as an entrepreneur and vendor of frozen orange juice. For a get-rich scheme, it had promise—future generations would regard frozen fruit juice as a near-miraculous concoction—but when the twenty-five-year-old Nixon rallied a group of local investors and accepted the title of president of "Citra-Frost," the science of draining the water from the juice and freezing the concentrate was still a decade away. Despite their best efforts, the Citra-Frost team was unable to bottle the juice without it deteriorating or spilling. The company also lacked capital. Dick worked furiously as usual, and Frank even showed up at night to squeeze the oranges. However, Citra-Frost failed, causing Nixon, his law company, and the investors to suffer financial losses. "You'll find people here," Bewley said decades later, who still "hate his guts because of that."

In September, after losing track of Pat over the summer (she had relocated without informing him of her new location), he wrote her a desperate letter at school. He needed to see you again—after class, before breakfast, Sunday, or whenever you could stand me!" She succumbed and gave him her address. "Social note — romantic?" She wrote sardonically. "In case I don't see you before, why don't you come early Wednesday…and I'll see if I can burn a hamburger for you."

Despite her resistance, they had much in common. She, too, had grown up on 10 acres in the countryside, working the farm and wishing to fly. She, too, had grown up with a turbulent father and a placating mother—an experience that caused them both, despite their other talents, to avoid personal confrontation. "I hate having a rage. I despise scenes. I just cannot be that way. Pat would tell her daughter Julie, "I saw it with my father." Dick had lost two siblings to TB, and Pat witnessed it claim her father. She and Dick skipped second grade, enjoyed their literature, participated in debate and school politics, and mounted the stage. They were never among the top students at school, but they were too intelligent and diligent to be overlooked.

They both had a chip on their shoulder. "The moneyed class come in and ask us to do their shopping," Pat wrote to an aunt after landing a job as a "collegienne"—a model and salesgirl—at Bullock's, a posh department store on Wilshire Boulevard, during her USC years. "They sit in luxurious chairs while we go all over the store and gather things for them to choose from….I drape the lovely velvet robes etc. around me, grin at the fat, rich customers and…they buy."

The wedding was a small ceremony (things were poor, and the bride had been orphaned), held on a Friday in June 1940 at the Mission Inn in Riverside. Dick only found out Pat's name was Thelma when they applied for their marriage license. She hadn't told him about her unhappy, hard background. He hadn't truly explained the Citra-Frost fiasco. "Pat still knows little about it and I prefer to handle it that way," he explained to Bewley.

Dick "thought often about his brothers' deaths," as his daughter Julie would write. "It may have helped him to talk about that anguish, but he was starting a life with a lady for whom death was a taboo subject, a pain so deep that it was sacredly, privately hers. "She pushed grief out of her consciousness, unwilling to open scars...Both would find it difficult in the future to break through their reserve and discuss their deepest feelings."

But what did that mean for a knight and his gypsy love? And so they went out together.

THEIR COURTSHIP took place during difficult times. Japan resumed its conquests in Asia, invading China, destroying most of Shanghai and Nanjing, and threatening Southeast Asia, Indonesia, and the Philippines. Between 1936 and 1939, fascists and communists took opposing sides in Spain's civil war, utilizing locals as proxy. Adolf Hitler sent his army into Austria in March 1938, amid pomp and pandemonium about the reunification of Germanic peoples, to claim it for the Nazi Reich. Throughout the summer, the Führer yelled and screamed, threatening war with Czechoslovakia if it did not surrender its German-speaking parts to the Nazis. Many people still remembered the horrors of World War I, and Dick and Pat were among the millions who applauded British Prime Minister Neville Chamberlain for appeasing the dictator and agreeing to the division of Czechoslovakia at a Munich summit meeting. "My good friends," Chamberlain informed his countrymen and the world, "a British Prime Minister has returned from Germany, bringing peace and dignity. I believe it represents peace for our time. Go home and have a lovely calm sleep.

Dick and Pat preferred peace and honor, and a good night's rest. They were only starting off, and the notion of American engagement in a battle of European quarrels was repulsive. "I come from a Quaker background. "I was as close to being a pacifist as anyone could be," Dick recalls. "I thought at that time that Chamberlain was the greatest man alive, and when I read Churchill's all-out criticism of Chamberlain I thought Churchill was a madman."

So the West slept as the empowered Nazis intensified their persecution of German Jews. Six months later, Hitler conquered the remainder of Czechoslovakia. In August 1939, the Germans struck a non-aggression pact with the Soviets, and in September, the two powerful bullies divided Poland. Chamberlain left office in disgrace, cursed in history with the title "appeaser." The war that followed claimed 60 million lives. The lesson of Munich would guide a generation: totalitarian hoodlums must be met with strength early on, before they gain power and momentum, and it takes a cataclysm to remove their fangs.

PAT KNEW Dick's desire to "accomplish great ends" was bound to lead to politics. They only had a year to do the things that young married couples do in peacetime—dancing and ice skating, cocktails, spaghetti dinners, and charades—before committing to a life of public service. Wonderful things were happening. The country prepared for war. Dick spoke at local service organizations in the spring of 1940, after learning that Whittier's state assemblyman was considering resigning. In the end, the incumbent stood for reelection, but Dick returned to the circuit in the fall to advocate for Republican presidential nominee Wendell Willkie.

Pat and Dick were still in California, planning to go east, when they received the news from Pearl Harbor while leaving a movie theater one Sunday evening.

The pair arrived in Washington a month later, on Dick's birthday, after driving across the country in snow and ice. The OPA's objective had shifted from combating inflation to planning and implementing a massive rationing regime during wartime. Dick worked on rubber and tire laws. He lasted three months. He did well in the job, earning swift promotions and more compensation. His responsibilities were expanded to include fuel and other key goods. But he grew to despise bureaucratic backbiting and opposed the New Deal's left-wing bent. He had several exemptions from the draft, including his employment, wife, and Quaker beliefs, yet he felt obligated to resist fascism. It was a risky move, but joining and entering officer candidate school promised a good battle. Combat was a great leveler: from Alexander Hamilton to Ulysses S. Grant, military service provided hitherto unattainable chances to men of low resources and social standing. And no one with Dick's ambition could deny that military service would be an almost unavoidable prerequisite for postwar leadership.

After an ideal final vacation in New England with Pat, Dick reported to navy officer training school at Quonset Point, Rhode Island, in August 1942. He spent time in Iowa (where the Californians experienced a Midwest winter with weeks of subzero temperatures and appreciated the boxes of citrus fruit his parents mailed them) before the navy decided to send him to the front.

The Navy's demand for bodies gave him an opportunity. He received instructions to report to the South Pacific in May 1943. In June, he arrived in the Solomon Islands, a line of islands off Australia's northeast shoulder. He sailed from San Francisco after saying goodbye to a stoic Hannah and a sobbing Frank at Union Station in Los Angeles. Dick and Pat toured San Francisco while waiting for his ship to depart, savoring the city's famous specialties, but neither was in the mood for merriment. "We've been to all the eating places," he informed Bewley, yet "are really too much on edge to enjoy it very much."

DICK'S STINT IN Ottumwa rescued him from the most intense fighting of the Solomons campaign: the struggle for Guadalcanal, which resulted in an American victory in February 1943. Nixon came as the Allied forces launched an onslaught, island-hopping toward Rabaul, the Japanese bastion on New Britain. The South Pacific War was famous, with battles at Henderson Field, Iron Bottom Sound, and the Slot, generating Broadway characters such as Nellie Forbush and Mister Roberts. Other navy officers who served there included John Kennedy, Ben Bradlee, Harold Stassen, and John Mitchell, as well as a Marine lieutenant named Joe McCarthy, all of whom would cross Nixon's path after the war.

Nixon served as an officer in Admiral William "Bull" Halsey's South Pacific Air Transport Command (SCAT). His tour began in rear-echelon safety, but by the autumn and winter of 1943, Dick had persuaded the navy to send him "up the line," and he saw duty on Guadalcanal and Vella Lavella before moving to the front on Bougainville, where the counterattacking Japanese were still bombing and shelling the American invasion forces. "He wanted to get into something where the smell of combat was closer," one of his supervisors, Carl Fleps, said.

By all accounts, he performed admirably and was popular among his men. However, several people noticed traces of strain in his attitude. There were flashes of Gloomy Gus. "Nixon always seemed to be two people: one, very quiet, very much in the background, and actually somewhat morose," Dole told me. "When the chips were down, it was as if he were electrocuted. He knew exactly what to say and how to say it, so he became lively and smiled."

Pat had stayed on after Dick's troop ship had left San Francisco. She got work, and eventually became an analyst for the OPA. Their correspondence during the war years depicts a loving couple braving the storm. "All of me loves all of you all the time," he wrote, assuring her when they first parted ways. "I certainly am not the Romeo type and you are so beautiful."

Dick asked her to have her portrait taken and forwarded to him. He was ecstatic with the results. He explained to her that the other males on Green Island couldn't believe he had such a wonderful female. "Everybody raved—I'm not sure how I rated! (I agree.)," he wrote. He sent her stuffed koala bears for her birthday, wrote her a letter from a cargo jet ten thousand feet above the Pacific ("I love you just the same up here as down below"), and described the sunsets he saw without her.

"I can't think of much to write about other than our pleasant moments together, which began the day we met in February 1938. Do you remember how you treated me then?! Laguna, Mexico City, Havana, Panama, Washington, D.C., Maine, Boston, Charlotte, Chicago, and even Ottumwa—what a fantastic five years. He wrote, "I love you always."

However, it was not all sighs and laughter. The months apart put a strain on the partnership. Pat rediscovered her desire for freedom. "I have to admit that I am pretty self-reliant, and if I didn't love you, I would feel very differently," she cautioned him as he prepared to leave. "These many months you've been away have been full of interest, and if I hadn't missed you so much and had been free, I could have been quite happy.

The navy assigned Nixon to the Alameda Air Station on San Francisco

Bay, then summoned him to the East to study and enforce federal contract laws. Dick and Pat were eating dinner at Bookbinder's restaurant in Philadelphia when they learned that Franklin Roosevelt had died and Harry Truman had become president. Nixon was in New York when he saw General Dwight Eisenhower being honored in a ticker tape procession. Then it was straight to Baltimore and the letter from Herman Perry.

Chapter 4: A Kind of Man the Country Needs

Dick and Pat arrived in January 1947 to a frigid and cold capital. On their previous visit to Washington, they had been fortunate in renting an apartment in Alexandria on their first day. Fortune was not happy this time, and they spent weeks in a hotel with baby Tricia before finding a duplex in the Park Fairfax section of nearby Virginia. His office turf was no grander: seniority determined workspace allocation, and Representative Nixon was consigned to the fifth level of the ancient House (now Cannon) office building.

The conflict had started with Poland's collapse. The war was finished, but the Poles were not free. Neither were the Czechs, Hungarians, or the oppressed peoples of the Baltic and Balkans. By October 1945, the United States military was developing contingency plans for a surprise attack on the Soviet Union with twenty to thirty nuclear weapons. The greatest of warfare did not cease; it simply cooled.

In early 1946, George Kennan, a US expert on Soviet behavior, wrote a famous dispatch—his "long telegram"—to Washington from the American Embassy in Moscow. He described the Soviet Union as an arrogant, dictatorial, and imperialistic state. Its leaders would invariably portray others as enemies to justify "the dictatorship without which they did not know how to rule, for cruelties they did not dare not to inflict." They were "committed fanatically to the belief" that there could be no coexistence, according to Kennan, and determined that "our society be disrupted, our traditional way of life be destroyed, the international authority of our state be broken."

As Nixon settled into his new role in Congress, the threat of Communism loomed large, both at home and abroad.

As Perry predicted, the new congressman was tested quickly—on an issue deemed critical by home-state real estate interests. During the 1946 campaign, Nixon joined Voorhis in full-throated opposition to the Whittier Narrows Dam, a flood-control project near his hometown, to get votes. The resulting reservoir would flood areas of nearby El Monte, uniting the community against it. "I shall oppose construction of the Whittier Narrows Dam to the limit of my ability," Nixon had originally pledged. Once elected, he did not back down. "I honestly believe the dam should not be built," he told Perry. Furthermore,

Nixon had the means to prevent it. Competition for federal cash was fierce, and the appropriators had plenty of alternative projects to fund—where local congressmen were supplicants rather than adversaries.

However, almost immediately following the election, Perry's status as Nixon's mentor led a swarm of local landowners, business boosters, and municipal leaders to the banker's office, where they browbeat, begged, and coerced the congressman to reconsider his mind. They claimed road and house construction had stalled. The Los Angeles Chamber of Commerce, the U.S. The Army Corps of Engineers, Senator Bill Knowland, and the politically connected oilman Ed Pauley were among those urging Nixon to back down. He discovered that a syndicate of investors had purchased land downstream, which would skyrocket in value once the dam was finished.

NIXON was also pleased with his committee responsibilities. Speaker Joe Martin recognized the value of supporting a new talent from the West. Nixon was given a position on the House Education and Labor Committee, whose members were working on the Republican majority's top legislative priority—the Taft-Hartley Act, which would limit the power of organized labor. He also received a seat on the House Committee on Un-American Activities. Both were excellent platforms for extending themes he had used in the 1946 campaign, namely the need to reduce labor and combat Red subversion. "He was one of the few who got an extra committee also—Unamerican Activities—so he is pleased about that as they will have the duty of cleaning up the Communist forces," Pat's family emailed him.

With Republicans in control of Congress, the labor law advanced quickly. It was their signature domestic achievement: a reversal of union privileges provided by the New Deal's historic Wagner Act. The Taft-Hartley Act authorized the president to declare a cooling-off period and postpone strikes that affected the national interest; outlawed sympathy strikes and boycotts; authorized right-to-work laws; limited union political activity; and, in a later ruled unconstitutional section, required union officers to submit signed affidavits to the government stating that they were not Communists.

On the midnight train to Washington, they shared a sleeper car and sat around—the ambassador's son and the shopkeeper's son—discussing their interest in global politics. Kennedy admired the man who defeated Jerry Voorhis, and Nixon was interested in the Choate, Harvard, and Palm Beach alumnus. "Neither of us was a backslapper, and we both were uncomfortable with boisterous displays of superficial camaraderie," Nixon used to say. "He was shy, but it was a natural instinct to protect his privacy and emotions." I recognized these characteristics because I shared them." Soon, Dick and Pat were attending parties at Kennedy's Georgetown townhouse. When John Kennedy married Jacqueline Bouvier, the Nixons were invited to the ceremony.

THE UNITED STATES emerged from World War II as a military and economic powerhouse, with global domination to rival ancient Rome. Despite being home to only 7% of the world's population, it produced 62% of its oil, 57% of its steel, and 80% of its autos. The motherland was unharmed, the industry and farmlands remained intact, and the number of losses was thankfully low—there would be no shortage of capable, battle-tested leaders in the postwar period. The rest of the world provided a study in contrast. Germany and Japan were in ashes. Even the victors—the British, French, and Soviets—had suffered horrific losses throughout the war, including a deadly winter and a strange drought that followed. Winston Churchill described Europe as "a rubble-heap, a charnel house, a breeding ground of pestilence and hatred." In February 1947, the British informed Truman that they could no longer secure the eastern Mediterranean. If Greece and Turkey were to be saved from Communism, America would have to do so.

Truman chose to act. "Mr. President, if that is what you seek, there is only one way to obtain it. Senator Arthur Vandenberg, a Republican from Michigan, recommended him to make a personal appearance before Congress and terrify the hell out of the country. Nixon was in the chamber on March 12, when the president spoke to a joint session of Congress, declaring America's willingness to defend lesser nations from Communist assault. It became known as the Truman Doctrine. A few weeks later, Truman started a federal Red Hunt, a loyalty investigation of government employees. Congress joined the president in passing the National Security Act of 1947, which established the Central Intelligence Agency, the National Security Council, the Department of Defense, and other elements of the national security state.

Nixon supported Truman's proposal for $400 million for Greece and Turkey, despite the reservations of certain Amateurs in California. They were members of a Republican wing known as "the Old Guard" led by Ohio Senator Robert Taft, who advocated for a noninterventionist foreign policy and a limitation in government reach and powers. Their isolationist feelings grew after Secretary of State George Marshall suggested in a June 5 address at Harvard that the United States would have to rescue the rest of Europe as well. The ungrateful socialists of Europe should be left to their "suffering," not bailed out by the "so-called Marshall Plan," wrote a half dozen of Nixon's early supporters. Truman's policy was "right down Stalin's alley."

In another letter, Herman Perry was succinct. "We will just be pouring the money down a rat hole to help the undeserving in Europe and tax the people in the United States to death," according to Perry. "Frankly, I trust that in the future you will be extremely careful in getting too far involved in this bungling thinking."

The Marshall Plan was a defining issue that Nixon couldn't avoid. In early July, Truman called him to the Oval Office and massaged him. On July 29, Nixon opened his morning paper to discover that the Speaker had appointed him to a select bipartisan committee that would travel to Europe, led by Massachusetts Republican Representative Christian Herter, to study circumstances and report back to the House. Nixon was suddenly at the center of a nationwide debate over the use of American power. A misstep, and his career may end right there.

Nixon addressed the basic question posed by Edmund Burke in his speech to Bristol electors. Did he owe his constituents obedience or judgment? Six months into his first term in office, Nixon was confronted with yet another moral quandary, this time involving more than a California water project. His performance may determine the destiny of freedom.

The Herter Mission left New York on the Queen Mary liner in late August. Pat and his dad wish Dick farewell from the dock after seeing the popular Broadway musical Oklahoma! The congressman wrote to his wife from the middle of the ocean, bragging about the ship's luxury while insisting on his hard labor. It was a refrain he'd use during the six-week journey, as he recounted the glories of London, Paris, Berlin, Athens, Rome, Naples, Pompeii, Venice, and other destinations, praised the delicious meals and wines, and generally talked about his exciting experience.

Yesterday, we drove from Milan to Turin for almost three hours. We visited rice growers, manufacturers, and the famed Martini Rossi vineyard, where we had lunch. The lunch consisted of cold ham, ravioli, chicken, fruit, and cheese, accompanied by several types of wine, champagne, and brandy.

As for Nixon, it was a difficult journey. His letters to Pat concealed the hazards and left out the most graphic occurrences. He visited Germany's cemeteries, went to the front lines of the Greek civil war, and witnessed bloodshed as Italians fought Yugoslav Communists on the streets of Trieste. He was a member of the "Jenkins Raiders" subcommittee, which was assigned to southern Europe and named after its commander, Ohio Republican Representative Thomas Jenkins. Their motto—"Don't stay too long in one place"—reflected the tempo. The American correspondents Nixon met during the trip admired him. "Nixon came up where the action was while the others…stayed down in the fleshpots of Athens," recalled the Baltimore Sun's veteran war journalist Phil Potter. "There was a curiosity and an energy to him."

We stood in the great hall of what was once Hitler's Reich Chancellery, and as we looked at the ruins and realized how much destruction a dictator had caused for himself and his people as a result of his totalitarian aggression, small thin-faced German boys tried to sell us the medals that their fathers had won during the war.

Economic activity was slowing, but it was due to starvation rather than communist coddling. Workers were given extra servings of food to boost production at mines and factories, but often snuck it home to keep their families fed. It was the same at the special soup kitchens that the Allies established to feed youngsters.

Nixon, of course, was affected by the suffering of mistreated tuberculosis patients. Representative Eugene Cox of Georgia, a staunch conservative, donated all of his sweets, soap, and extra clothing to a group of German children after witnessing the eldest, a ten-year-old, deliver a prized piece of chocolate to her tiny sister. In

Greece, Representative James Richards of South Carolina handed over his wallet to a young woman who told the delegation that during torture, the Communists had severed one of her breasts.

Trieste's port was a contested city—a "free territory" on the Adriatic separated by Communist and Western armies, similar to Berlin. During their mid-September tour, Nixon witnessed the Red methods firsthand. He left his hotel to get a better look as a column of Communists marched, yelling in song, arms raised and fists clenched, causing violence and disorder. Two spectators were killed as he watched—a woman who was thrown to the ground and struck her head on a curb, and a guy decapitated by a grenade. Nixon traversed the city, documenting the bloodshed. His colleagues dubbed it "Nixon's Charge."

At the Yugoslav border, Nixon learned a lesson from Lieutenant William Ochs and the twelve US infantrymen under his command, who refused to surrender to a column of two thousand Yugoslav soldiers armed with artillery. No guns were fired, and the Yugoslavs soon backed down. Nixon believed that the Communists would probe for weakness but retreat if confronted with resolve.

The Communist intimidation made an impression, but it did not detract from Nixon's belief that if the Europeans received the aid Marshall promised, they would fight for freedom. Empty tummies, not bayonets, posed the menace. That was also the analysis that Nixon received from the top-tier advisers Herter had enlisted to brief the mission—the State Department's Charles "Chip" Bohlen, future CIA chief Allen Dulles, and General Lucius Clay, the Allied commander in Berlin—all the way down to Rosetta Rubsamen, a Foreign Service officer at the US embassy in Italy who served as Nixon's guide in Rome.

Nixon arrived home in mid-October. His reconnection with Pat was a happy one, and his daughter Julie was born nine months later. His tenure on the Herter committee left him with no qualms about the necessity for immediate action, and an unwavering belief that, for political and policy reasons, he needed to sell George Marshall's plan to the naysayers back home. Yellow legal pads were brought out. He outlined his ideas for a speech that he planned to deliver several times in the coming weeks.

Nixon warned his Amateur friends about the dangers of "blank checks to inefficient, weak, and corrupt governments," but there was no mistake where he stood in the conflict between isolationists and internationalists. "We must remember that we are a part of the world and cannot bury our heads in the sand in isolation, because if we do, the cause of freedom and democracy will be lost, not just in Europe. "It will be lost here."

Nixon criss crossed his district to deliver that speech. His constituents listened, inquired, and many were persuaded. So it happened across the land. Both the House and the Senate approved the Marshall Plan after being endorsed by the Herter Committee. It contributed to the survival of Western Europe and is seen in postwar history as an American strategic, diplomatic, and humanitarian triumph.

At a Georgetown dinner party that spring, John Kennedy regaled a visitor with stories about the young congressman from California's sharp mind and admirable realism. Dick Nixon, Kennedy claimed, was the type of man the country required.

Chapter 5: A Tragedy of History

On Independence Day, 1948, Dick took Pat to Columbia Hospital in Washington, where she gave birth to a nine-pound, six-ounce girl the next morning. They named the baby Julie. It was a welcome and happy event for a couple who had been through difficult times, war, and campaigns. With a five-month congressional recess coming and no serious opposition to Dick's reelection, he and Pat anticipated spending more time together and reaping the benefits of a long vacation. They needed it to rekindle their marriage.

Newcomers have little time. Dick's winter and spring were dominated by the Mundt-Nixon bill, the Marshall Plan, and his reelection, while the Republican national convention in Philadelphia, which crowned Dewey as the presidential candidate, took up the early summer. Dick, a Stassen man, was confined to the galleries, but he liked dragging his father around; together, they examined an exhibit of that new miracle, television. Hannah arrived in Washington to help with the new baby, but she became unwell, leaving Pat with three children to care for: her mother-in-law, two-year-old Tricia and Julie.

The Communists refused to collaborate. In early 1948, the Russians completed their control of Czechoslovakia, which was marked by the death of Czech foreign minister Jan Masaryk, who jumped, fell, or was thrown from an upper-story window after failing to guarantee his country's independence. Talk of conflict with Russia flooded America's coffee shops and living rooms, and media reported on the United States' nuclear weapons tests at Eniwetok atoll.

As Congressmen returned to the glory of August in Washington, HUAC's leaders were still hobbling from the Condon catastrophe. The Truman administration, an unlikely source, bailed them out. In July, a federal grand jury investigating subversion accused twelve Communist Party officials in the United States. The Justice Department's win in the case emphasized civil libertarians' claim that the Mundt-Nixon measure was unnecessary, but also benefited HUAC by freeing up federal witnesses, whose evidence steered the committee in a profitable direction.

Bentley told her story to Senate investigators and then HUAC at a public session on July 31. She implicated a senior Treasury official,

Harry Dexter White, and a slew of other New Deal officials as Soviet operatives. When White and others refuted the claims, HUAC was once again chastised for incriminating people without giving them the opportunity to react. Staffer Robert Stripling took "a forlorn shot in the dark," subpoenaing Whittaker Chambers to back up Bentley's evidence.

The reporters at the press table looked up. This was news. Bentley did not mention Hiss. He was then president of the Carnegie Endowment for International Peace, a respected organization. He had been a key State Department official before and during the war, and Franklin Roosevelt's Sherpa at the Yalta summit, where Churchill, Stalin, and Roosevelt announced their postwar plans and promises. He was a midwife at a United Nations birth. According to the mumbling Chambers, Hiss was a Communist all along.

The liberal fascination with Communism faded as word of Stalin's purges reached America and the Soviet leader signed a nonaggression deal with Hitler to dismember Poland. However, the union between the two gangster statesmen did not survive long. By the time America entered the war in late 1941, the Nazis and Soviets were fighting on the eastern front. For Americans, Stalin became "Uncle Joe," an indispensable friend in the great war against Germany, Italy, and Japan. "To cross this bridge, I would hold hands with the Devil," Roosevelt told a friend.

Hiss arrived in Washington in 1933, at the age of twenty-eight, to join a team of outstanding socialist lawyers in the Agricultural Adjustment Administration, the New Deal organization tasked with addressing the rural problem. While at the AAA, Harold Ware, an agricultural specialist, enlisted Hiss and others in the Communist Party and created an underground cell. Hiss moved to Capitol Hill, where he served as counsel for a Senate probe into the arms business, before joining the Department of State. When Ware was murdered in a car accident, authority of the cell passed to a Soviet spymaster, who ordered Hiss and Chambers to steal information for Soviet military intelligence. Chambers abandoned the Communist beliefs in 1938, but Hiss continued espionage during the war years, rising through the ranks to become a prominent adviser to Secretary of State Edward Stettinius Jr.

It was difficult for Nixon to assess the intellect of the "unkempt, disorderly" Chambers on that August morning. He characterized the witness as "short, fat, so soft-spoken that it was often necessary to ask him to repeat what he said, his clothes un-pressed, his manner almost diffident."

Nixon had no objections when others suggested making Chambers' testimony public. He had joined his fellow lawmakers, the committee's staff, a parade of reporters and spectators, and the skittish witness (Chambers, not unreasonably, feared he was a target for assassination) as they marched across the street from the committee's offices to the spacious Ways and Means room in the new House (now Longworth) office building.

hiss now had a choice. He could invoke the Fifth Amendment's protection against self-incrimination. Or, like Chambers, he could hide behind half-truths. Yes, Hiss may have said, he had an early romance with Communism. Yes, he had paid his party dues. And, indeed, he had deceived his New Deal comrades. But he was a patriot who despised Hitler. Secretaries of state and Supreme Court justices would support him. His diplomatic record was perfect. It was so long ago. Hiss might have gotten away with it. Chambers played that hand, remained out of prison, and was posthumously awarded the Presidential Medal of Freedom.

Stripling described Hiss as a "big fish." He had more at risk than Chambers. He would undoubtedly lose his job, perhaps his career, and certainly his reputation. And HUAC would force him to play the rat, reveal names, or risk imprisonment for contempt, like the Hollywood Ten did. It was better to deny everything, Hiss determined. He wouldn't betray his cause. He'd brazen it out. He addressed a telegram to the committee, demanding an opportunity to defend his name, saying: "I do not know mr. chambers and, as far as i am aware, have never laid eyes on him."

HISS received his invitation to testify and turned his presence before the committee into a victory. The August 5 hearing was held in the enormous Caucus Room of the old House office building, where onlookers were fanning themselves as the ventilation system battled to keep up with the summer heat. The press table was filled with newspaper reporters, and the legislators on the dais appeared and went in a cloud of cigarette smoke. Alone at the microphone, Hiss faced the inquisition.

Hiss ended his day with a goodbye salvo. "I am not happy that I didn't have a chance to meet with the committee privately before there was such a great public press display of what I consider completely unfounded charges against me," he told the reporter. "Denials do not always catch up with charges."

After lunch, when the glum HUAC members met to discuss their options, "everyone was convinced that a great injustice had been done," Nixon remembered. Some suggested burying it and sending the entire issue to the Department of Justice to determine who was lying.

"The committee was in a state of panic. I must admit that I was inclined to do what the majority of the committee wanted: drop the issue and go on to something else," Nixon recounted. Nonetheless, he insisted that they remain the path.

"Only one dude. "Richard Nixon argued quietly but firmly against a shift away from the Hiss investigation," Chambers recalled. "He pleaded the necessity of reaching the truth."

It is difficult to find a term that accurately characterizes Nixon's chutzpah. He was a first-term congressman from a remote area with few institutions of learning or influence. His few powerful allies—Southern California's oilmen and the Los Angeles Times—were vested interests. Mentors including Christian Herter advised him to cut his losses. Berle and others feared Chambers was "a screwball."

Nixon did not risk it all on a whim. He had cause to assume Hiss was a Communist, as Father John Cronin had told him so.

Cronin was a Catholic philosopher, a warrior "in the defense of human dignity," as he put it. He supported civil rights for black Americans and the right of the working class to organize, and he became a staunch anti-Communist after witnessing the Reds penetrate the labor movement. He took up arms, investigating, raising the alarm in reports to his bishops, and acting as a conduit to the press and public for disgruntled FBI and State Department agents who "were so distressed by the misinformation and naiveté of the American public that they were desperately seeking outlets," he recalls.

Representative Charles Kersten of Wisconsin, a fellow watchman, introduced Cronin to Nixon in early 1947. The priest discovered that the new congressman was a willing learner. "A twenty-minute appointment was made," Cronin stated. "The actual meeting took two hours."

"The story told in Mr. Nixon's office was dramatic and possibly lurid," Cronin recalls. They reviewed "Communist espionage, particularly atomic espionage; Communist penetration into government, including influential sectors in the State and Treasury Departments; and the Executive Department's agonizingly sluggish response to genuine reports on this situation. Names mentioned in the conversation include Alger Hiss, Harry Dexter White, and many others.

Nixon believed that if he pursued Hiss, he could rely on Cronin and his associates for assistance. The priest would act as a go-between, gathering material from the FBI and relaying it to Nixon over the congressman's secret phone line.

Nixon was well aware that bringing Hiss down could cause significant political dividends. In 1950, California had a vulnerable US senator, Democrat Sheridan Downey, who was up for re-election. By the summer of 1948, Nixon had scheduled talks across the state, and Roy Day and others were making subtle questions about "the Senator deal."

At one point during the hearing, Nixon forced Hiss to declare that one of his mentors was Justice Felix Frankfurter, a Roosevelt Supreme Court appointee. Hiss had objected, citing the committee's carelessness.

On August 7, Nixon led a HUAC delegation to New York, where they summoned Chambers from his desk at Time to question him in a closed-door hearing at the federal courthouse on Foley Square.

"I grilled him for two and a half hours on everything a man should know about another man if he knew him," Nixon can still recall. He probed Chambers for information on Hiss and his wife, his home, hobbies, mannerisms, and habits. As the day progressed, it became increasingly plausible that Chambers was speaking the truth. The witness knew quite a bit about the Hiss family, including their home, cocker spaniel, and phrases of endearment. Chambers discussed an ancient Ford that Alger had loaned him with hand-operated windshield wipers, Hiss' boyhood job bringing water from Druid Hill Park in

Baltimore, and a prothonotary warbler that Hiss and his wife had observed while bird-watching.

"I never saw one," Chambers admitted, sounding envious. "I am also fond of birds."

Nixon and the others returned to Washington, where committee investigators corroborated much of what Chambers told them. "It was obvious that either Chambers knew Hiss and Hiss was lying," according to Nixon. "Or that Chambers had a very, very deep-seated motive which caused him to want to destroy Hiss, and he concocted a story after having studied Hiss's life." He resolved to know Chambers better. There were real and unfounded reports regarding the witness's mental health, drinking habits, and sexual preferences. "There was a gnawing doubt in the back of my mind," Nixon explained. "This was a bizarre tale." If Chambers held a grudge against Hiss, it was possible that he had spied on the family and documented the commonplace details of their lives. So the congressman drove to Westminster and spent hours talking with Chambers on the porch overlooking the fields. He met the witness's wife, Esther Chambers, and was startled by her dark complexion and strict Quaker demeanor. By the conclusion of the day, "I was not convinced that everything" Chambers had said about Hiss was real. I believed he had a reason for destroying Hiss, but after learning he knew him, I became sure.

Nixon sought allies, delivering transcripts of Chambers' testimony to William Rogers, the counsel for the Senate committee that had grilled Elizabeth Bentley, and Bert Andrews, the New York Herald Tribune bureau chief who had won a Pulitzer Prize for exposing excesses in Truman's loyalty program. With Congressman Charles Kersten on his side, Nixon traveled to New York to meet John Foster Dulles, Dewey's top adviser.

Nixon was gathering more than moral backing. He was asking the Dewey campaign for permission to proceed. Dulles was in an unusual situation; the venerable Wall Street lawyer was poised to become the next Republican secretary of state, but he had also suggested Hiss for the Carnegie Endowment position. If Nixon reveals Hiss as a Communist, Dulles may suffer the consequences. In such conditions, Nixon had little trouble getting an audience at Dewey's headquarters in the Roosevelt Hotel. Dulles was joined by his brother Allen and

Christian Herter. The young man from Whittier was conferring with the party elders, impressing them with his wisdom and winning their appreciation. After reading the testimony, the Dulles brothers shook their heads at the irrefutable proof of their buddy Alger's betrayal and instructed Nixon to proceed.

Nixon then took Stripling and Andrews to visit Chambers at his farm near Westminster. They, too, became believers—though Stripling suspected Chambers was hiding something.

It was time to put Hiss and Chambers in the same room. Nixon and McDowell resumed their journey to New York the following morning. They called Hiss to a closed-door hearing in a Commodore Hotel suite, where Chambers confronted him.

Hiss approached his old friend, fists clenched, and challenged him to repeat his allegations in public, where he would be subject to libel laws. "I challenge you to do it, and I hope you will do it damned quickly," the man remarked.

A HUAC employee grabbed Hiss by the arm and drew him away. He stormed out. The room was silent. Stripling then addressed Chambers, saying, "Hi-ya, Mistah Crawzli."

THE FINAL SHOWDOWN took place on August 25 in Washington, in the Caucus Room, in front of banks of television and newsreel cameras, cementing the image of the Hiss case in American memory. Spectators packed the seats and lined the walls, while hundreds of disappointed latecomers waited in the halls. According to the Evening Star, Washington's "society" found the dispute and attended "in the greatest of air-conditioned comfort." Representative Nixon's "blonde, good-looking wife, seated in the third row...hanging on his every word." Radio presenters spoke quietly into their microphones, and reporters handed bulletins to copy boys, who raced them to the newsrooms. "The air was heavy with the ominous and ultimate charges of modern history: treason, espionage, and insanity," said the Nation magazine.

It was the first House hearing broadcast on television. Nixon and Hiss had released their versions of the Commodore confrontation to the press, so each side knew what the other was going to say. It was a performance-based competition. Could Hiss reclaim the audience with his stance of wounded innocence? Could Chambers, with his plodding assurance, defeat a daring opponent?

Hiss and Chambers recreated their face-to-face contact for the cameras, and then Hiss took the witness stand. He was "a tall, well-groomed, handsome young man, adroit in manner, diplomatic in his speech," according to James Reston of the New York Times. Nixon's questions to the witness "were detailed and often acidic."

Chambers' status as an informant earned him disdain. He had to persuade the people that he wasn't crazy or filled with hatred. He needed to portray his activities as a sacred mission, a noble responsibility. The remarks that followed would reverberate throughout the years.

"The story has spread that by testifying against Mr. Hiss, I'm working out some old grudge, or motives of revenge or hatred," Chambers replied slowly, sadly. "I don't detest Mr. Hiss. We were good friends, yet we were caught up in a tragic historical event.Mr. Hiss represents the hidden adversary against whom we are all battling, and I am fighting. I testified against him out of sorrow and empathy, but in this historic time, I couldn't do differently.

The hearing had begun at 10:30 a.m. It finished at 8 p.m. Andrews described it as a "vicious battle," with "spine-tingling moments," and as "one of the most tensely dramatic congressional hearings in America's history."

Hiss had wowed with his array of notable mentors and associates. His remark appeared well taken. How could he have been an advocate for Communism? How could he have pushed such harmful policies without all those wonderful guys recognizing and objecting? There were two options. The first theory was that Chambers was lying, which became increasingly unlikely as more details of his testimony were revealed. The alternative was that Hiss was more than just a Communist sympathizer; he was actually a spy. The fundamental soul of espionage is to penetrate without raising suspicion. If Hiss had openly supported the Soviet Union's goals, he would not have been trusted with the knowledge he stole. Hiss's famous colleagues' attestations did not exonerate him; rather, they highlighted his exceptional spy skills.

Why hadn't Chambers informed Congress about the entire nature of Hiss' activities? He maintained, both then and later, that compassion restrained his hand. He was fighting Communism, he claimed, not his former pals, whom he intended to protect from the misery of trial. Perhaps, but to expose Hiss's espionage, he would have to reveal his own. Chambers was astute, serving the story in manageable chunks. "He sits and lights his pipe, he is cold and calculating, and he knows exactly what he will do in three weeks hence," Stripling told me. By the time he confessed to his own treason, Chambers was a right-wing hero with allies like Nixon to defend him.

HISS HAS MADE A GOD-AWFUL MISTAKE. He sued Chambers for slander, assuming that if his old friend had evidence of their wrongdoings, he would have presented it. During the pretrial proceedings, Chambers was directed by the court to divulge any material in his possession. He contacted his wife's nephew, who had concealed a lumpy packet of microfilm and paperwork for him under a dusty dumbwaiter over a decade ago. Chambers kept the microfilm but gave the records to Hiss's stunned lawyers, who handed them over to the government. They were typed duplicates of top-secret materials and handwritten notes, indicating that Hiss was a Soviet agent.

Nixon and Stripling went to a Capitol Hill restaurant for lunch, when Stripling suggested they go meet Chambers. Nixon was to leave for New York the following morning, where he and Pat had a ship to catch. He couldn't cancel the cruise on the eve of their departure. Pat would never forgive him.

"I am so goddamn sick and weary of this case. I don't want to hear any more about it, and I'm off to Panama! "The hell with it, you, and the entire damn business," he said to Stripling.

So proceeded their lunch: Nixon in a frenzy, torn between competing commitments, and Stripling seething from the reprimand. None of them loved his meal. The standoff lasted as they walked back to the office, and it wasn't until Stripling, headed out the door with car keys in hand, made one more plea that the congressman gave in. "Goddamn it," he replied, "if it will shut your mouth, I'll go."

They traveled down the now-familiar path to Westminster in hushed stillness. They arrived just in time for milking and had to wait for Chambers to finish with his cows.

NIXON WAS TOO SMART to deceive himself in that way. On his way out of town the next morning, he stopped at the HUAC offices and instructed Stripling to subpoena any evidence Chambers still had. Dick and Pat boarded a boat and sailed away.

Stripling issued Chambers with the subpoena and dispatched two HUAC detectives to retrieve whatever was hidden in Westminster. At the Chambers property, they fumbled around with flashlights in the dark until the witness saw a carved-out pumpkin in his garden, reached inside, and produced the microfilm cans.

"I think this is what you are looking for," he said.

Investigators delivered the footage to Stripling the next morning. He commandeered a men's room to serve as a darkroom and requested an enlarger. He soon began calling HUAC members across the country to inform them that the committee had discovered proof of espionage. The microfilm included confidential government documents. Chambers and Hiss were not only communists; they were also spies.

Despite their heated disagreements, Stripling remained loyal to Nixon. He acknowledged that, when others had given up, the California congressman kept the cause alive and deserved to be present for the accolades. "It was Mr. Nixon's case...""And he had gotten on a boat," Stripling explained. He notified Nixon aide Bill Arnold and the Tribune's Bert Andrews, who showered the steamer Panama with telegrams.

NIXON'S HOUR OF VICTORY was tainted by a blunder that nearly cost Chambers his life. As they prepared to present their findings to the press, a photographer asked Nixon and Stripling if they had verified the film's normal numbering to ascertain its manufacturing date. Stripling contacted an Eastman Kodak lobbyist, who relayed the question to the company's headquarters and returned with bad news: the film was made after 1945, not during Hiss and Chambers' collaboration. The authenticity of the images was questioned, and Chambers' story about the dusty dumbwaiter appeared to be a fraud. They believed "we had been taken," Nixon recalled.

The hiss case had been "broken." The federal prosecutors who found Elizabeth Bentley and indicted the Communist Party leadership have called Chambers and Hiss to testify.

Chambers retracted his previous lies. They were actually Soviet agents, not, as he had claimed, simple Communist supporters. He told the grand jury how Hiss smuggled secret records home at night, where his wife, Priscilla, typed out copies, which Chambers handed on to their Soviet spymasters.

The statute of limitations for espionage had expired, but Hiss and Chambers risked imprisonment for perjury. The case against Chambers was clear-cut, but Nixon defended him, accusing the Truman administration of pursuing a strong witness to conceal its shortcomings. And if Chambers was prosecuted with perjury, Nixon contended, the evidence against Hiss would be irreparably weakened. "You can't indict your main witness for perjury and expect the other case to stand up," he noted.

Nixon was loyal and protective. When Chambers revealed his homosexuality to the FBI, Nixon met with Esther Chambers, calmly counseled her, and made no judgments about her husband's past behavior or sexual orientation. "She said imaginative creative people wanted to explore all things & defended C that way—but was obviously disturbed," Nixon wrote in his diary. "Nevertheless, she was behind him 100%."

"I told her I wanted her to tell C I wished him well…and that a lot of people were behind him," Nixon recounted. "She seemed immensely pleased."

The Justice Department summoned Nixon to the grand jury, where prosecutors demanded proof of his claims of a White House cover-up. He instantly yielded. If that was how people read his words, Nixon apologized. He hadn't meant any harm. "I certainly have no evidence to back that up," he said. However, under rising public pressure, the Truman administration began to see things Nixon's way. On December 15, Hiss was indicted for perjury. Chambers, the witness, wasn't. Years later, Nixon would enjoy recalling his role in Alger Hiss' trials. He had "won the Hiss case in the papers," he would boast his White House advisers. "I had to leak stuff all over the place."A Congressional committee wields two weapons. It ruins a man's reputation in public. And if it turns over its files to the Department of Justice for prosecution, the poor bastards will be prosecuted," Nixon recalled. "I did it to Hiss."

Richard Nixon repeatedly astounded Washington during his first two years there. The "handsome, strong-jawed Republican freshman," as one newsmagazine described him, had helped drive the Taft-Hartley and Mundt-Nixon bills through the House, given critical support for the Marshall Plan, and sought to limit HUAC's excesses. Nixon then revealed a high-ranking Soviet spy, while others remained silent. According to analyst Fulton Lewis, this was "undoubtedly the most brilliant record...by any young congressman in a great many years.".

Stripling once chastised his young ally. Stripling scolded Nixon for going "limber tail" during the Hollywood Ten probe. He had distanced himself from Thomas and the others while things were bad, but now he was taking the spotlight. "I don't think you realize you're not in the bush league," Stripling replied. "You're in the majors now. "You cannot undermine the committee."

Karl Mundt's administrative assistant also filed a complaint. "It was understandable that you should seek honor for yourself...and perhaps play down and ignore the contributions of others," W.E. O'Brien wrote to President Nixon. "But when you joined in a slur on the committee methods...that was going...too far."

and these were Nixon's buddies. For weeks, the Hiss case dominated the national news. He had clashed with President Truman, questioned the liberal establishment, matched wits with a New Deal idol, and emerged victorious. If he expected universal applause, he was going to be disappointed. As with the campaign against Voorhis, where Nixon took the topic of anti-Communism beyond what many considered fair play, his zeal overcame him, exposing him to vengeance.

Laurence Duggan, Alger Hiss' friend and former State Department colleague, leaped or fell from the sixteenth-floor window of his midtown Manhattan office on December 20, following an FBI questioning. Mundt and Nixon held a midnight press conference to take credit for HUAC's involvement in exposing Duggan as a Red Agent. According to reports, he was one of six State Department personnel who had previously worked for the Soviet Union. When the press inquired about the names of the other accused spies, Mundt remarked, "We'll release the others as they jump out windows."

It was Christmas time. Duggan, whether a communist or not, was a gentle soul who left a wife and four children behind, and his death brought back thoughts of Harry Dexter White, who died after being insulted by HUAC the summer before.

Nixon and Mundt were ridiculed. "At a stroke [the committee] has undone months of genuine effort...to correct past excesses and bring its procedures within the limits of reason and fairness," the newspaper revealed. A "dead man's character is being destroyed," stated CBS reporter Edward R. Murrow in his evening program.

The Hiss case—the story of White and Alger, the papers in the pumpkin, the broken-down Ford, and the yellow-chested warbler—went beyond the typical political dispute. It was controversial and personal. Andrews had warned Nixon in the telegram, bringing him back from the water. documents are incredibly hot. The link to his appears to be certain.my liberal friends don't love me anymore. nor you.

Just as it formed Nixon, the Hiss case affected the political climate throughout the early days of the Cold War.

It was an "epitomizing drama," Chambers remarked. "The two irreconcilable faiths of our time—Communism and Freedom—came to grips in the persons of two...resolute men," according to his words. "With dark certitude, both knew...that the Great Case could end only in the destruction of one or both...just as the history of our times...can end only in the destruction of one or both of the contending forces."

Chambers was never short of theatrics, but plainspoken Democrats understood the risks. According to House Speaker Sam Rayburn, there was "political dynamite" in the Communism problem. "Don't doubt that."

The Hiss case instilled guilt, or at least defensiveness, in individuals on the left who had dabbled in radical ideologies as adolescents. It alarmed the liberal society that "the primitives," as Dean Acheson described the right's rabble-rousers, could use disastrous witch hunts to undermine Roosevelt's legacy.

The Hiss case served as a rallying point for Republicans, bringing together Bob Taft's Old Guard, young literati such as William F. Buckley Jr., Senator McCarthy's blue-collar supporters, and an emerging crop of Sunbelt activists whose conservative passion, once harnessed, would lead to Republican disaster, rebirth, and triumph before the end of the century. The case inspired them all, fueled their anger toward the Ivy League elite, and reaffirmed their fears that postwar reversals in Eastern Europe and China were the result of treason and betrayal.

It would also send Richard Nixon to the United States Senate.

Chapter 6: The Great Train Robbery

Richard Nixon's defeat of Helen Douglas was not without cost. In his battles with Voorhis, Hiss, and Douglas, Nixon defeated three New Deal aristocrats. Bryce Harlow, a Republican strategist, noted that the left now saw him as "a threat to liberalism." "He was tough." "He enjoyed rolling in the dust."

"Voorhis was the darling of Washington, D.C." "The media, liberals, and leftists of the day all adored Jerry," Harlow added. "So when Nixon arrived, he was already marked. "The Washington press disliked him before they met him."

Nixon subsequently rose to prominence by "unfrocking Alger Hiss—a most unsettling business, once again, for the liberal establishment," according to Harlow. "He beats a left-wing woman from California."Now the Washington jackals had a firm grip on him."

It was not only Washington. The Senate contest had also tarnished Nixon's reputation in California. Douglas and her backers spent the final six weeks of her campaign attempting to make Nixon's character the central issue. She failed, but her argument was memorable, earning her the nickname Tricky Dick.

Nixon's family overheard the muttering. Dick's uncle Oscar Marshburn felt his aggressiveness came from his debate training. "Perhaps his remarks were misconstrued, or maybe he became overly ambitious. "I don't know," Marshburn replied. He may have implied something he couldn't confirm.... from the vast group that was supporting Helen Gahagan Douglas, these things could be regarded as dirty."

Nixon was sworn in a month early, on December 4, 1950, after Sheridan Downey, who was leaving to work as a lobbyist, resigned to offer his replacement a few weeks' seniority in the Senate. Nixon's successor in the House of Representatives was his protégé, Pat Hillings. As a senator from a large and distant state, Nixon's salary, expenditures, and office allowances increased. He loaded his third-floor rooms in the Senate office building with new assistants, most notably a thirty-three-year-old secretary named Rose Mary Woods, whom he had met while working on the Herter expedition. The males on Nixon's staff came and went throughout the years, while the ladies frequently stayed for decades. Woods and other secretaries grew to revere "the Boss," as they nicknamed him, and became known as his "vestal virgins." According to advance man Aylett Cotton, they were "dedicated...to the same degree that a nun is dedicated to God." The war had created new opportunities for women, and while many left when the lads returned home, others remained in the workforce. More than a handful became executive secretaries, administrative assistants, or alter personalities for powerful men. Woods was one of such women. She had gone to Washington from Ohio to work for the government during the war, stayed, and eventually became Nixon's personal secretary. Woods was more than simply a typist, though there were many of those. He was also a gatekeeper, a detailed person, and a valued secret keeper. Their friendship was constantly tested. Pat admitted to Helene that the daily grind and responsibility were exhausting. "We are so busy that we don't find the time for any close friends and just fun." When Pat became angry and refused to speak to him, Dick begged Hannah to come and plead his cause. "Not speaking?" Woods informed one of Nixon's cousins, recalling the couple's disagreements, that there were times when Pat locked him out of the house.

When the Senate was not in session, Nixon traveled the country, giving addresses in twenty-one states. His itinerary increased his paycheck and introduced him to appreciative Republican audiences in Akron, Wichita, Des Moines, and other exotic destinations. Temptation accompanied success. Aides recalled Nixon and his pal Bill Rogers in town with a group of young females.

Sheridan Downey, an ulcer sufferer, brought Nixon a book called The Will to Live by Dr. Arnold Hutschnecker, who specialized in treating the physical manifestations of modern diseases such as worry and stress. The New York doctor accepted Nixon as a patient and would advise, soothe, and tend to him on and off for the remainder of his life. He advised him to limit his alcohol consumption, avoid hard-to-digest foods, and engage in regular exercise. Over time, Hutschnecker would prescribe a variety of tranquilizers to help Nixon relax, stimulants to get him going, and barbiturates and other medications to help him sleep.

The doctor also listened carefully as Nixon discussed his background and home life. Hutschnecker was not a licensed psychiatrist, but he gradually developed his own views regarding his patients' psyche. He occasionally made indiscreet references to them in interviews or writings.

The psychiatrist believed Nixon was so engrossed in his work that he was masking serious insecurity. Frank had been demanding, while Hannah was distant and frequently absent. Nixon struggled with conflicting childhood emotions—his desire for his mother's affection and attention, and the hurt he felt when Hannah denied it. "He did have this tension," Hutschnecker explained to Nixon historian Jonathan Aitken. "The root cause of it was his drive, his ambition, his insecurities." Hutschnecker concluded that Dick thought he owed everything to his mother, including his great intelligence, achievement, and goals. His life was driven by a desire to show his mother that he was a nice son. He couldn't be a loser because that would entail disappointing his mother."

A crisis occurred in the fall of 1951, possibly resulting in the chest pain and near-blackout mentioned by Hutschnecker in his notes. "Dick is more mentally tired than I have ever seen him," Pat informed Helene. "The doctor told him he would have to get away and also take it easier." Hutschnecker advised Nixon to take regular doses of the therapeutic sunshine of his childhood. Pat took Dick on vacation to Sea Island, Georgia. "It was a real rest for Dick, but not long enough," she informed Helene. Following Christmas, Nixon traveled alone to Florida. On a previous trip, Senator George Smathers had connected him with a high school acquaintance, a Cuban American businessman called Charles "Bebe" Rebozo, who could take Nixon out on his boat. Rebozo and Smathers were well-known in the Capitol for providing recreational activities to senators from Florida. Smathers' close friends included John Kennedy and Lyndon Johnson. Nixon was not like other party politicians. "Don't ever send another dull fellow like that down here again," Rebozo reportedly told Smathers. "He doesn't drink whiskey, he doesn't chase women, he doesn't even play golf."

But, over time, Nixon and Rebozo formed a lasting bond. "He had a depth and genuineness about him that didn't show through because of his shyness, but I saw it," Rebozo said, recalling their first meeting. "I knew he'd return and we'd be pals. I can't explain why, other than to suggest that it was probably the attraction of opposites. He's a genius. I just bumble through.

"Bebe knew that I was somewhat of a loner, that if I wanted his opinion I'd ask for it," Nixon recalls. "He's never one that wanted to sit down at the throne and have me confide in him."

In spring 1952, the Nixons and Drowns traveled to Hawaii. Including Christmas break, it was Dick's fourth therapeutic trip in six months.

EVEN IF NIXON HAD CONCERNS ABOUT McCarthy, they did not prevent him from joining his committee—a seat the chairman created by replacing the insufficiently aggressive Senator Margaret Chase Smith. In his first Senate speech, Nixon engaged in some Red-baiting of his own, criticizing Harry Truman for removing General Douglas MacArthur. "The Communists and the stooges for the Communists are happy, because the president has given them exactly what they have been after: General MacArthur's scalp," he commented. Nixon pushed the US to escalate the Korean War and bomb China's supply lines.

However, Nixon was hardly a loutish partisan. In an exchange of letters, he defended the Berkeley school board's authority to host Paul Robeson, an accused Communist, at the local high school. "I do not believe that we should follow the example of the totalitarian nations through the suppression of a free expression of ideas," one critic said to Nixon. He gained press attention when, while using the committee's investigative powers to expose some of the Truman administration's corruption—officials had accepted fees, freezers, and mink coats from businessmen seeking favors—he declared that the Republican and Democratic national chairman, each of whom was implicated in various shady acts, should both resign. The evenhandedness would cost him—Republican chairman Guy Gabrielson survived and was barred from giving a keynote speech at the upcoming national convention in Chicago—but it would also help Nixon avoid a minor scandal when it was revealed that the Republican campaign committee had laundered a $5,000 donation for him with the assistance of a shady influence peddler.

The bug in Nixon's bowl was Earl Warren, who aspired to be president but despised the shady method of obtaining the title. In this, he resembled Eisenhower, and both were more sophisticated than they appeared. They had both survived destitute boyhoods—Warren in Bakersfield and Eisenhower in Abilene—and achieved success through steely purpose hidden under veneers of rectitude. Neither were ideologues. Each preferred to consider himself a statesman rising above the fray, both for political and personal reasons.

He "was a man who wanted everyone to support him when he was running for office, but never wanted to give anyone else any help when the other fellow was running....It was all for Warren," according to Earl Adams, a friend of Nixon's. "If he saw anyone coming on up from the ranks and developing power, he would devise ways to cut the fellow down."

Warren's strategy was to keep the California delegation united behind him, expecting that neither Eisenhower nor Taft would be selected on the first ballot in Chicago. But Nixon wanted Ike to secure the nomination, ideally with his assistance. Throughout the spring of 1952, Nixon had regular contact with the general's political commanders, including Dewey, Senator Henry Cabot Lodge Jr. of Massachusetts, Ike's campaign manager, and delegate hunter Herbert Brownell Jr., the most skilled Republican strategist of his time. It was all conditional, but they informed Nixon that if he acted as a "fifth column" in California, he stood a good chance of becoming the general's running mate.

California's seventy delegate candidates were to be chosen at the state's Republican primary election in June. Only New York's delegation was larger. Nixon couldn't defeat Warren with an Eisenhower slate because the governor was too powerful, owing too many favors, and had chits to trade. Furthermore, Nixon's supporters were divided. Some of his admirers, like Dana Smith, Roy Day, and Chotiner, backed Ike. Others, such as Bernard Brennan, respected Governor Warren as the party's leader. And a vociferous part of Nixon's team, including Herman Perry and Tom Bewley, supported Taft; many of them joined Representative Thomas Werdel of Bakersfield, who was gathering the state's conservatives to embarrass Warren, with whom they had been warring for years. "There were a few of us who had some actual principles and kept to them, knowing that we couldn't do anything with Nixon or Warren because neither had any true principles. "They were both open field runners," said

Keith McCormac, a Werdel organizer.

Given the chaos, Nixon's best option was to form a Solomonic coalition with Warren and Bill Knowland, another potential vice president. They agreed to work together to defeat the Werdel slate, each naming one-third of the state's delegates to the convention. Warren followed along because, according to custom, law, and honor, all of the delegates on the slate were bound to him as a cherished son unless he released them. Nixon was satisfied with the agreement, which allowed him to pursue his own agenda while doing what he could for Eisenhower. In a statement issued just before the June 3 primary, Nixon dismissed Warren's chances of obtaining the nomination and guaranteed California Republicans that "once Governor Warren releases the delegation, we shall be free to look over the field and select the man best qualified."

Warren-Nixon-Knowland won by a two-to-one margin. But Nixon quickly prodded the governor with another banderilla tactic: notifying his constituents that Warren's chances were slim and asking them, via a poll he mailed out, whether they chose Eisenhower or Taft as an alternative. When a few last-minute changes were made in the delegation, Brennan made sure the replacements were Nixon supporters. Despite Kyle Palmer's warning, Nixon was doing everything he could to derail Warren's ambitions.

Eisenhower's magnetism, along with Nixon's words, provided Ike with the necessary second victory. California's seventy votes were still legally tied to Warren in the nomination balloting, but in the critical credentials challenge that night—the victory Ike needed to secure those southern ballots—Californians voted sixty-two to eight to seat the Eisenhower delegates. It was a scathing struggle played out on national television, with an iconic scene of Taft's spokesman, Senator Everett Dirksen of Illinois, waving a finger at Dewey and declaring, amid tremendous booing, "We followed you before, and you led us to defeat."

As the delegates took a break for lunch on Friday, Ike's men conducted a meeting of several dozen party officials in a parlor at Eisenhower's headquarters in the Conrad Hilton. Some took off their coats, and many smoked cigarettes or cigars. The smoke-filled conversations reminded New Hampshire's Sherman Adams of "a Philadelphia ward committee discussing the selection of a candidate for alderman." Brownell and Dewey worked effectively, as if picking the running mate was an open topic, allowing numerous cheerleaders to espouse the merits of good gentlemen such as Taft and Dirksen. Only after the field had been whittled down did Dewey, who was chairing the conference, inquired, "What about Nixon?" and proceeded to answer his own question. They discussed briefly and voted; no one disagreed, and after congratulating themselves on their afternoon's labor, Brownell picked up the phone.

In the years to follow, Dick and Pat and their friends would recount stories about how astonished they were, and how Nixon was taken off guard—literally—by the phone call informing him that he had been chosen. "Wake up, Dick! "It's you," Hillings was supposed to have exclaimed after answering Brownell's call in Nixon's hotel suite. Pat was having lunch at the downstairs coffee shop with Helene Drown and Phyllis Chotiner. When the news came on the restaurant's screen, she took a piece of her sandwich out of surprise. Indeed, the final word must have shaken the gypsy and her knight. They had risen from obscurity to national prominence in six years.

However, they were not completely unprepared. Earlier that year, they had spent an evening discussing the vice presidency with the indefatigable Alice Roosevelt Longworth, who told them all about her father, who hated the job but was given the presidency when William McKinley was slain. And Nixon needed his nap since he had spent the night before in deep discussion, attempting to persuade his hesitant wife to accept Ike's proposal.

And then it occurred. Nixon hurriedly changed, bypassing a shower and shave, and went to see Ike for a little awkward fifteen-minute conversation. Will he join the crusade? Ike asked. "You bet," answered Nixon. He then made the long journey back to the convention hall, where he found the breathless Pat. "I'm amazed, flabbergasted, weak, and speechless," she told journalists. The band performed "Anchors Aweigh" when Nixon entered the hall. He penned sentences for a brief, forgettable victory speech while sitting with his Californians, who covered him from intrusive reporters and well-wishers. He was named by acclamation. The Californians cheered. Pat kissed him repeatedly.

Eisenhower had met with Taft to mend the party's schisms, and Nixon regarded it as his responsibility to advance the reconciliation process. Nixon's acceptance speech lavishly praised Taft and the Old Guard, leading some of Ike's supporters to believe he demonstrated too much independence and too little thanks. They were on the podium during primetime, Nixon holding Eisenhower's hand aloft and Pat smiling in a striking pattern dress with coin-like spots. Pat left the next morning for Washington, leaving Dick with the thousand political intricacies that required his attention.

Chapter 7: A Candidate for the Little Man

In one and a half hours of television, Richard Nixon did more than salvage his career; he reset the equation of American politics.

For eighty years, from the end of the Civil War to the outbreak of World War II, the Republican Party was recognized as a breeding ground for swinish businessmen and Wall Street financiers, according to its opponents. Republicans may appeal to the general population by conjuring the holy Lincoln, offering military heroes like Ulysses S. Grant and Teddy Roosevelt, or painting Democrats as dangerous radicals. However, as the Democratic Party absorbed the Populists in the 1890s, there was little debate in American politics as to who advocated for the little guy. Franklin Roosevelt championed "the forgotten man" and railed against "unscrupulous money-changers" and "financial oligarchies."

RUARK WAS NOT ALONE. Others saw the signs of realignment. In 1952, Whittaker Chambers wrote Witness, his autobiographical tale of descent, recantation, and redemption. His dismal embroideries resonated at a period when Albert Einstein warned of "general annihilation," High Noon was in theaters, and En attendant Godot was ready to make its Paris debut. An excerpt from Witness appeared in the Saturday Evening Post, which sold an additional half-million copies that week. It became a noir gospel for the right, a depiction of America emerging from adolescence and confronted with evil both at home and abroad.

Nixie, the kind and nice, was too cagey—had too exquisite a talent for political devilry—to pass up such a golden opportunity. He knew how to connect with the petit bourgeoisie, in part because he shared their origins, values, dissatisfactions, and animosity. "The Fifties were not the Eisenhower years, but the Nixon years," liberal columnist Murray Kempton would write after the decade had ended. They were the periods "when the American lower middle class in the person of this man moved to engrave into the history of the United States, as the voice of America, its own faltering spirit, its self-pity and its envy, its continual anxiety about what the wrong people might think, its whole peevish, resentful whine."

Nixon's actions contributed to hostility. When Hiss was convicted, he questioned the liberal meritocracy's patriotism in a speech sent to thousands of followers. "Men like Alger Hiss...come from good families, are graduates of our best schools," he remarked in an email. The mutual distrust would continue. Late in the decade, Nixon's advisers tasked Rita Hauser, a young New York lawyer who had been charmed to him, with polling East Coast intellectuals. She answered with a pessimistic outlook. "The net feeling as to Mr. Nixon's campaigns is that they did dupe, and thus were 'dishonest' or lacking in campaign due process," Hauser had written. "From this flows the strong feeling that Nixon is unprincipled, non-trustworthy, a man without a firm moral base."

Nixon's inherent opportunism liberated him from convention, according to political journalist William White, and "his antennae are remarkably acute—matchlessly acute among national politicians." His appeal was "the quintessence of the modern spirit of revolt from the aristocratic principle of the leader." It is this trait of being in tune with what ordinary people are thinking that gives him such an advantage."

Ike had spent four years of war restoring order and unity to his divided allies. He was confident. He knew how to lead, and through those seemingly endless mediations, he learned how to persuade and distribute his charm. He was one of the few military men who could transform battlefield reputation into political success. Korea needed to be fixed, and Ike appeared to be the man to do it, especially after he promised, in mid-October, "I will go to Korea."

However, the Communist danger remained in the headlines—Julius and Ethel Rosenberg would be executed the following summer—and Nixon was deployed by Eisenhower's managers to instill dread in people as a more respectable, temperate Joe McCarthy. The temperate part didn't come naturally. Nixon's childish enthusiasm during a World Series game they saw in New York astounded Brownell. The Yankees defeated the Brooklyn Dodgers in extra innings, leaving the ranting vice-presidential candidate exhausted and Brownell perplexed. Nixon brought the same zeal to the campaign, hitting out against "Adlai the Appeaser"—who had a "Ph.D." from Dean Acheson's cowardly college of Communist containment." In mid-October, the Republicans gave Nixon another primetime spot on national television to chastise Stevenson for testifying as a character witness for Hiss during the spy's

1949 trial. Nixon explained that he was not questioning Stevenson's devotion, but rather his judgment.

In late October, in Texarkana, the "Tricky" side of Dick made its most significant appearance when, with calibrated malevolence, he called Harry Truman and his colleagues "traitors to the high principles in which many of the nation's Democrats believe." Truman, Rayburn, and others were convinced Nixon had accused them of treason—and never forgave him. Truman called Nixon a "shifty-eyed goddamn liar," and Speaker Rayburn told colleagues that of all the guys he dealt with in Congress over the last half-century, none had such a cruel, deceptive, or hateful countenance as Nixon.

Ike won 55 percent of the popular vote to Stevenson's 44 percent, and 39 of 48 states and 442 electoral votes. Stevenson even lost Illinois, and Republicans managed to maintain slender majorities in both the House and Senate.

Nixon had no illusions about his role in Ike's win; he understood that the people had voted for a hero. As a joke, one day he switched places with a tall, skinny news reporter and laughed from the press bus as the newsman played his part, sitting next to Pat and waving to audiences who thought they were witnessing the real Nixon. Dick continued his pattern of escaping on Election Day, heading to the beach with Bill Rogers and playing touch football with a group of Marines. The results were later delivered to him and Pat at the Ambassador Hotel in Los Angeles. Aylett Cotton assisted an ailing Frank Nixon. "He didn't seem to show great jubilation over his son's election," the Nixon aide said. "It was more or less a tiring, grim satisfaction."

The "Inquiring Photographer" [sic] from the Washington Times-Herald caught Tricia on the street outside the Nixon residence. "He's always away," Tricia explained. "If he's that renowned, why can't he stay at home?"

The hostility between Nixon and the mechanisms through which American political leaders communicate would have far-reaching effects. It also provides insight into the man. Nixon's chaotic childhood left him desiring order. In his teenage public speaking competitions, he spoke out against opposition. His Quaker background gave him a strong feeling of privacy. His insecurity made him susceptible. The press was none of these things—snoopy, wild, and irreverent. Nixon was "so goddamn shy that it was just painful for him," according to Earl Mazo, a reporter for the New York Herald Tribune. "Newspaper men were part of an inquisition to Nixon. We were representatives of a hostile world, trying to tear him down and find out what he wanted to hide—in a personal way." It wasn't very political. It was aiming to depict him as a poor and clumsy youngster. "He was more than anything else."

According to James "Scotty" Reston, a New York Times reporter, "he was never one of the boys....He always had that sense that if people knew him, then they would not like him." "He had so much to hide, and he would never give of himself. Reporters sense that and they push."

Nixon had learned in his earlier elections that good publicity could be purchased by buying ad space in California newspapers or kneeling to powerful figures such as Kyle Palmer and the Chandlers. "Kyle allowed Nixon to think that Nixon could have special treatment—that he could have a kind of special deal," she recalled. The result was corrosive, and ultimately a disservice. It left Nixon with a jaded view of the game, believing that it was rigged and that newscasters were whores.

Nixon's fears were confirmed by the Hiss case. He had come to Congress, bravely shouldering and capably performing a patriotic duty, only to be mocked by left-wing periodicals, columnists and cartoonists. "In the Hiss days, aggressive and militant activity against Communism was very de trop," said newspaper executive and Eisenhower confidant William Robinson. "It was downright anti-liberal and put you in a very bad light at the Press Club bar." Nixon discovered that, while journalists claimed to value fairness and truth, as mortals, they desired influence and power. Nixon believed that his enemies on the editorial pages of the Washington Post and other liberal newspapers would never forgive him for proving them wrong about Alger Hiss, because he had not only triumphed, but humiliated them in the process.

Nixon was a practical man who took well-wishers' suggestions to schmooze and carouse with the press. He hosted reporters for drinks in his office and appeared at the press club bar. But he was terrible at small talk and seemed overly serious and awkward. "Nixon would phone and say, 'Let's go face the enemy,' indicating that he intended to go to the National Press Club. "There he would tease a drink in the bar, trying hard to be 'one of the boys,' among reporters dedicated largely to his extermination," recalled a sympathetic newsman, Walter Trohan. "These sessions did not help him."

"These newspaper guys just don't understand a guy that doesn't drink and chase women," Nixon told Lyman Brownfield, a law school classmate.

THEN CAME THE Checkers event, which reinforced Nixon's belief that he was held to a different standard. "Press men temperamentally and traditionally are skeptical and cynical," he'd claim. Nonetheless, "when it is a public official who has been in what to most of them is the contemptible business of Red hunting, this feeling is particularly strong."

Nixon had put his trust in Peter Edson and the other reporters who first inquired about his political slush fund. But then he watched, baffled, as a single dishonest headline in a liberal newspaper sparked national outrage. The extent and fury of the assault, the savagery of his interrogators, and the betrayal by those he thought were friends had seared the Nixons, pushing Dick to tears on several occasions and sending Pat, frightened, into solitude with the Drowns.

Following Nixon's Checkers speech, the Republican ticket surged in the polls; reporters grew tired of taunting Nixon, and the attention shifted back to Ike and Adlai. But a few commentators—just enough to irritate him—remained on Nixon's case. Herblock was a never-ending source of frustration. Nixon's attacks on Democratic "traitors" prompted a Post cartoon comparing Nixon to McCarthy, with both men wielding brushes and buckets of tar. The chipmunk-cheeked Nixon of early cartoons suddenly sported a five o'clock shadow, signaling the beginning of his change into the sewer-dwelling scoundrel of the many Herblock cartoons that followed. "It was the opportunist, the political thuggery in him," the cartoonist said years later.

Nixon had barely learned how to navigate the Capitol when he was stung by Pearson and retaliated in a letter to House colleagues in the summer of 1947, blasting the journalist as a "arch character assassin and truth distorter." So the game began. In 1952, Pearson slashed

Nixon many times per week. Some columns were accurate. Nixon's office had certainly intervened with the State Department to assist Dana Smith, the slush fund custodian, in avoiding a gambling obligation incurred at a Havana casino. He had also helped Smith get a $500,000 tax credit. And, certainly, Nixon lied when he told the nation at the Checkers speech that Pat was born on St. Patrick's Day. Her exact birth date was March 16. The columnist discovered favors Nixon's office had done. Many were routine constituency services, but one intercession—for an unscrupulous Romanian industrialist named Nicolae Malaxa—smelled of influence peddling. Malaxa, whose entry into the United States was barred by American immigration officials due to his past as a Nazi collaborator, had engaged Nixon's old legal partner, Tom Bewley, to assist him in obtaining US residency and federal funding to develop a pipeline plant in California. Bewley was promised "a substantial fee" if the facility was built, and he and Herman Perry were appointed officers and directors of the firm. Malaxa received assistance from Nixon's office, as one might expect.

The effect was cumulative and long-lasting. Other journalists picked up dubious claims, embellished over time, and repeated as facts in books and articles. "Some of the mud stuck," Nixon explained. "Many people who under no stretch of the imagination could be called politically partisan…wondered whether there was 'something wrong' as far as my personal integrity."

Mazo was surprised when, at the conclusion of the decade, he was offered a book deal to write a brief biography of the vice president. "I was a Democrat, as are most reporters. "And I despised Nixon," Mazo remembered. "I wanted to cut him up, but I wanted to do it honestly, so I started researching."

"I found out that so much of what I knew to be total fact, had been rated as fact, even written as fact, was just total horseshit," Mazo claimed. "At least half of the established facts concerning this individual were complete fabrications made up out of whole cloth. Never occurred. Never occurred. They began in a column and grew and grew.

In the abstract, Washington reporters realize that CEOs use vice presidents as hit men to keep their own cuffs clean. They understood that throughout the 1952 campaign, Nixon merely did what Ike wanted. Nonetheless, many were "blinded by their emotional attachment to Stevenson," Nixon stated. Adlai has his way with the shiv. But he was clever, literate, and well-protected by the reporters who covered him. "We all loved Adlai," Mazo added. Later in the decade, James Reston told an associate that Stevenson was "the only one who speaks with the voice of a philosopher, poet, and true leader." Their connection was insufficient to turn journalists against Ike, the popular hero, but it was more than enough to turn the press on the clumsy, beetle-browed Nixon.

THE CHECKERS SPEECH was Nixon's epiphany. It taught him how to outwit the press. He could appeal to voters directly on television. "He saw that night what television can do and he was in awe…he was absolutely spellbound," Ted Rogers told me afterwards. "He saw the ratings, and he changed. "He was the electronic man."

From that point forward, Nixon "didn't give a damn about the regular press," according to Rogers. If an errant reporter disrupted the motorcade or the press plane, Nixon would yell, "Fuck them." Let's go. "They're the enemy. We don't need them." The press caught up on this and responded. Nixon was upset and enraged when, following the debate over whether he had called Truman a "traitor," reporters began bringing tape recorders to his campaign rallies.

Nixon's closest advisers at the time—men like Rogers, Bassett, and Chotiner—all attributed painful changes in their boss's demeanor to this specific period in his life. The misery of the Hiss case combined with the agony of the financial issue weighed heavy. The new vice president retreated, lost faith in others, and viewed the world with distrust. "A serious young man," Bassett remarked, "became a political megalomaniac."

Chapter 8: The New Nixon

In the early evening of September 24, 1955, the increasing crowd of reporters and cameramen outside the Nixon residence on Tilden Street was woken from their mumbling and smoking. Pat and Tricia had appeared at the front entrance. Perhaps there was something to report. The nation was jolted that dreary Saturday by announcements informing people that Dwight Eisenhower had suffered a heart attack. The liberator of Europe, severely ill, lay gasping in an oxygen tent at a Denver hospital. Nixon, at forty-two, has a good chance of becoming president of the United States. As Pat and Tricia distracted the reporters, Nixon and Bill Rogers slid out the kitchen door and over a neighbor's grass to Bill's wife's Pontiac. "The coast was clear," Nixon recounted, "and we made it to the car in a run."

The Nixons had attended a wedding Saturday. They had no idea that Ike had resigned on his twenty-seventh hole of golf on Friday, made it through supper and an evening with friends before being struck about 2:30 a.m. The president had been in a bad mood for much of the year, exacerbated by the Quemoy and Matsu crisis, and preparations for a Geneva summit. The summit had gone well, but Ike struggled to get back into gear afterward. "The veins stood out on his forehead like whipcords," his doctor recounted, after the president's round of golf on Friday was cut short by signals from Secretary Dulles.

Eisenhower's seventy-four-year-old physician misdiagnosed the president, claiming dyspepsia. It wasn't until 2:30 that afternoon—5:30 p.m. in Washington, twelve hours after his coronary—that the 64-year-old president was transported to the hospital and the country was notified. The Nixon family had returned home. Pat was changing clothes, and Dick had picked up the newspaper, when the phone rang at 5 p.m.

Rogers had arrived in a taxi and found Nixon pallid, red-eyed, and dazed. They huddled in the den, with only a few moments to talk before the news spread around the globe. Dick realized he hadn't informed Pat. They entered the kitchen and told her what had happened. She implored them not to scare her girls.

There are few instances that speak to Nixon's marriage like this. Nixon did not engage his wife in his deliberations—or, at first, his thoughts—

after learning of Ike's heart attack. Pat's immediate reaction to the news was to think about her children.

The Nixon phone wouldn't stop ringing. Reporters arrived. The house was soon lit up with spotlights. This was Washington at its most macabre. Even if Ike survived, Nixon was now "heir to one of the greatest responsibilities and political opportunities ever presented to so young a man in the history of the Republic," the New York Times reported the next morning. They were "in a better position than anybody else to get the Republican nomination" in 1956, which is "if, as seems almost certain, the stricken President retires at the end of his first term."

Nixon felt a target pinned to his back. "My every move, gesture would be watched, interpreted and misinterpreted for the slightest sign that I was moving to 'take over,'" he'd recalled. He wanted space to ponder, so the back-door bolt led to the Rogers home in adjacent Bethesda, where they met with Jerry Persons, the White House liaison to Congress, and took calls from the president's staff on the Rogers kitchen phone.

With Attorney General Brownell out of the country, Deputy Attorney General Rogers was asked for opinion on a prospective delegation of authority. What did the Constitution state? "I haven't the faintest idea," Rogers stated. He advised calling a scholar. "We can't do that," Nixon responded. "If the vice president and the deputy AG don't know what the Constitution says, we will look like a couple of idiots." They searched the house and eventually discovered a copy in the Farmer's Almanac.

In the days that followed, Nixon demonstrated sagacity and self-control. Ike progressed but experienced unsettling setbacks. The president was weak, worried, and melancholy, and he spent weeks in bed. His advisers and associates, frightened and aware of the president's power, kept a wary eye on Nixon. Rumors kept the capital and its press corps busy.

Eisenhower issued notes directing Nixon to head cabinet and National Security Council sessions while reminding the vice president that Dulles had the power to manage foreign policy. The secretary of state was in post-summit negotiations, and the last thing he needed was Nixon's rant about Communists. But Ike's caution was unnecessary.

The vice president was carrying out his duties with compassion, declining to take the president's chair and talking with White House personnel and cabinet officials in their offices rather than summoning them to his.

"Throughout this whole terrible episode, your straightforward dignity and visible unselfishness and loyalty has been superb," remarked C. D. Jackson, a former White House aide. Nixon touched each chord with tact and stability, instilling confidence both domestically and internationally. Skeptics were converted. "Nixon is behaving like a model vice president," wrote Jack Anderson in a memo to Drew Pearson. Dulles, soothing a worried world, was grateful.

However, Nixon had been in Washington almost a decade. He was now a city dweller, aware of the political ramifications like everyone else. On October 3, Frank Jorgensen submitted a proposal to secure the California delegation for the 1956 convention, and a list of nominees for a "Nixon for President" committee. California Governor Goodwin Knight and Senator Bill Knowland, confident that Ike would retire, attempted to outflank Nixon. Rose Mary Woods took careful notes and relayed directions as Murray Chotiner, Kyle Palmer, and other supporters plotted and schemed on Nixon's behalf. Father John Cronin, an unpaid consultant and speechwriter, issued Nixon a lengthy paper in mid-October describing the actions he should take to secure the Republican nomination. Cronin cautioned against arrogance and encouraged stealth: "It is critical that the President and his immediate advisers believe your primary concern is to assist in the crisis, with no indications of independent excursions for political purposes."

Nixon felt confident. His promise to Pay to forsake politics was forgotten. On November 11, Ike was greeted warmly at National Airport upon his return to Washington. "The whole town was bustling with excitement," Nixon recounted. "The river glittered blue in the late fall sunlight, and thousands of smiling faces lined the streets of the nation's capital. "Washington can be a beautiful place."

A beautiful place, yes—sometimes. For at the nation's capital, the cynics' song rings true, and no good deed is unpunished. So Nixon quickly discovered. Eisenhower emerged from post-coronary depression eager to run for reelection—and to remove Nixon from the ticket.

In early October, Nixon visited Ike at a Denver hospital. "It hurt like hell, Dick," the president said, retelling the incident of his heart attack. The encounter with death compelled Eisenhower to ponder his succession. Nixon was usually on Ike's lists, but he was never number one. Eisenhower praised Nixon's skill during the fall crisis, but complained to others about Dick's immaturity. Nixon had an excessive amount of political hacking. Too much of an opportunist. He hadn't grown.

Eisenhower's ambiguity was highlighted in a letter he wrote to Nixon that summer. As he went for the Geneva conference, Ike outlined Nixon's responsibilities, cautioned him against overreach, and directed him to follow Adams' lead. "Dear, Dick. I hope you will hold a Cabinet meeting while I am gone. I would also hope that you would have the weekly [congressional] 'leaders' meeting," Eisenhower wrote. "Of course, if the majority of the individuals concerned would prefer to omit one of these meetings, I do not expect you to embarrass yourself by insisting on it."

So Nixon was stunned when, on the day after Christmas, Ike brought him to a White House meeting and offered that, instead of serving as vice president, he spend his second term in the cabinet. It would be beneficial for him, Eisenhower stated. Nixon would gain executive experience by leading the Pentagon or another large department.

The suggestion made sense. William Howard Taft and Herbert Hoover ascended to the White House through cabinet positions, whereas Martin Van Buren was the last vice president to replace a healthy president in 1837. Nixon had never managed anything larger than his office crew. Riding herd on the joint chiefs, defusing interservice rivalries, and signing off on weapons purchases was a significant improvement from hounding Rose Woods to keep up with the mail. He would resemble a young executive rather than Ike's hatchet guy. As the weeks passed, Eisenhower sweetened the bargain by also offering Dulles the position of secretary of state.

However, Nixon realized—as Eisenhower should have, must have—that the president's heart attack had warped public opinion. By reassigning his vice president to the cabinet, Ike would be indicating that he questioned Nixon's ability to accept the post in dangerous times. That's how the press and public would interpret the move. In fact, Eisenhower informed Nixon—in a moment that appears designed to embarrass the vice president—that the wise play may be to remain on, betting that a sexagenarian with a poor heart would not live until 1960. "I can only assume that if he puts it this way, this must be his way of saying he'd prefer someone else," Nixon said to Republican Party Chairman Hall.

Nixon was right. Hall understood exactly what Ike preferred. The president invited him to the Oval Office to discuss possibilities. What about Ohio Gov. Frank Lausche, a Democrat and a Catholic? They would create political history. Or Robert Anderson, a conservative Texas Democrat, former secretary of the Navy, and presidential ambassador to the Middle East whose abilities Eisenhower often praised?

It was 1952, redux. Ike wanted Nixon gone, but he left it up to him to slash his own throat to minimize the political damage. Those scars had never entirely healed. Nixon, who was always sensitive, insecure, and watchful, detected a trap—most likely created by Adams, Clay, and others. Nixon's humiliation was not yet complete, as his suffering became public. He was ignored when Ike invited his senior political lieutenants to a meal and talk about the 1956 campaign. "Ike went along" with Nixon's adversaries. "If the fellows could organize [the coup], it was alright with him," said Hall's deputy, Lou Guylay, summarizing the vice president's time in purgatory.

Ike's handling of the vice president shocked Senator John Kennedy, Nixon's friend and future opponent. Eisenhower "won't stand by anybody," Kennedy warned Arthur Schlesinger. "He is quite chilly and vain. In reality, he's crap." Nixon was in "absolutely indescribable anguish," according to Bryce Harlow. Tension was evident. Nixon was in and out of hospitals, whining about stress, drinking, popping uppers and downers, and fleeing to Florida for therapeutic expeditions on Rebozos yacht. During one long retreat from Washington, Nixon used Woods as a conduit to keep Hutschnecker updated on his progress. He complained about experiencing "up and down" phases, even on vacation. "On Wednesday, which was the 8th day here, I did not feel so hot." His uneasiness lingered, whether he worked hard or forced himself to relax. "I don't see any relation to how you feel to what you do."

Hutschnecker responded, via Woods, that "the lack of an immediate aim at this moment is problematic. He can't construct. He's not sure which way to go. This is a fatal condition of frustration." He urged Nixon not to become overly reliant on the narcotics, and the dangers of mixing them with alcohol. "The danger of these other things" is that they "create something similar to mental depression. You grow listless. "We want a state of relaxation, not this other listlessness," Hutschnecker stated. Additionally, "if you are very tense and you take another drink I am afraid you would lose control."

Eisenhower never liked me. "He's always been against me," Nixon told Hall. But he refused to crawl, and Ike dared not fire him, especially after Nixon's friends planned public displays of adoration among voters in early primary states. In New Hampshire, where Senator Styles Bridges was an enemy of Sherman Adams and thus a supporter of Nixon, an orchestrated write-in effort netted Nixon more than 22,000 votes.

Finally, in late April, Nixon reached his breaking point. He produced withdrawal notes, and as he expected, word spread to Hall and others. Consternation arose. Hall confronted Ike and told Nixon to discontinue the Eeyore act. Nixon requested an appointment, formally notified Eisenhower that he intended to remain on the ticket, and Ike appeared happy. Instead of posing with Nixon, the president sent Hagerty to deliver the news.

In the end, the Republican delegates chose Ike as their nominee, with Nixon as his running mate and possible successor. After seven months as the presidential piñata, Nixon lived to earn the prize. However, there was little celebration. In line with that unpleasant spring and summer, Frank Nixon's death drew his son away from the Republican convention in San Francisco. Dick flew to Whittier, where, in this most painful hour, the press exposed the depth of its hostility for Nixon and earned a little more of his. To ensure that the family was not exaggerating things for sympathy, the reporters sent one of their own to the sickroom to confirm that Frank was actually dying. Nixon agreed to let them do it. Jim Bassett was impressed by Nixon's dissociation while on the death watch with his boss and listening to Frank's final gasps. Dick flew back to San Francisco, where he delivered his acceptance speech and inaugurated the campaign. He returned a few days later and was present on September 4, when his father died. Hannah maintained her composure. She "put her little head down, said her prayers, grit her teeth together, and that was it," Nixon's old Whittier secretary, Evlyn Dorn, would recall.

That fall, Ike had good prospects. The decade had turned for the better. Consumer culture flourished and the economy boomed. "The U.S. is more prosperous than ever before," Time declared. Europe and Japan were rebuilding, but China was still hiding behind its bamboo barrier. Ike informed a friend that while the United States would confront competition for economic primacy one day, there was nothing to worry about just now. Americans manufactured their own steel, automobiles, telephones, and televisions. Labor demanded more salaries and benefits, while management shrugged, agreed, and walked to the golf course. The vehicles on the roadways were gigantic, finned behemoths propelled by guzzling V8 engines. Gas was a quarter per gallon. Boomers would remember their childhoods as happy times. Or at least white kids would.

Stevenson highlighted the possibility of Ike dying in office on the day of the election, apologizing for the "distasteful" duty (but still going on). "Every piece of scientific evidence we have, every lesson of history and experience, indicates that a Republican victory tomorrow would mean that Richard Nixon would probably be President of this country within the next four years," Stevenson warned the nation's citizens. "I say frankly, as a citizen more than a candidate, that I recoil at the prospect of Mr. Nixon as custodian of this nation's future, as guardian of the hydrogen bomb, as representative of America in the world, as Commander in Chief of the United States armed forces."

Nixon campaigned in thirty-six states in a DC-6, full of his usual frenzied enthusiasm. He had wooed reporters with over fifty press conferences, determined to dispel the "horror image" of a gutter-dwelling hatchet guy. His typical anti-Communism was set aside in favor of "a non-polemical, balanced discussion, with no comments on Democrats as such, no figures of subversives purged from government, etc.," according to an internal campaign memo. He would engage with academia and churches, broadcast his support for civil rights, and seduce pundits. The idea was to make his listeners think: "This is a sound, thoughtful, mature, statesmanlike approach. "Surely we have nothing to fear from such leadership if Providence decides to shorten our President's life."

"We had to show the country that he didn't have horns," one assistant explained. However, The New Yorker noted that it was difficult to clothe Marilyn Monroe as Mother Hubbard while maintaining the romantic sizzle. Nixon "has lately been laboring with great zeal to remove any possible reasons for being unloved," reported Rovere from Washington. "There are some people here who think that the new Nixon is an authentic creation."

There were fissures in the veneer. When his staff organized his presentation before a group of hostile student editors at Cornell University, Nixon returned to his plane and burst in fury. "He went for me like a caged animal," Ted Rogers recalled. "He was shouting at me; screaming at me; [they] had to pull him off." Mutiny rumors circulated as morale plummeted. Bassett addressed Nixon. "What scares the hell out of me is that you would blow sky high over a thing as inconsequential as this," he informed his manager. "What in goddamn would you do if you were president and get into a really bad situation?"

Despite being witnessed by the press, the incident was not widely covered. Finally, the method proved successful. News reporters referred to his "maturity." Stevenson complained that the "new Nixon" had "put away his switchblade" and "now assumes the aspect of an Eagle Scout."

Nixon took the oath of office for a second term on January 20, 1957, in the East Room of the White House, which was mostly empty. Senator Bill Knowland, the Republican leader, swore him in, and Chief Justice Warren administered the oath to Eisenhower. (Had the Californians been armed with rapiers, the day could have ended in Shakespearian bloodshed.) Pat stood by Dick's side, with Hannah, Julie, and Tricia watching. Then they all went to the dining room for sweet buns and coffee. It was a Sunday, Lord's Day, and the speeches and pomp had been postponed until Monday, when news cameras caught the president's grandson David stealing an enraptured glimpse at Julie as they stood in the reviewing box at the inauguration procession. He was attracted by the black eye she had from a sledding mishap that week. They married in 1968.

IKE SOON had the Nixons traveling. Nixon was flown to Africa in March, when he met Reverend Martin Luther King Jr. while attending Ghana's independence ceremonies. The young civil rights leader urged Nixon to speak out against segregation. Ike's top priorities were to maintain peace and prosperity. But, just as McCarthyism had presented a moral challenge during their first term, the emergence of a tremendous civil rights movement would put Eisenhower and his vice president to the test in their second. In each situation, Ike avoided confrontation as much as possible, relying on steady progress and the goodwill of the American people. In both cases, gradualism would fail, forcing him to take a more assertive posture. And Nixon? He delayed his feet in the McCarthy battle, but when it came to civil rights, he would take the lead.

Chapter 9: The Desolate Night of Man's Inhumanity

The African American struggle for justice dates back to the founding of the Republic; to the abolitionists of the early nineteenth century; to the 180,000 black troops who helped end slavery by serving in the Union Army; to the sorrows of Reconstruction; and to an abominable Supreme Court decision—Plessy v. Ferguson—which upheld segregation in 1896. In the early twentieth century, a few black leaders and white liberals fanned the flame, but a southern Democratic-dominated Congress failed to implement anti-lynching legislation, safeguard black voting rights, or ensure fair housing and employment prospects.

The Second World War, with its ruthless use of manpower, reenergized the civil rights movement. Thousands of black families relocated north to work in the factories. They bought property in New York, Chicago, Detroit, and other cities, crowded schools, and used their voting rights. Millions of African Americans served, including many on critical combat missions. And after the war was done, having bled to defeat racial supremacists abroad, blacks north and south were in no hurry to bow down to bigots at home.

Following the war, the revived movement took three paths: through the courts, Congress, and public protests that turned streetcar lines, lunch counters, buses, and schools into battlegrounds for freedom. The New Deal's social programs had enticed millions of black Americans to join the Democratic Party, and Harry Truman had issued an order to desegregate the military forces, but the first tangible successes in all three areas occurred during the Eisenhower-Nixon administration. A Republican president, a Republican attorney general, a Republican chief justice, and a Republican-Northern Democratic alliance in Congress reacted to civil rights advocates' cry of conscience and unwavering fortitude. In the Eisenhower administration's councils, Richard Nixon was a proponent of equality.

When it came to settled law, Ike fulfilled his responsibilities. He carried out Truman's directive to desegregate the armed services, even on Southern military posts, where squads of soldiers worked on weekends, painting over the "whites only" signs and presenting their comrades with a fait accompli on Monday morning. The federally run District of Columbia and Veterans Administration buildings were desegregated. When the Supreme Court issued the Brown decision, which outlawed segregation in public schools, the president swallowed his disapproval and enforced the ruling.

Ike was unhappy with Brown's decision. He informed his secretary, Ann Whitman, that he would have preferred a more gradual approach, first desegregating graduate schools, then colleges, and finally public secondary and elementary schools.

"As you know, the reason I so earnestly support moderation in the race question is because I believe two things," he wrote to Atlanta newspaper editor Ralph McGill. "The first is that unless America realizes the concept of individual dignity and equality before the law, we will not be fully deserving of our boundless opportunities. Coercive compliance alone cannot achieve 100% compliance in areas where public opinion is strongly opposed. "This generalization was true under the carpet-bagging government of the South, under the Prohibition Amendment and the Volstead Act, and it is still largely true within the four deep South states."

Eisenhower sought unanimity and enraged civil rights leaders by labeling them as "extremists" with white supremacists. But, as time passed and he experienced the South's unwavering hatreds, the president found himself driven, against his will, into a more aggressive position. He did not blow a moral trumpet. However, his judicial appointees were courageous and excellent, and the decisions they issued worked in his favor. And, despite being stripped of vital powers by the Democratic Congress, Ike's two civil rights measures served as templates for subsequent major legislation.

Eisenhower's political problems with civil rights were, to a large measure, his own fault: he insisted on nominating individuals of high principle to the Department of Justice, the Supreme Court, and the federal courts in the South. Chief Justice Warren, Attorney General Herb Brownell, and federal justices Elbert Tuttle, John Minor Wisdom, Simon Sobeloff, and Frank Johnson all shared attributes such as integrity, courage, and a strong sense of justice. Ike saw the political advantage of portraying himself as a hostage of circumstances and harbored his own doubts, but he had numerous opportunities to reverse course on civil rights and never did. Following the Brown decision (which prompted 101 senators and representatives, all but two of whom were Democrats, to sign a "Southern Manifesto" in support of segregation), Eisenhower appointed two northerners to the Supreme Court, John Harlan and William Brennan, who were civil rights advocates.

Toward the end of 1955, Brownell directed his aides to develop a civil rights measure. The Justice Department need legal tools to investigate crimes such as the Till lynching, protect voting rights, and enforce school and university desegregation. After much haggling with the White House, the law was divided into four sections. Part I established a Civil Rights Commission to investigate discrimination; Part II established a civil rights division within the Justice Department; Part III empowered the federal government to sue, seek injunctions, and win contempt charges in a variety of civil rights cases; and Part IV included specific voting rights protections. In cabinet sessions, while others were skeptical, Nixon supported Brownell.

Nixon's initial contribution to the passing of the 1957 civil rights act occurred at a critical parliamentary juncture—the time Congress convened in January.

The South was known for ingenuity. For decades, southern voters had been electing Democrats to the House and Senate and returning them year after year, allowing them to build power through seniority. Many became chairman, eager to incorporate civil rights legislation into their panels. The ultimate line of defense was in the Senate, where a long-standing distrust of arrogant majorities necessitated a two-thirds vote to stop debate before the Senate could proceed with a roll call. As long as southerners stayed together, they had enough votes to filibuster and debate a bill indefinitely.

The Senate governed itself and, theoretically, could change the number of votes required to break a filibuster. However, the South had the benefit of a parliamentary refuge, as the rules could only be amended by majority vote at the start of a Congress—otherwise, it required an almost impossible two-thirds tally. And, because one-third of the senators were chosen at once, the southerners argued that the Senate was a permanent body that was always in session. The filibuster would continue—unless Vice President Nixon, who was sitting in the chair and presided over the Senate, issued a ruling stating otherwise.

For a politician with national ambitions, the outcome was unknown. Ike had won Texas, Virginia, Florida, and other southern states—and Nixon would enrage white southerners if he overturned the filibuster. Southern blacks who were prevented from voting would be unable to express their gratitude.

So goodness would be its own reward, together with any contribution a virtuous deed made to the perception of a "new" Nixon. He gave it a lot of consideration, had a eureka moment, and got out of bed to write down his decision. He did the right thing. When Congress convened and the civil rights movement proposed new rules, Nixon issued an advisory opinion stating that the Senate was a new body and could amend the rules with a simple majority vote.

It was a "thunder striking" moment, Time reported. The southern leaders were forced to scramble. With much arm-twisting, Majority Leader Lyndon Johnson of Texas and Senator Richard Russell of Georgia gathered fifty-five votes to table the resolution. However, that was fifteen votes less than the South had obtained the last time the Senate voted on the filibuster. Southerners had been warned of the consequences if they continued to abuse their status. Russell stopped the tactic, and civil rights leaders declared the day "historic."

Nixon had announced himself. No other administration official besides Brownell would match the vice president's current level of work on the bill.

Two Republican presidential candidates, Nixon and Minority Leader Bill Knowland, were now shepherding the legislation and courting black voters in Electoral College powerhouses like New York, California, Illinois, and Pennsylvania. However, the top Democratic candidates, John Kennedy and Lyndon B. Johnson, were competing for Solid South support by proposing gutting amendments. Both voted to send the bill to Eastland's abattoir. To entice others, Johnson offered committee assignments, labor support, and, to western Democrats, southern votes for a federal water and power project.

Russell launched the floor debate by attacking Part III as a despotic "devil's broth"—an "instrument of tyranny" masquerading as a voting rights measure, giving the federal government broad new powers to "put black heels on white necks." When pressed by the press if Russell's allegations were true, Eisenhower shocked the civil rights movement by admitting that he "didn't completely understand" what the measure would achieve and inviting the senator to the White House to explain it.

King's advice guided Nixon's decisions on the bill. They met in June at Nixon's Capitol office. "The Vice President was highly impressed with Reverend King and believes the President would appreciate chatting with him. He is not, he claims, a man who believes in violent and vengeful pro-Negro measures, but rather supports an evolutionary but progressive march forward," wrote White House staffer Max Rabb to Sherman Adams. It was a heartening affirmation for King, whose status had alienated several elder civil rights leaders.

After seeing Nixon's work in legislative wrestling that summer, King returned the compliment. "Let me say before closing how deeply grateful all people of goodwill are to you for your assiduous labor and dauntless courage in seeking to make the Civil Rights Bill a reality," stated Mr. King. "This is unquestionably an expression of your commitment to the highest commandment of the moral law. It also reflects your political knowledge...With guys like you in such significant positions in our country, I am confident that we will soon rise from the dark and dismal night of man's inhumanity to man into the bright and glittering daybreak of freedom and justice for all."

The press concurred. "Through the fight," the magazine Time observed, "Vice President Nixon punched hard for a meaningful bill." But the most reliable indicator of Nixon's effectiveness may have come from Russell, who caustically predicted on the Senate floor that, with the 1960 election just around the corner, Nixon would continue to press the administration "to apply the great powers of the law to the Southern states at such places, in such time, and manner as the NAACP, of which the Vice President is the most distinguished member, may demand."

Russell once told a pal he planned to keep segregation for two hundred years. His summer triumphs seemed like Pyrrhic victories now. In the Little Rock showdown, he sent a crazed telegram to the White House accusing Eisenhower of using "strong armed totalitarian police state methods...copied from the manual issued by Hitler's storm troopers" against "inoffensive and peaceable American citizens," squandering any moral high ground he had claimed during the Senate debate.

Eisenhower spoke to the nation on television. The country, having seen the president's forbearance and heard his cry for justice, turned against the South. Ike was behaving like Lincoln's heir. Black Americans' civil rights would be preserved, even if it meant using rifles and bayonets. "The alternative to supporting the law in such a situation is to acquiesce in anarchy, mob rule, and incipient rebellion," Eisenhower warned Mississippi Democrat Senator John Stennis.

Nixon supported Ike. The president may have saved the Little Rock children from a brutal lynching, Nixon told a press conference. In the fight for black Americans' rights, "there is, here, a very real moral issue," he stated. Ike had fulfilled his duty protecting the country from constitutional anarchy.

Nixon's loyalty was not without consequences. He had gone too far with some of his fans, who, like him, were looking forward to the 1960 election. He "has a good chance of picking up a lot of convention votes in the southern block, but such statements will make it hard for those who wish to support him to do so," a Republican from Florida said. "He could have let Ike take the rap on this one down here and save a lot of good votes that he might need."

Chapter 10: The Field of Pending Battle

It is difficult to pinpoint a single day or event that marked the start of the paroxysm known as "the Sixties." The Montgomery bus boycott and the collapse of Dien Bien Phu were forerunners of seismic events to come. The Little Rock crisis was another tremor. Elvis Presley dominated the pop charts that summer, while Jack Kerouac's Beat classic On the Road was published. However, if one had to choose a moment that "forever separates the old from the new"—as an NBC commentator proclaimed at the time—it could easily be the evening of October 4, 1957. Ike was in Gettysburg, preparing for his fifth round of golf that week. Millions of his countrymen were at home, watching the premiere of Leave It to Beaver, a sugary television depiction of American life. But high above, orbiting the planet every 96 minutes, was a silver Russian beach ball singing beep beep beep in the key of A-flat at 18,000 mph.

KENNEDY was, in many respects, Nixon's antithesis. He was wealthy, a playboy, charismatic, and Harvard-educated, and an obliging press obscured his less desirable attributes. The two men shared enough characteristics—demanding fathers, aloof moms, the death of brothers, navy duty in the South Pacific, and a desire for glory—to form a bond. "Poor brave Jack is about to perish. "Oh God, don't let him die," Nixon pleaded as Kennedy escaped death on an operating table in 1954. Four years later, he informed a former staffer, Christian Herter Jr., that he could not campaign for him in the Massachusetts attorney general race since Kennedy was competing for reelection to the Senate that year. Nixon stated that the press would expect him to endorse Kennedy's Republican rival, but he would not. "I know Kennedy," Nixon stated, "and I have a high esteem for him. "That would be difficult for me."

The Kennedys had fewer scruples and plotted to bring down Nixon's main strategist. Murray Chotiner was subpoenaed, taken before a Senate committee, and interrogated by Robert F. Kennedy, the committee attorney and senator's brother, on allegations that he used his influence on Nixon to solicit high-paying, disreputable clients. Evidence of influence peddling was present and embarrassing, albeit not proven criminal. Nixon released Chotiner, and he was blacklisted in national politics. Nixon would be without a key counsel throughout his 1960 presidential campaign. Chotiner had outlived his usefulness.

JOHN KENNEDY FACED SIGNIFICANT POLITICAL OBSTACLES. He was young—he turned forty in May 1957, and his wife Jacqueline was twenty-eight in July—and a Roman Catholic. His health was questionable, his womanizing was well known in political circles, and his performance in Congress was disappointing. Liberals criticized his bleak stance on civil rights. His father, Joe, a corsairing millionaire, had embarrassed himself by advocating appeasement in the face of Nazi aggression while serving as the United States ambassador to Great Britain prior to World War II. After the war, Joe and his family loved Joe McCarthy.

However, when Adlai Stevenson left the decision of his running mate to the Democratic convention in 1956, Kennedy had waged a lively, unconventional campaign and nearly won the election. The experience persuaded Joe, Jack and Bobby that obstacles could be overcome.

For Kennedy, Sputnik's beeps were like manna. Ike appeared impervious on the matter of national security. The Democrats could now launch an attack from the right, claiming that the doddery old general had left the country exposed. Nixon quickly recognized the threat. At the NSC meeting on October 10, after hearing CIA director Dulles downplay the Soviet triumph and Ike expressing his joy with the US space program, Nixon gave a dose of reality, urging his colleagues to brace themselves for a political inquisition. Things got worse before they got better. The Vanguard rocket, intended as the American response to Sputnik, rose feebly for a few feet before exploding on its launch platform in December.

Nixon's march to the Republican nomination was marked by difficult ascents, humiliating stumbles, and subsequent displays of tenacity. His first big break bordered on catastrophe. In the spring of 1958, a mob ambushed his convoy in Caracas, Venezuela, disrupting his otherwise routine trip to Latin America.

Dick and Pat had left National Airport on April 27, a cold and dreary day. "We'll see you in three little weeks," Julie told them. In Uruguay, there were anti-Nixon protests. "Initially, I was unconcerned about this. "Every country has crackpots, Communists, and other America-haters," he recalled. By the time they reached Peru, the "crackpots" had formed. At a welcome reception at the American embassy, Nixon was advised that the next day, a hostile mob would approach him at the University of San Marcos. The United States ambassador outlined the vice president's options. If Nixon fled, the United States could be humiliated. If he charged ahead, he may earn points for daring, but he might also ignite a violent clash, for which he would be held responsible. "It was a momentary feeling of unreality," Nixon recalled. In the nearby Great Hall, Lima's aristocracy were seen dancing, conversing, munching, and sitting. The laughter and occasional wisps of talk filled the room where my associates and I sat so seriously, assessing the field of upcoming war."

Nixon exited his vehicle at San Marcos and, accompanied by Sherwood, some local police officers, and his interpreter Vernon Walters, stepped into a shouting, sign-waving mob. "I want to talk to you," the vice president yelled. The crowd initially gave way, but then its organizers regained control. "Mr. Vice President, they are throwing some stones and fruit at us," Walters informed him. "I know," Nixon said. "Our exit has to be slow and dignified." A pebble cracked one of Sherwood's front teeth. Another peeked over Nixon's shoulder. They backed away.

"By now I was excited, of course, and I felt the excitement of battle," Nixon recalled. "I stood up in the back of my convertible, with Sherwood holding my knees to keep me from collapsing, and I shouted to be heard above the crowd: 'You are cowards! "You're afraid of the truth!"

The American correspondents in Nixon's entourage wrote flattering reports, and Eisenhower sent a cable of congratulations. U.S. ambassador Theodore Achilles, a career diplomat, wrote to Nixon: "I express my deep regret at having to recommend your exposing yourself to such unpleasantness and possible danger, but I would certainly do it again, and with more certainty than before, now that I have seen how you handled it...."'"The reporters and I couldn't help but admire you.

Nixon and his entourage traveled to Ecuador, Colombia, and Venezuela. Two days before arriving in Caracas, Nixon learned that the CIA had discovered rumblings of an assassination plan. On May 13, a large gathering greeted him at the airport in Venezuela. "Mr. Vice President, they're not friendly," the interpreter said. Demonstrators spit on them from a balcony and a nearby barrier as the pair stood at attention for the Venezuelan national anthem. Dick had been spit on in Peru, "but now Pat was having to submit to this filthy indignity, and this second baptism for me was far worse than the first," he remembered. "If the sky wasn't so clear and the day so bright you might have thought it was raining." Nixon decided to destroy his suit. Pat's outfit was soiled, and Sherwood was enraged, throwing an elbow at a demonstrator. Pat stretched across a barricade and softly grabbed a young woman's hand. The girl ducked aside, stunned and somewhat embarrassed.

Nixon was supposed to conduct a wreath-laying ceremony at a statue of Simon Bolivar, but a barrier on a vast city street brought his caravan of limos (some borrowed from a local funeral parlor) to a standstill. "Things began to happen," he recalled. "Here they come," Sherwood announced.

Pat sought to console the Venezuelan minister's wife, who was nearly in tears. The Secret Service detachment sprinted alongside the cars, pushing the demonstrators away. "Many were obviously teenagers. Mostly boys, with a few girls. "But they all had a look of pure hatred," Nixon said. "And interspersed through the youngsters were the tough case-hardened Communist operatives." The automobile began to rock. Sherwood and another agent drew guns. "I think we'll have to get some of these sons of bitches," Sherwood was saying. "No," Nixon replied. Unless they pull him out of the automobile. "If it got that bad, I knew it all would be lost anyway," he told me.

And suddenly, like cavalry, Venezuelan police broke through the traffic gridlock. The press vehicle and automobiles darted into an open lane and accelerated away. Dick and Pat took stock of their situation in the courtyard of the American embassy, which was guarded by Marines. "There was no great emotional reunion," Hughes recounted. "Just an…'Are you okay?' 'Yes, are you okay?'…sort of a situation." Hughes was more upbeat. "This is American soil," he said, "and a little bit of heaven."

Only afterward, away from the press and embassy officials, did the Nixons express their dread to one another. "That's when they realized it was a near-death experience," their daughter Julie explained.

According to press accounts from Lima and Caracas, the vice

president remained calm under fire while defending his country's reputation. Nixon was overjoyed by the enthusiasm of the gathering, headed by Ike, that gathered at National Airport to welcome him back to Washington.

The fall was as foul as the spring was sweet. The 1958 election was a disaster for the Republicans, undoing all of the party's postwar gains and leaving it demoralized and outnumbered to a level not seen since Franklin Roosevelt's first term. The Sputnik controversy was followed by a mid-term recession, growing unemployment, farm-related problems, and allegations of corruption at federal institutions. Sherman Adams was accused of accepting a vicuna coat and other presents from Bernard Goldfine, a New England industrialist. Eisenhower couldn't bring himself to fire his chief of staff, so Nixon and others were sent to persuade Adams to fall on his sword. Nixon despised personal confrontations. Ike noted that telling Adams to go was "the most difficult single assignment I undertook" for him.

In the fall of 1957, Knowland said he would run for governor, regardless of Knight's ambitions. The choice was haughty and terrible. To avoid a destructive primary, Nixon and newsman Kyle Palmer forced Knight into running for the now-open Senate seat instead. The governor resisted until Republican contributors threatened to withhold campaign cash. It was all played out in public, with Mrs. Knight and Mrs. Knowland remarking that Goodie had "a macaroni spine." Among the shenanigans, Knowland supported a right-to-work legislation that unions opposed. Propelled by organized labor and the faltering economy, Attorney General Edmund "Pat" Brown defeated Knowland by a million votes, and Knight lost the Senate race by nearly the same percentage. The Republican Party, which had dominated California politics for decades, was crushed. Nixon might console himself—after all, two competitors had stabbed daggers into one another's throats—but he now had to fight for his own state in 1960. "They just pulled the rug from under Knight," Brown cheerfully recounted. "Mrs. Knight despised both Knowland and Nixon. There was much animosity in the Republican Party. "Everybody hated everyone." Nixon's melancholy was not improved when he tripped on the ice (again) that winter and fractured two ribs.

The Republicans took one taste of champagne from the 1958 results—

but even that was ashes for Nixon. In a battle of robber baron children, Nelson Rockefeller, a bon viveur, arts patron, and presidential candidate, defeated Averell Harriman and was elected governor of New York. Nixon's Republican nomination adversary was no longer the plodding Knowland, but "Rocky"—a dynamic extrovert whose name was linked with unlimited money, and who participated in the criticism of the administration's laziness. "Bets at even money are already being made that the vice president is through and that the 1960 Republican nomination is Mr. Rockefeller's," wrote Richard Rovere in The New Yorker. Nixon was particularly upset when Rockefeller flew to a family ranch in Venezuela for a post-election vacation. Rocky cabled his support for Nixon during his trip to Caracas. He now told the Latin American press, "No tengo nada que ver con Nixon."

THEN, SUDDENLY, Nixon was summiting. During talks in Geneva, the Soviet Union and the United States agreed to hold "exhibitions" of each other's cultural, economic, and scientific achievements in the spirit of the World's Fair. High-ranking Soviet ministers visited the pavilion's opening in New York in the summer of 1959, and Nixon was tasked with launching the American display in Moscow.

PUBLICITY AND BUILD-UP HAVE BEEN EXCEPTIONALLY WELL RECEIVED EVERYWHERE I'VE GONE. This is the most important trip of your life. Nixon's luck held. He had been invited "to extend the usual social courtesies," he'd recall, but "what caught and held the interest of the world was a series of bizarre circumstances which ran the gamut of high drama to comic opera."

Nixon performed his typical iron-clad cramming for the trip, and a second plane packed with journalists accompanied him to Moscow. He had trouble sleeping the first night and got away shortly after daybreak to explore a farmers' market with Sherwood and a Soviet police interpreter. His first visit with Khrushchev established the tone for their discussions: he discovered the premier fondling a model of a Soviet rocket, much like Charlie Chaplin did with a globe in The Great Dictator.

Stop sending Soviet tanks into West Berlin. His tantrums and tirades, coming from a leader with nuclear weapons, were intended to unnerve Western opponents.

Nixon had been briefed on 132 issues. Anyway, "all the briefings in the world could not have prepared me for Khrushchev's unexpected, unpredictable conduct," according to him. The premier's initial shot was typical: a graphic criticism of Congress' ratification of a "captive nations" resolution calling for the freedom of Eastern Europe. If the United States desired constructive discussions, he advised Nixon not to poison the terrain. "People should not use the toilet while eating," Khrushchev warned. "Fresh shit stinks."

The official record removed the remark, as well as Nixon's retort: "The Vice President noted that he had also grown up on a farm and that he knew that if anything smelled stronger than horse shit, it was pig shit." Mr. Khrushchev responded, "Human shit smells the worst."

Nixon didn't fare badly—or much better—when he and Khrushchev continued their conversation a few minutes later at an exhibit of a "typical" American kitchen. But he got a big break from the US press corps, which was rooting for their guy in this heavyweight bout, and Nixon won this round of what became known as the "kitchen debate." The images confirmed the verdict. The two presidents had been waving fingers at one other all day, but the front pages of America portrayed Nixon jabbing Khrushchev's chest or slicing with his hand to make a point. They made Nixon appear strong, as if he had defeated a confused Soviet big guy.

Nixon went on to explore the country, from Leningrad to Siberia and the Urals. He was granted half an hour on Russian television to address Soviet citizens. He resisted the impulse to lash out at the government-sponsored hecklers along the way, whose goal, he informed Ike, was "to provoke me into some angry and ill-considered reactions." It was Also Khrushchev's goal. When Nixon mentioned his childhood and the Nixon market, Khrushchev spat on the memories. "All shopkeepers are thieves," the premier declared. Nixon's only mistake (after warning his staff to limit their alcohol consumption) was to drink too much vodka at an embassy event following his address, revealing his lack of self-confidence once more by boorishly badgering the other guests for compliments.

"He was pleading for reassurance, and, as nearly always happens, the confirmations and slightly sycophantic replies and comments from his staff did not help," remembered a US envoy, Vladimir Toumanoff. "His uneasiness was too deep, he was too intelligent, and I believe he had played the same scene too many times and for too long to deceive himself. His nervousness seems to increase."

Dick and Pat concluded their tour with a stop in Poland on the way home, where hundreds of thousands of applauding and adoring Poles showered them with flowers. Aside from the Cold War drama, Nixon's tour made little difference to the state of US-Soviet ties. Its primary legacy was political. Nixon came across as forceful and statesmanlike.

ROCKEFELLER WASN'T HAPPY WITH Nixon'S SUCCESS, and the bickering between the two prompted an annoyed president to handcuff his two ambitious cubs. He recommended Rocky take the second position on the Republican ticket in 1960 in exchange for Nixon's vow to serve one term as president and then support Rockefeller in 1964. Ike attempted to remain neutral, telling the White House press that "there are a lot of darn good men" who could succeed him. He longingly remembered Bob Anderson.

Nixon faced no other Republican contenders. There was energy and unrest on the right, where vestiges of the Old Guard were joined by militant Sunbelt conservatives, East Coast anti-Communists, and tax-hating suburbanites. Senator Barry Goldwater of Arizona championed the idea, but the revolution was still years away. Nixon sensed the energy and spent years attempting to harness it without becoming subsumed. So the action shifted to the Democrats, where John Kennedy used his charm and good looks, his father's wealth, and a variety of ruthless tactics (having Franklin Roosevelt Jr. accuse Kennedy rival Hubert Humphrey of avoiding military service in World War II) to defeat the Minnesota senator in the Wisconsin and West Virginia primaries. With money, strength, and nerve, Kennedy and his lieutenants rallied the party's big-city rulers and enough northern and western delegates to stave off an 11th-hour challenge from Lyndon Johnson, the South's champion.

After losing to Kennedy on the first ballot at the party's Los Angeles convention, Johnson shocked everyone by accepting JFK's invitation to be his running mate. It was a watershed moment—and bad news for Nixon, who had intended to follow Eisenhower's lead and seize Texas and other southern states from his opponents. The Democrats now had a presidential candidate who could sing one song on race and faith in liberal, Catholic, and African American precincts up north—while his running mate wandered the South, winking at white Protestant Democrats, assuring them they had nothing to fear, and bawling, as he did in one Virginia town, "What's Dick Nixon ever done for Culpeper?"

Karma may be terrible. Johnson's acceptance of the second position was influenced by his mentor Sam Rayburn's strong antipathy for Nixon ("that ugly fellow with the chinquapin eyes"), whom the Speaker believed had labeled him, Harry Truman, and other Democrats as traitors. Unfortunately, for Nixon, Nelson Rockefeller did not foster such hatreds—or party allegiance. When Nixon attempted to replicate Kennedy's success by asking Rockefeller to accept the vice-presidential candidacy, winning New York and possibly other northeastern states for the Republicans, Rocky declined.

The Cold War hostilities had eased in early 1960. Khrushchev's behavior alarmed Americans, but Ike realized how much of it was bluster. The CIA's top-secret U-2 spy planes had kept him informed of the Soviet Union's true capabilities. When Eisenhower joined Khrushchev at a summit meeting in Paris in May, he understood the "missile gap" was a hoax. However, Ike had made a mistake by ordering one final U-2 mission. The Soviets shot down the jet and apprehended the pilot. Khrushchev used the incident to humiliate the US president. It was a "debilitating, painful, and depressing rejection by an authoritative father figure," as Dr. Arnold Hutschnecker, Nixon's physician for tension-related and psychosomatic sickness, would remark, and a new source of contention between the president and his insecure apprentice.

"Eisenhower was not deliberately snubbing Nixon," said Herb Brownell, but added, "I don't think Nixon was ever convinced of that."

Chapter 11: Nixon vs. Kennedy

As he left the Republican convention in Chicago for his fifth national campaign (1952, 1954, 1956, 1958, and 1960) in nine years, Richard Nixon had a slim lead in the polls, tremendous strengths, and significant shortcomings. With no military icon on the Republican ticket, there was every reason to believe that the Eisenhower victories were outliers, and that the 1960 race would be more like the barnburner, Truman vs. Dewey, in 1948. "To win, our ticket needed eight to ten million Democratic votes, plus 55 to 60 percent of the independent vote," campaign director Robert Finch recounted. Ike had finished it. Could Nixon?

Nixon's most enticing quality was experience. For eight years, he attended cabinet meetings, served on the National Security Council, and protected Cold War secrets. He was forty-seven, young enough to match the vigor of the forty-three-year-old Kennedy, and he had traveled the world, advising with foreign leaders and confronting Communists in Caracas and Moscow. His advisers and the media they groomed kept repeating the same theme. The escalating tensions following the U-2 incident reminded voters of the importance of experienced leadership. In October, Khrushchev visited the United Nations, removed his shoe, and smashed it on his desk in rage. The Nixon campaign goal, according to his pollster Claude Robinson, was to "help voters make up their minds that Kennedy is immature and that in this time of crisis, the country is better off by calling on the experience of Nixon-Lodge."

The Republican Party remained the vehicle of business, which, while ensuring a sufficient treasury, shifted the party's agenda away from working families. The Democrats had a three-to-two edge in registered voters, and Republicans struggled in many regions to recruit persons to do such basic jobs as disseminating material, regulating local election processes, and guarding polls.

The future lay in the Sunbelt and suburbia. While California continued to flourish at a rapid pace, the remainder of the South and Southwest lagged behind, as the wonders of central air-conditioning extended slowly through the arid regions. In the 1960s, the Electoral College would resemble those that brought Roosevelt and Truman victory. Between 1932 and 1960, newcomers brought ten new electoral votes to California, primarily at the expense of the Northeast. However, the Rust Belt states of New York, Ohio, Pennsylvania, Michigan, and Illinois, together with Texas and California, would still decide the 1960 election. Suburban development had weakened Democratic bosses' clout, but their urban machines remained formidable. Even Nixon's home state, due to the 1958 disaster, would present a problem.

Rockefeller's exit had pros and cons. Without a Republican opponent,

Nixon had watched glumly as Kennedy dominated the headlines that spring, piling success on top of victory and generating excitement. Nixon's own campaign polls showed him leading all other Democratic contenders by double digits but losing to the "charismatic" Kennedy.

The economy betrayed Nixon as well. When the White House rebuffed his requests to stimulate the economy with additional federal spending, unemployment rose, indicating a looming recession. Over 450,000 people lost their jobs in the weeks leading up to the election. "When you have good times, you don't get credit, but when they are bad, you get all the blame," his economic adviser Arthur Burns cautioned Nixon. "The decline in government spending this year…is just plain stupid."

Nixon and Leonard Hall, the former Republican Party chairman who was advising the vice president, made a personal pitch to Like to have the Pentagon order military aircraft to support California's struggling aerospace industry. The president declined. "That goddamned old fool," Nixon fumed to Hall as they left. "If I had been sitting in that chair and wanted to keep my successor there I'd spend the whole goddamned treasury."

The general election was conducted in stages. August was a draw, with Nixon in a hospital bed and Kennedy engrossed in a special summer session of Congress. The first revolutionary event came on the night of September 12, when Norman Vincent Peale and a group of Protestant leaders made headlines by warning that a Catholic president would do the Vatican's will. Kennedy addressed the religion problem during a ministerial meeting in Houston. He appeared to be the embodiment of reason, while his interrogators resembled pinched, sour roundheads. The Kennedy campaign took the tape from the showdown, purchased television time, and aired it repeatedly. California Democrats then claimed that the pastor of Nixon's East Whittier church had likewise supported "scurrilous literature" disparaging Catholicism. They urged Nixon to reject the leaflet. Another day passed, and the national Democratic Party leader, Senator Henry "Scoop" Jackson of Washington, alleged that Peale's attack was instigated by the Nixon campaign. Jackson asked that Nixon apologize for injecting "religious hate" into the race. He claimed that Protestant clerics promote hatred both in person and by mail. "Religion has become an issue."

Graham's concerns appeared to be exaggerated over time. "Contrary to rumors, Catholic support of the Nixon-Lodge ticket appears to be rising" and "bigotry may have less influence than one might think," Nixon's pollster, Claude Robinson, informed him in October. Nixon was not fully persuaded. "The religious issue helped Kennedy more than it hurt him," he concluded in a post-election memo. According to Gallup, Nixon received barely 22 percent of the Catholic vote, a historic low for a Republican.

When it came to religion issues and other breaking news, Nixon shut himself off. "The vice president has no kitchen cabinet or small elite circle of close advisers," Finch told a gathering of Republican officials. "He is his own campaign manager."

Nixon consulted few, if any, advisors on crucial issues such as whether to debate, parlay with Nelson Rockefeller in New York, or honor his hasty commitment to campaign in all fifty states. Finch noted that his supper with Rockefeller was entirely his own choosing. "It was never even discussed as a remote possibility" and caused "terrible havoc" in the party and campaign.

Nixon frequently fell flat on his face while serving as both a candidate and a manager. He scarcely slept throughout the Chicago conference, and he and the staff relied on "jolly pills" to get through each day's schedule. After one engagement in Fresno, Don Hughes discovered Nixon basically sleeping on his feet. As Hughes put the fatigued candidate to bed, Nixon opened one eye and remarked, "It will be alright…God is on our side." On other nights, Haldeman found Nixon absent from their hotel and tracked him down to "flea-bitten" coffee shops. The strain triggered the now-familiar outbursts of fury. In Iowa, Nixon vented by forcefully kicking the automobile seat in front of him. Its irate inhabitant, the devoted Hughes, abandoned the damaged seat and the automobile and marched along the road. Nixon lost his cool again at an otherwise successful telethon in Detroit on election night, striking adviser Everett Hart. Hart was furious and quit the campaign. "I was really mad," Hart recounted. "I had had a rib removed where I had had open heart surgery, and that is where he hit me."

After a few weeks, he started nitpicking again. "I do not think it is effective to say at the end of a program—'Vote for Dick Nixon on election day.' I would prefer to have Richard Nixon," Finch was telling him. "I understand that there are instances when a less formal salutation is appropriate, but when discussing how people vote, use the name that will appear on the ballot. In this scenario, Dick Nixon sounded flip and undignified.

The next turning point—and the single most crucial event in the 1960 presidential campaign—was the first televised debate, held on September 26 in Chicago. Neither man stumbled; there were no embarrassing gaffes to be played and repeated on the next day's news. They both demonstrated command over the subject: domestic affairs. The panel of reporters disputed Nixon's claim of experience by throwing Ike's comment—"Give me a week and I might think of one"—at him, but he handled it effectively. Nixon's supporters, including many radio listeners, felt he had won. In fact, Nixon probably lost the election and debates. Television had betrayed him. The studio lighting was poor. His clothing was not dark enough and ill-fitting. His hair was trimmed too short, which accentuated his receding hairline. He fidgeted in his seat. His gaze wandered furtively. He was seen on camera using a handkerchief to wipe away sweat on his upper lip and chin.

It was a terrible ending that no amount of makeup could have remedied. A college debate judge might have totaled the points and ruled the match a tie, because Nixon had performed like the captain of the Whittier College debate team. However, by the end of the night, the American people had analyzed Kennedy and concluded that he was on par with Nixon. According to the Gallup Poll, 43 percent of those polled thought Kennedy won the debate, 29 percent thought it was a tie, and 23 percent gave it to Nixon. "Kennedy was bursting with confidence, witty and full of bounce. "People thought the vice president appeared tired and less confident," noted pollster Robinson in an internal campaign report. Kennedy had responded to questions about youth, stature, and experience. He had stared down the guy who had challenged Khrushchev.

Before the debates began, Robinson assured Nixon that the vice president would make Kennedy appear like a valedictorian "at Podunk College." During the four televised debates, Kennedy did come across as "the shy young sheriff," as Marshall McLuhan, an early scholar of the medium, told an interviewer. Nevertheless, Nixon, "with his very dark eyes that tend to stare, with his slicker circumlocution, has resembled more the railway lawyer who signs leases that are not in the interests of the folks in the little town."

The debates concluded on October 21. In that four-week period of the campaign, Kennedy had turned a few-point deficit in the Gallup poll into a narrow lead, which a fawning press corps saw as a sign of an impending landslide. With all of the advantages of a Democratic candidate—urban machines to boost turnout, a registration lead, and the assistance of liberal-leaning reporters—the fight appeared to be all but over. But Nixon refused to capitulate. He campaigned like a berserker in the last two weeks; his party rallied around him and, with Eisenhower's assistance, outspent the Democrats in news coverage and broadcast advertising.

The polls' trend lines changed direction. Nixon was closeton a point. Kennedy became weary of the idea that, like Truman in 1948 (or Bill Mazeroski, whose walk-off home run for the Pittsburgh Pirates sent the New York Yankees to baseball Hades that fall), Nixon would win it in the final turn at bat. But the Fates gave Nixon a final curveball. He decided not to swing. The election results were so close—possibly the closest ever, depending on how they were measured—that his lack of nerve, or what he referred to as scruples (as if any remained in either candidate in the final week of the election), may have cost him the presidency. For, despite all the talk about youth and religion, race ruled the final innings.

Back in the spring, when the campaign started, the civil rights issue was as thorny as ever. The Solid South had not been truly solid for Democrats since the 1944 election. With a Catholic leading the Democratic ticket in 1960 and blacks fighting for their rights, the Republicans were faced with a Faustian deal. "The prospect for the Republican high command is…tantalizing in the extreme," White told CNN. "If they adopt a civil rights program only moderately more restrained than the Democrats', the South can be theirs for the asking; and with the South, if it comes permanently to Republican loyalties, could come such solid addition of electoral strength as would make Republicans again, as they were for half a century, the majority party of the nation." The unexpected moment arrived on October 19 when

Martin Luther King Jr. was arrested at a sit-in in the Magnolia Room, a Five days later, a state judge sentenced King to four months of hard labor at the state penitentiary in rural Reidsville, citing an old traffic violation. He was carried away at night, shackled. King's pregnant wife, Coretta, family, and associates were terrified that he might be assassinated on the way to prison or in his cell. It was a reasonable fear.

According to pollster Lou Harris, Kennedy's popularity among black voters remained at 62 percent throughout the fall, similar to Stevenson's success in 1956. However, with the impending recession and the King incident, "the Negro vote soared for Kennedy" in both the North and South in the last days. Harris described it as "the most dramatic upturn for the Democrats on the presidential line," with double-digit gains or larger in New York City, Chicago, Memphis, and Atlanta, and rural Texas and Virginia. "Their Martin Luther King gambit paid off handsomely," William Safire wrote to Finch in a postmortem study of the campaign.

Kennedy did a better job of bridging the race divide than Nixon by selecting Lyndon Johnson as his running partner and making that phone call to Coretta King. He received the large turnout he needed in the northern cities but, with Johnson's assistance, still won seven of the eleven Confederate states, including Texas, Georgia, the Carolinas, and Louisiana.

Robinson was destroyed, and King left the race with a fresh perspective on Richard Nixon. "I'd known Nixon longer. "He was supposedly close to me and would call me frequently for advice," King recalls. "However, when this moment arrived, it was as if he had never heard of me. So this is why I thought him a moral coward, unwilling to take a daring move and danger."

Whatever the reason, Eisenhower's shortened schedule paid Nixon dearly. The president was "knocking our block off," as Kennedy told a pal. JFK had a horrible feeling, as if he were "standing on a mound of sand with the tide running out." No one was more grateful than Kennedy when Ike's appearances were cut short.

As Election Day approached, Nixon still had a chance. On October 28, pollster Robinson informed him that they had a solid lead in states with 130 electoral votes, primarily in the West, Midwest, and outer South, while Kennedy had won states with 151 votes, including New York, much of the Northeast, and the inner South. Robinson's scorecard contained multiple inaccuracies, but the substance was correct. The campaign would come down to nineteen states where the candidates were deadlocked or separated by one or two points, including the crucial battlegrounds of California, Ohio, Texas, Illinois, Pennsylvania, and Michigan. With 269 electoral votes required to win, Nixon would have to divide the smaller states with Kennedy while capturing four of the six large ones. Organized labor was strong in Pennsylvania and Michigan, so "California, Texas, Ohio, and Illinois are the key to a Nixon victory," Robinson wrote. Nixon flew to California in the early morning hours of Election Day, where 25,000 people greeted him at the airport with fireworks and torchlights. He and Pat had two hours of rest before leaving for Whittier to vote.

Across the continent, at Hyannisport, Nixon's remarks provided a welcome respite on a night when laughter had turned to sadness. Kennedy's popular vote lead had vanished in the hours following midnight, like a spindrift on the coast. It was likely to be one of the tightest elections ever, and the New York Times stopped the presses to revise its headline from "Kennedy Elected President" to "Kennedy Is Appearing Victor." California would not be given (to Nixon) for several days, and Hawaii was determined in a recount by 115 votes.

Kennedy captured Pennsylvania and Michigan. And then-Mayor Richard Daley of Chicago called to inform him, "Mr. Reston captured the night's drama in the Times, stating that "with a little bit of luck and the help of a few close friends, you're going to carry Illinois." Although Kennedy was declared the winner in Minnesota at noon Wednesday, the election could still be thrown to the House of Representatives. However, with Minnesota gone, Nixon yielded.

So concluded the closest election in American history. Both candidates went to bed without knowing who had won. Nationwide, Kennedy would receive 34,221,000 votes and Nixon 34,108,000. Nixon lost just one percent.

Chapter 12: The Greatest Comeback

On November 22, 1963, John F. Kennedy was shot and murdered while riding in an open vehicle through Dallas. His motorcade slowed as it approached the Texas School Book Depository building, from which Lee Oswald, a deluded Communist who had relegated all of his rage at his bleak life to a mail-order rifle and his Marine Corps marksmanship, fired three times from a sixth-floor window, striking the president in the throat and skull.

Nixon had left Dallas that morning, having spoken with a group of soft-drink bottlers. He had landed at Idlewild Airport and was in a taxi on his way to his new Manhattan home when a pedestrian yelled out the terrible news. The doorman at his building confirmed it. His adversary had died, and the fetch was no longer necessary. Hannah Nixon got the California news. Her initial impression was that, if not for a few thousand votes, Richard would have been in that car, with Pat alongside him, covered in gore.

In June 1963, Nixon moved to New York to lay down and bleed for a time. He had brought his name and rainmaking potential to a Wall Street law firm that was later renamed Nixon, Mudge, Rose, Guthrie & Alexander, thanks to enthusiastic corporate bosses who made it clear that their legal business would follow. Los Angeles was a land of lotus eaters. However, "New York is very cold, very ruthless, and very exciting," Nixon told the Los Angeles Times. "It is a place where you can't slow down."

Nixon practiced litigation by taking a privacy case to the United States Supreme Court. He learned that corporate law was not his destiny, finding it "degrading" and "terribly difficult" to solicit and represent business owners. However, one of his biggest clients, Pepsi-Cola, was looking for new markets overseas, so his interests coincided with theirs. He could traverse the capitals of Europe and Asia, interviewing American ambassadors and foreign leaders for hours at a time and documenting their responses on foolscap pads. On a trip to Finland, he hopped on a train to Moscow to knock on the door of an old rival. A servant informed him that ousted Premier Khrushchev was not present.

Much of what Nixon discussed with his international contacts involved Southeast Asia. For a while following the Cuban missile crisis, hope had supplanted fear. The Soviets and Americans stepped back from the brink of war and negotiated an agreement to prohibit above ground nuclear tests. However, the Cold War persisted, and Kennedy's administration was an incomplete image when he died. The CIA assassination schemes in Cuba and elsewhere persisted—when Lyndon Johnson took office, he was shocked to discover that "we had been operating a damn Murder Inc. in the Caribbean," he told a former aide—and there were sixteen thousand US forces in Vietnam.

In the years following the fall of Dien Bien Phu, the Communists strengthened their grip on the North and tried to destroy South Vietnamese President Ngo Dinh Diem's administration. In the United States, there was a broad bipartisan consensus—from liberals like Congressman Tip O'Neill to conservatives like Cardinal Francis Spellman and Senator Barry Goldwater—that Southeast Asia needed to be spared from the Communist juggernaut that appeared to be about to devour all of Asia. Henry Cabot Lodge Jr., Nixon's 1960 running mate, agreed to serve as John Kennedy's ambassador in Saigon.

Three weeks later, Kennedy was shot. Johnson and his legislative captains pushed the stalled liberal agenda—Medicare and Medicaid, the Civil Rights Act of 1964 and the Voting Rights Act of 1965, government aid to education, a war on poverty, and a Keynesian tax cut—through Congress in the wake of the assassination. "These are the most hopeful times in all the years since Christ was born in Bethlehem," Johnson proclaimed during the 1964 national Christmas tree lighting ceremony. Americans were unified to an extent "unmatched in the history of freedom," he remarked.

However, the inherited agenda included Vietnam. In August 1964, Johnson requested wide war-making powers from Congress, citing an unsubstantiated confrontation between American and North Vietnamese vessels in the Gulf of Tonkin. The vote was 416 to 0 in the House and 88 to 2 in the Senate. During his presidential campaign, LBJ promised not to "send American boys nine or ten thousand miles away from home to do what Asian boys ought to be doing for themselves." It was a lie. By the end of 1965, there were 184,000 American boys in Vietnam, twice that number en route. Johnson had initiated "Rolling Thunder," a bombing campaign that would use more high explosives than any previous conflict combined.

As he moved through the political wilderness, Nixon began studying philosophy, reading or rereading Edmund Burke, Machiavelli, and his favorite, Friedrich Nietzsche, who advised: "What does not destroy me makes me stronger." He agreed. He thought that hardship, rather than material comforts, gave life significance.

The assassination of John F. Kennedy weakened Nixon's decision to boycott the 1964 presidential election. Within days, he had canceled a scheduled book contract and was meeting with his political advisors. Over martinis, a friend tried to persuade him out of it, questioning why he would put himself through the stress and work. "I understand the fucking Commie psyche. Nixon replied, "But they don't know mine." "I honestly believe I can do something. I truly feel I can contribute to peace."

When Goldwater was defeated by a write-in vote for Lodge in the New Hampshire primary, he couldn't resist the itch, and unfriendly Republicans expressed their feelings about his divorce and remarriage to a woman who abandoned her four children for him. Nixon made it clear that he was available—as an anyone-but-Goldwater candidate or a peacemaker who could appeal to all parts of the party. He arranged to have his name entered as a write-in candidate in the presidential primaries, went on a high-profile tour of the battleground states, and embarked on a twenty-four-day trip through Asia, visiting Saigon, accusing Johnson of timidity, and recommending that the United States drop more bombs on Vietnam. Senator J. William Fulbright, the Democratic chairman of the Foreign Relations Committee, had called for a review of US policy toward China. During a visit to Hong Kong, Nixon criticized "naïve, woolly-headed thinking."

On his 52nd birthday, Nixon sat in his New York study and made a list of resolutions for 1965, including setting tremendous goals.Take daily rest.Take brief trips...Awareness of all weaknesses...Make better use of time.Start writing a book.Consider golf or other forms of everyday exercise.Articles or talks about controversial new global and national concerns. Then he laid down his yellow foolscap, turned off the light, peered into the fire, and began planning his path to the presidency. He would occasionally hesitate during the next three years, most notably when he contemplated the impact—the "emotional disaster"—that another campaign could have on his family. However, he eventually concluded that "politics was not just an alternative occupation for me." "It was my life."

Hannah Nixon spent her final years in California, apart from her famous son. Cozy Whittier has been changed, overrun by suburban smog and expansion. She furnished her little home with memorabilia from his political career and maintained her work ethic as long as she could, upsetting Dick by refusing nursing care.NIXON aspired to geopolitical genius, but his attitude toward Vietnam in the early 1960s was never more than ordinary. Until surveys revealed mounting popular displeasure, he was a vocal and relentless advocate for escalation. For Nixon, like most men of his time, the Munich lesson was unchangeable. "What had been true of the betrayal of Czechoslovakia to Hitler in 1938 was no less true of the betrayal of South Vietnam to the Communists," he made clear.

He repeatedly demanded more time, troops, and explosives. During his travels to Saigon, he opposed plans for a negotiated settlement, claiming that anything less than full triumph "would be a defeat or a retreat," for which the Democrats should be held accountable.

In 1966, Nixon returned to the road, campaigning for Republican congressional candidates nationwide. It was his ninth major campaign in sixteen years, and this one proved successful.

On the day of the election, Johnson traveled to the Philippines to meet with Asian leaders and suggested a cease-fire that included the mutual departure of American and North Vietnamese soldiers from South Vietnam. Nixon opposed the president and the idea. "Communist victory would most certainly be the result," he told me. Johnson rebuked Nixon, calling him a "chronic campaigner" who will kill men to achieve his goals.

In 1967, the number of American forces in Vietnam had risen to 500,000, with 100 deaths each week. "We face more cost, loss, and agony," Johnson stated during his State of the Union address. "For the end is not yet."

Johnson sought to fight the war on the cheap, both in terms of resources (the government ran a deficit) and people, avoiding the politically risky step of calling up the reserves. However, the draft, which was handled inequitably and drew 350,000 young men every year, exposed ordinary America to the realities of war. As did the returning casualties. The war correspondents' coverage in Saigon became increasingly suspicious. And so, with the assistance of new communications satellites deployed in the early 1960s, did the nightly television news. By the end of 1967, dissident liberal Democrats and emotional college students were traveling to New Hampshire to support antiwar contender Senator Eugene McCarthy, a Minnesota Democrat.

Johnson's administration published glowing reports of military triumph. Intelligence analysts who questioned the ads found superiors altered or ignored their reports. As 1967 progressed into 1968, the CIA identified indications of an impending enemy onslaught to coincide with the upcoming Tet celebration. American commanders relocated their forces to the northern and western borders, but as the North Vietnamese froze U.S. soldiers in place at remote outposts like Khe Sanh, the Viet Cong struck back in the cities. The historic capital of Hue fell, and the Communists slaughtered 3,000 political and civic leaders. Suicide squads targeted American positions in the center of Saigon. Bay Tuyen and Ut Nho, who led seventeen other Communist guerrillas into the US embassy compound, breaching the wall, besieging the building, and killing five guards before being killed by American reinforcements, may have delivered the war's single most significant psychological blow. Their bold assault was replicated across South Vietnam, with over a hundred cities, towns, and hamlets targeted. On February 2, 1968, the news of Nixon's presidential candidacy shared the front page of the New York Times with a photograph of a Vietnamese police commander wielding a gleaming, snub-nosed pistol to perpetually execute a Viet Cong captive amid the mayhem in Saigon.

Johnson's credibility was supposed to have a gap; now it was a chasm. The Pentagon said it will require another 206,000 troops to win the war, on top of 525,000 already authorized. Young males, along with their partners and families, performed the math. On March 12, McCarthy received 42% of the vote in New Hampshire. By St. Patrick's Day, Robert Kennedy, whose dislike for Johnson was mutual, had entered the campaign.

Clark Clifford, the new defense secretary, informed Johnson that the nation's political and commercial leaders wanted no more of this "hopeless bog." A bipartisan group of "wise men"—elder statesmen from prior administrations—now urged the terrified president to abandon hope of triumph and haggle for whatever he could rescue. In a nationally televised speech on March 31, Johnson ceased bombing in parts of Vietnam, called for peace talks, and revealed his decision not to run for reelection.

History was moving in dizzying leaps. Martin Luther King Jr. was one of the war's critics, viewing the conflict through a moral lens—the US government, he said, had emerged as "the greatest purveyor of violence in the world"—and a racial lens: white versus yellow, with black soldiers doing a disproportionate amount of the killing and dying.

African American aspirations have risen for decades, resulting in frustration. In 1964, there were race riots in Harlem, Bedford-Stuyvesant, Rochester, and Philadelphia, and the following summer, five days after Johnson signed the Voting Rights Act, a routine drunk-driving stop sparked a riot in the Los Angeles neighborhood of Watts, killing 34 people. More riots, with comparable fatality tolls, occurred in Newark and Detroit during the summer of 1967.

To the ordinary white voter, "the Negro, for whom the past fourteen years represented a unique era of progress, showed himself to be, not only ungrateful, but sullen, full of hate and the potential for violence," cautioned Harry McPherson, a Johnson assistant, in a note to the president. "The crime rate continued to rise; the number one 'public' problem for millions of people became physical fear; the administration seemed unable to do anything about this; or in the eyes of some whites, it was unwilling to offend the Negroes upon whom it depended for votes."

Everything was just a prelude to the indignation, sadness, and violence that followed King's killing on a balcony at the Lorraine Motel in Memphis on April 4, 1968. The country was still reeling from Johnson's resignation; now it watched as the Eighty-Second Airborne fixed bayonets and deployed machine guns to protect the White House and Capitol from crowds torching the neighboring business district. After some deliberation—remembering Kennedy's call to Coretta

King in 1960, but knowing that a similar gesture would be dismissed as expedient in 1968—Nixon paid a private visit to the widow and her family in Atlanta. He also attended the funeral, but it "won no votes," he told Haldeman when he returned.

America was reeling, and the battering was far from over. On the night of King's assassination, after paraphrasing Aeschylus to a devastated audience of black Americans, Robert Kennedy was killed as he left the celebration of his victory in the California primary. In six months, a liberal movement that had been "Clean for Gene" in New Hampshire, boasted of its "flower power," or campaigned for a Kennedy restoration had been wiped out. Radicals and nihilists took control. "The New Left seems to have read nothing and relies entirely on the proposition that feeling and acting are all that matter; the deed will eventually produce the doctrine; the act of revolution will lead to the program," said Arthur Schlesinger, Jr. in his diaries. The outrage peaked at the Democratic convention in Chicago in August, when Mayor Daley's cops gassed and beat demonstrators in the streets outside the convention hall, and was matched by a raw display of power within, as Johnson and his captains stifled dissent and ensured that Vice President Hubert Humphrey received the Democratic nomination.

As the world went insane around him, Richard Nixon demonstrated touch and timing in his campaign for the Republican candidacy. The ever-loyal Rose Mary Woods had followed Nixon to California and back to New York, serving as his personal secretary. His new law partner, Leonard Garment, an outstanding attorney and jazz pianist, joined him during a midlife crisis. Old hands Haldeman, Ehrlichman, and Finch had returned to their regular occupations but remained on call. Patrick Buchanan, the first outsider hired, disguised his fake combativeness with degrees from Gonzaga High School, Georgetown University, and Columbia University's graduate school of journalism. Buchanan was a multi-talented professional who worked as a bodyguard, speechwriter, and press liaison. For a decade, he also served as Nixon's link to the conservative movement.

Another desk in Nixon's outside office was set aside for "Miss Ryan," who assisted Woods with her job, exchanged cigarettes with Buchanan, and dreaded what was ahead. Over Christmas break in

1966, Julie's exhausted mother told her "flatly, almost tonelessly," that she couldn't take another presidential campaign. Tricia was distraught, unable to sleep at the prospect. Pat fled to California alone with the Drowns for three weeks in the summer of 1967. They were invested in Dick's comeback, as were many of his friends. They informed her that he was about to fulfill his lifelong wish. How could she oppose him? Pat and her girls had taken "the awful decision" to support him once more when the calendar flipped. Their lives would be horrible, anyway. "If I had to practice law the rest of my life," Nixon was telling his buddies, "I would be mentally dead in two years and physically dead in four."

According to White, Nixon's greatest challenge was the "image of a loser" that remained from the 1960 and 1962 elections. To counter the notion, Nixon ran in all Republican primaries. "If we can lick the can't-win thing, we've got it made," Price told his boss in a campaign message.

The violent turns of 1968 shook moderates and conservatives alike, even card-carrying liberals. Humphrey appeared to be a gasbag, and Wallace a monstrosity. Nixon came to be seen as a comforting, stolid centrist with foreign policy experience who could provide him an advantage and bring some reason to the chaos in Southeast Asia. He spoke movingly about the need for "the lift of a driving dream" to revitalize America.

Dick Schaap, a superb feature writer, was tasked with writing about Nixon for New York magazine, the hipster bible. He expected to find Old Nixon, the one whose "name was invoked to frighten little liberal children." But Nixon "fell short of being the personification of evil," Schaap said. Schaap argued that the left had lost faith after sacrificing their hearts to Lyndon Johnson, and he now appeared as an appealing underdog, similar to the New York Mets' attitude. "Instead of seeing opposing views as black and white now, they see them more often as black and grey." So what if Nixon employed racial code terms like law and order. "Nixon is merely playing the game," Schaap stated. "And if it is a dirty, degrading game—and it is—he did not invent it."

Mailer maintained a feeling that the current Nixon was a ruse—that "the young devil had reconstituted himself into a more consummate devil, Old Scratch as a modern Abe Lincoln." But he hoped it was not true. "It might even be a measure of the not-entirely dead promise of America if a man as opportunistic as the early Nixon could grow in reach and comprehension and stature to become a leader," according to Mailer. "For if that were possible in these bad years, then all was still possible, and the country not stripped of its blessing."

The challenge to Nixon's candidacy came from a group of moderate Republicans led by Rockefeller and Michigan Governor George Romney, and (after defeating Pat Brown in 1966) Ronald Reagan, the newly elected governor of California. Rocky had no friends on the right. While conservatives adored Reagan, many in the party still cringed at the recollection of the Goldwater scandal and thought the former movie star lacked gravitas and experience.

Romney dropped out of the race two weeks before the New Hampshire primary, giving Nixon the decisive victory he needed to disprove his reputation as unelectable. As in 1960, he was regarded as a pragmatist—tolerated if not particularly favored by his party's antipathetic wings, but a hero to its middle, with a huge wad of IOUs accumulated during all those years of Podunk rallies and peas-and-chicken Lincoln Day feasts. He appeared to have secured the Republican candidacy before a single vote was cast, unless Rocky and Reagan formed a cynical anti-Nixon alliance.

Which, of course, is what happened in 1968, the year of wonders.

Rocky had the press's favor, a plausible pattern, New York's delegates, and the funds to mount a spectacle. However, he had previously wavered—renouncing the race in the winter and then changing his mind in the spring. Reagan was the bigger threat. The 57-year-old California governor was Goldwater without the crust—a herald of conservatism whose cheerful, almost supernatural certainty energized his supporters and disarmed critics. The right may appear quiet, but a flame still burns in millions of hearts, and Reagan possesses the abilities to fan it.

Reagan saw the South as the key to stopping Nixon. The Republican Party's development in the region was slow but steady in the postwar era, as the Democratic Party, after years of failing to address the horrors of segregation, fractured over race and lost control of a territory it had dominated since Reconstruction. Eisenhower acquired Virginia, Tennessee, Texas, and Florida in 1952, and Louisiana in

1956. Nixon nearly matched him in 1960, winning Florida, Virginia, and Tennessee while coming close in Texas and the Carolinas.

"Ike's campaign was really the first campaign that made a two-party area out of the South," said former Republican chairman Leonard Hall. Young veterans returning from World War II, dissatisfied with the way Democratic judicial gangs controlled their neighborhoods, had turned to General Eisenhower's party as a more appealing avenue for their ambition. By 1968, Republicans like John Tower and George H. W. Bush of Texas, Linwood Holton of Virginia, and Howard Baker and William Brock of Tennessee were capitalizing on the Democratic disarray to win over converts in the growing southern middle class. However, just as the South was the key to the nomination, so was Strom Thurmond—and Nixon had that key in his pocket. The South Carolina senator had changed somewhat since the day in 1948 when he and his Dixiecrats stormed out of the Democratic convention to protest the platform's small nod to civil rights. Thurmond switched parties in 1964, becoming a Republican. He was still concerned with segregation, but not entirely. He was a staunch anti-Communist, and military spending was a key economic driver in his state. So was the textile industry, which was protected by federal trade regulations.

Thurmond mostly wanted to win. He'd seen what happened in 1964 and dreaded the possibility of four more years of liberal programs, liberal taxation, and liberal federal judges. Nixon could rally the Republican Party and was willing to make the necessary concessions. Their feud over the 1957 civil rights bill, in which Nixon defied the segregationists and Thurmond staged the Senate's longest filibuster, is now forgotten. "Strom is no racist," Nixon told reporters visiting South Carolina in 1966. "Strom is a man of courage and integrity." Nixon said the South needs empathy and understanding. Southerners "didn't want to be treated like national pariahs, they wanted recognition, their right to be heard," he told White.

The first topic posed by the delegates addressed compulsory busing, the most recent method of racial integration. Integrating schools in the rural South was a relatively simple task, but busing black students from the poorer sections of Richmond, Charlotte, or Atlanta—or Detroit, Boston, or Los Angeles—to white neighborhoods was a politically explosive, expensive, and questionable proposition.

Frequently, it triggered a "white flight" that undermined support for public education systems. In Boston, the number of white students in public schools decreased from 45,000 in 1974 to 16,000 in 1987. Even among black parents, the cure had only a narrow majority of approval in public opinion polls. Nixon was courting southern and working-class whites, and busing was anathema to them.

"My feeling is this: I think that busing the child—a child that is two or three grades behind another child—into a strange community…I think you destroy that child," Nixon said to the delegation from the south. The country needed to get about the job of "building bridges to human dignity" rather than "trying to satisfy some professional civil rights group, or something like that, by busing the child from one side of the country to the other."

Nixon had previously supported the Civil Rights and Voting Rights Acts, and in 1968 he endorsed the Fair Housing Act. He refused to compete with Wallace in the Confederacy's main states. "Forget the Goldwater South," Nixon instructed his advisors. "You can't just echo Wallace," he replied. "You've got to be more sophisticated." What became known as "Nixon's southern strategy" was actually subtle. He stuck with Bush, Baker, Brock, and other moderates, preaching a low-tax, pro-business message, emphasizing national defense, praising traditional values, opposing busing, and targeting Southern suburbs—and minority communities in northern cities—with appeals for law and order.

Haldeman captured Nixon's private thoughts during a July meeting. "RN has emotional access to lower middle class white—not fair [to call them] racist—but concerned re crime & violence, law & order," Haldeman wrote in his note to himself. The Roman Catholic minorities—"Irish, Ital, Pole, Mex"—were "afraid of Negroes," and should be targeted after the convention. "Need a stronger N position on this operationally—must do something," Nixon informed Haldeman. "Must dry up Wallace vote."

Nixon, his followers believed, stood between Wallace and the presidency. While there was undoubtedly some justification in this, to his aides, he was Horatius, astride the bridge, repelling barbarians of all colors.

Whalen was a conservative, but many liberal thinkers shared his anxieties. "We would be hiding our heads in the sand," wrote Lippmann's columnist, "if we refused to admit that the country may demand and necessity may dictate the repression of uncontrollable violence....It is better that Mr. Nixon should have the full authority if repression should become necessary in order to restore peace and tranquility at home....Repression of some sort may be unavoidable."

So, in his lectures and magazine pieces such as "What Has Happened to America?"" and "If Mob Rule Takes Hold in the United States," Nixon reiterated the winning thesis from all those teenage speaking contests in Whittier: liberty is not a ticket to license, violence, and anarchy. The majority had their rights. "There can be no progress without order, no freedom without order, no justice without order," declared the president.

It was enough to cost Nixon, among other things, the backing of his old friend Jackie Robinson. Nonetheless, Nixon took care not to inflame. To concerned Americans, he was proposing peace and harmony, not more divide. Intentional division occurred later, during his presidency. The rioters depicted in Nixon's campaign posters were white, and the criminals he condemned in his speeches were pornographers, drug dealers, lax judges, and organized crime dons, not slum children. Political scientists Richard Scammon and Ben Wattenberg observed that his campaign was characterized by "social stolidity," rather than racial anger. He stood for stability, "stopping history in mid-dissolution," observed Garry Wills, who accompanied Nixon on his campaign that year.

In the decades that followed, Nixon's liberal critics would dismiss the previous century—in which progressive icons such as William Jennings Bryan and Franklin Roosevelt refused to support anti-lynching measures and other civil rights remedies for fear of offending Dixie Democrats—and begin the clock on the political exploitation of racism with the 1968 campaign. There was some of that, but Nixon also talked with wisdom and dignity. In a national radio broadcast, he asked: "Are we to become two nations, one black and one white, destined for irrepressible conflict?""

"The answer is no," Nixon said. "Only if we can light hope...can we have peace," stated President Nixon. "We must move with both compassion and conviction to bring the American dream to the ghetto."

And, speaking to an audience in a rich Philadelphia suburb, Nixon stated, "You are fortunate, but you are aware that there is terrible poverty in America's great cities." There are impoverished folks. There are others who haven't got the same opportunities as you."

"You can't be an island in the world," Nixon advised them. "You can't live in your comfortable houses and say, 'Well, just as long as I get mine, I don't have to worry about the others…' This isn't going to be a good country for any of us to live in until it's a good country for all of us to live in."

Nixon was a master of the rhetorical tightrope.

Furthermore, Nixon still had the bag of IOUs. "I was the southern chairman for him in 1968," Brock said. "I worked across the country for him, partly because I owed him. He approached me [during Brock's early campaigns] when no one else would. And I respected that." In the past, Mississippi's Clarke Reed had urged Reagan and Nixon to assist strengthen the Republican Party in his state. Nixon had appeared, but Reagan had not. "Perhaps you had better try where you have a few favors owing," Reed urged the California governor.

The uprising fizzled. In 1964, the conservatives "had our shot at a candidate who totally met our qualifications, and that candidate got six states," Louisiana committeeman Tom Stagg told reporters. "We've had our way. Now, shall we win one?" Reagan left the field, looking forward to another day. Rockefeller slunk home, his third presidential campaign having ended like the others.

Nixon chose Maryland governor Spiro Agnew, a beautiful mediocrity from a border state, as his running mate. Ward Just, writing for the Washington Post, described Agnew's appointment as "perhaps the most eccentric political appointment since the Roman emperor Caligula named his horse a consul." Despite the tinseled folders of politics, Nixon showed a particular chutzpah by describing Agnew as "a statesman of the first rank."

Appointing Spiro Agnew shows Nixon at his worst. It was a cynical nudge, a race-baiting wink, and a disastrous mistake. Nixon's first "presidential" decision—the selection of a running mate—was a fiasco. "What appealed most to Nixon was Agnew at his public worst—administering a demagogic public tongue-lashing to black leaders in Baltimore after the riots following the death of Martin Luther King," according to Novak. At that time, "in the absence of any vetting process, nobody suspected that Agnew was one of the most crooked politicians in America."

NIXON'S acceptance speech, written in seclusion on the Atlantic shore in Montauk, New York, the week before the convention, exemplified both calculation and refinement. Again, he addressed his "forgotten" Americans. Over time, he referred to them as the "silent center," "the great Silent Majority," and, subsequently, the "New American Majority." They were warriors in a conservative revolution that began in resistance to the New Deal under Taft and Eisenhower, erupted with Goldwater in 1964, swelled during Nixon's presidency, and prevailed at the end of the century. They were self-made men "in an age when self-made men were not honored for the agony of their creation," Wills wrote. They were people on whom Nixon relied in 1946 ("Richard Nixon is one of us"), and they were the target audience for his Checkers address in 1952.

The vast silent majority lived south of the Potomac and west of the Appalachians, or in densely packed ethnic communities in northern cities. The country's advertising firms, hawking soft drinks and vehicles, portrayed them as steadfast, the salt of the earth, driving Chevys, hunting and fishing, watching NASCAR or football, or playing summer softball. On Sundays, they dressed up and attended church, bowing their heads, holding hands, and saying grace before meals. They donated their time to the Boy Scouts, Rotary, and Jaycees. They respected Old Glory. They laughed alongside Bob Hope and praised John Wayne. Their sons volunteered to fight in Vietnam. It's no accident that Norman Rockwell's portrait of Richard Nixon hangs in Washington's National Portrait Gallery. "The Irish, Italian, Polish Catholics of the big cities—these are our electoral majority—they, and the white Protestants of the South and Midwest and rural America," told Buchanan's manager.

Nixon had a pivotal role in the realignment of American politics in the late twentieth century. In 1968, he and the "forgotten" fell under siege. They couldn't relate to those other Americans, restless in their riches, who gathered on colleges from Cambridge to Berkeley, in Manhattan newsrooms, or in the lanes of the Hollywood hills, seeking not comfort but witless uniformity in ancient ways and traditions. The stylish applauded emancipation. They wore their hair long, experimented with recreational drugs, and embraced new fashion, sex, music, cinema, and art trends. Their films celebrated outlaws—Bonnie and Clyde, Cool Hand Luke, and The Graduate—and they appeared to have boundless sympathy for individuals who defied the System. They had first marveled at, then welcomed, the civil rights movement, before moving on to promote a variety of new rights for women, homosexual Americans, atheists, artists, criminal defendants, and welfare recipients. "The man who works hard, pays his taxes, rears his children—the man who has always been the hero of the American folk mythology—now finds himself living in an era where the glorified man is the antihero: morose, introspective, unconcerned with God, country, family or tax bill," according to Scammon and Wattenberg.

When we look at America, we see cities covered in smoke and flames. We hear sirens at night. We see Americans dying on distant foreign battlefields. We witness Americans hating each other, fighting, and killing each other at home.

As we witness and hear these events, millions of Americans scream in anguish. Did we come this far for this? Were American lads killed at Normandy, Korea, and Valley Forge for this?

Hear answers to those questions.

It's another voice. It's the quiet voice amidst the chaos and shouting. It is the voice of the vast majority of Americans, the forgotten ones—the non-shouters and non-demonstrators.

They are neither bigoted nor sick, nor are they responsible for the crimes that afflict the land. They are black and white; local and foreign-born; young and old.

They work in American manufacturing. They manage America's enterprises. They work in the government. They supplied most of the dead troops for our freedom.

They energize the spirit of America. They elevate the American Dream. They provide steel to the backbone of America. They are good, respectable individuals who work, save, pay taxes, and care.

Nixon promised to bring peace to all good and moral people. Not just any peace—not a quick escape. But peace with honor. He claimed that honorable and respectable people had been misled by their leaders.

For four years, the world's strongest nation has been engulfed in the Vietnam War with no end in sight.

The world's richest nation struggles to govern its own economy.

The nation with a strong tradition of the rule of law is experiencing unparalleled lawlessness.

Unprecedented racial violence has torn apart a society recognized for its equality of opportunity.

When the President of the United States faces hostile demonstrations abroad or in major cities at home, it's time for new leadership.

To them, Richard Nixon declared, "I am one of you." In his personal ascent to the apex, and his enormous fall and subsequent rise, he portrayed himself as an embodiment of the American Dream, which he promised to restore during a Nixon presidency.

Tonight I glimpse the face of a child. He lives in an excellent city. He is Black. Or he's white. He is Mexican, Italian, and Polish. None of this matters. What counts is that he's an American child.

That child in that huge metropolis is worth more than any politician's pledge. He embodies America. He's a poet. He is a scientist, an excellent teacher, and a proud craftsman. He is everything we have ever wished for and dare to imagine.

My fellow Americans, America's long black night is about to end.

It was a long night. At 1:30 a.m., Safire was summoned to Nixon's suite, where he found the candidate in a familiar pose: recovering from a huge moment, nursing a drink, eager to talk, and running on adrenaline after nearly no sleep in 36 hours. "None of them could write a speech like that," Nixon said of his Establishment opponents, "and they hate me for it." An hour had passed, Safire wrote in his diary, and Nixon was "nodding, eyes closing, holding on to the same drink"—his fears on full show. "They won't like the speech, will they?" Nixon asked. "The New York Times and the guys. "Fuck them."

He described Rockefeller and Lindsay as elitists. They were unable to talk to the American heartland about an "impossible dream," but he and Ike" could. We both started from nothing. "We're emotional,"

Nixon explained. "They call me intelligent and cool with no sincerity and then it kills them when I show 'em I know how people feel."

It was around 3 a.m. when Safire said good night, leaving the candidate dizzy with exhaustion, resting against a wall, still too wired to sleep, and asking the Secret Service if there was anywhere open where he could buy a sandwich and a glass of milk.

Nixon had learned something in his fifty-five years. He had given presidential candidacy serious consideration, examined the problems in his 1960 campaign, and taken steps to improve them. For the general election, he gave Mitchell and Haldeman genuine authority. Nixon couldn't resist the impulse to scribble down memoranda about the operation ("We need to mention crime in every speech"), but he tried not to be the politician who obsesses over every minute detail.

In exchange, the campaign sought to establish a comfortable, controlled climate. Nixon's program was thorough, and the operation was precise. "We should continue endeavoring to keep the day of telecast uncluttered for RN…and provide him with sufficient time at the studio to be alone for ten minutes, in a cool room, collecting his thoughts, just prior to air," a single note stated.

Haldeman went even further when Robert Kennedy was assassinated, suggesting that Nixon discontinue all personal appearances. "Eliminated would be all rallies, large public functions, press-the-flesh campaign techniques, plunging through crowds, whistle-and-prop stops," the advertisement's writer stated. "Instead, utilize the mass communications media." They never went quite that far, but Haldeman and his advisers did express their views on television that fall. Nixon's calendar would be reduced to only one notable event every day. Their rested candidate could then perform to his full potential—relaxed, on his feet, and conveying genuineness.

"The greater the element of informality and spontaneity the better he comes across," according to Price. "We have to capture and capsule this spontaneity—and this means shooting RN in situations in which it's likely to emerge, then having a chance to edit the film so that the parts shown are the parts we want shown." The discussion resulted in highly effective "man in the arena" events. The campaign produced ten hour-long television presentations in which Nixon appeared on a circular stage surrounded by the audience and took questions from a panel of voters.

Color television, tanning sessions and expertly applied cosmetics helped restore Nixon's body tones. Lights were directed toward the shadows around his eyes. Nixon had a fear of being televised from the left. The cameramen were trained, and the studio was cold, to reduce his perspiration. Pat and the girls were placed in the audience, providing moral support and a homey atmosphere. The questions were not filtered, and he fielded topics ranging from anti-Semitism to civil rights, the Vietnam War, and relations with the Soviet Union.

NIXON began the fall campaign with a significant advantage over his opponents. In early September, he envisioned a landslide that would give Republicans control of Congress. A young staffer, Alan Greenspan, created an Election Day simulation based on polls that showed Nixon winning 461 electoral votes to 11 for Humphrey and 66 for Wallace, who was mounting a third-party campaign on the American Independent Party banner. Nixon's campaign took a downturn. According to one aide, it suffered from "platitudinous wishy-washiness." Buchanan described it as "programmed, repetitious, and boring."

Nixon knew it wouldn't last—that blue-collar Democrats who supported Wallace would return to the Democratic Party if its contender showed the least signs of life. Humphrey did so in a speech in Salt Lake City on September 30, when he created a sliver of space between his views on Vietnam and that of the Johnson administration. The press desired a struggle and—reverting to form at the prospect of a Nixon victory—hailed Humphrey's tiptoe as a watershed moment. Liberal benefactors reached for their wallets, and Humphrey's campaign manager, the competent Lawrence O'Brien, got the wheezing party machinery moving. Labor leaders emphasized the link between increased salaries and Democratic electoral success.

Nixon rejected Hatfield and other opponents, instead opting for "peace with honor." Wallace contributed to his own demise by picking retired air force commander Curtis LeMay as his campaign mate, reminding voters of his incompatible qualifications for the presidency. At a news briefing, Wallace stood by glumly while the hawkish LeMay recited paeans to nuclear warfare. Wallace was forced to intervene and stop him, and LeMay only later realized his mistake. He had not wanted to appear "as a drooling idiot whose only solution to any problem is to drop atomic bombs all over the world," he told the reporters. "I assure you I'm not." Soon, Michigan, New York, and Pennsylvania returned to Democratic control, and Humphrey began to close a 15-point polling advantage.

The North Vietnamese, meanwhile, had suffered greatly during the Tet Offensive. Their Soviet quartermasters, preferring to deal with President Humphrey, pressured them to be accommodating. To improve Humphrey's chances and keep Nixon out of the White House, Soviet Premier Alexei Kosygin wrote to Lyndon Johnson that summer, offering a bargain. If Johnson halted all bombing of North Vietnam, Moscow would pressure Hanoi to participate in meaningful discussions. "I and my colleagues believe—and we have grounds for this—that a full cessation by the United States of bombardments…could promote a breakthrough," according to Kosygin. The prospects had never looked greater for a peaceful resolution to the conflict, which had already killed 30,000 American lives.

Johnson flew to Manila on election night in 1966 to promote the prospects for peace. Now, following a post-convention briefing at the LBJ Ranch in which Johnson informed Nixon there was reason to be optimistic, "I knew what was coming," Nixon remembered. Big events, such as a breakthrough in Southeast Asia, may "change people," he feared. "Events could cut down a lead as big as ours."

THE KEY TO A SETTLEMENT was the Communists' unwavering insistence for an increasing share of power in South Vietnam. Doves like Kennedy and McCarthy were willing to consider forming a coalition government with the Viet Cong. However, getting President Thieu to participate would be difficult—if not impossible—given Nixon's insistence on his refusal.

Nixon used Anna Chennault and South Vietnamese ambassador Bui Diem as go-betweens to convince Thieu that if he helped elect a Republican president, Saigon would benefit more. Anna was the Chinese-born widow of Claire Chennault, the American commander who organized the Flying Tigers, a squadron of American pilots that fought the Japanese in China during WWII. She was a well-known hostess, a Nixon fundraiser, and a Chinese lobby grandee with friends in Asian palaces. Some nicknamed her the Dragon Lady, others the Little Flower. Thieu was easily persuaded. He delayed his feet, the press reported on his intransigence, and Johnson's idea quickly became an election-year Hail Mary.

"We could stop the killing out there," Johnson told his friend Everett Dirksen, the Republican leader in the Senate. "They've implemented a new formula: wait for Nixon. And they slaughter four or five hundred people every day while waiting for Nixon."

Thieu's opposition stifled the bombing halt's political appeal. Haldeman's notebooks from the 1968 campaign show Nixon personally directing the shady backstage negotiations with a foreign country in violation of US law.

"Keep Anna Chennault working on SVN," Nixon told Haldeman at the height of the plot.

In the backdrop of their midnight phone calls, Haldeman could hear Nixon playing the "Victory at Sea album—loud." Nixon handed him Chennault's most recent report on how the Thieu government and the US commander in Saigon, General Creighton Abrams, had reacted to the prospect of a bombing halt: "D. Lady says Abrams screamed like a stuck pig." According to Haldeman's notes, Nixon also asked, "Is there any way to monkey wrench it? Anything RN can do," as well as Nixon's recommendation that Rose Woods call Louis Kung, another nationalist Chinese figure, and get him going "on the SVN—tell him to hold tough."

A New York businessman who discovered the idea alerted the White House about Nixon's plans. The United States government eavesdropped on conversations between the South Vietnamese embassy in Washington and Thieu's office in Saigon. Johnson had "The Dragon Lady" under watch. The FBI tracked the phone calls made by Agnew's campaign workers.

Rostow encouraged Johnson to "blow the whistle" and "destroy" Nixon. To expose the Republican campaign's deception on the day of the November 5 election, Johnson would have to reveal the surveillance of both a military ally and the domestic political opposition. The scandal would tarnish the next presidency and, possibly, cause a disastrous breach with South Vietnam. Neither

Johnson nor Humphrey were willing to pay the price. Johnson did not have proof of Nixon's direct involvement. A skeletal version of the Chennault affair leaked immediately, but the records and White House tapes that proved the story were kept locked away at the Johnson presidential archives. Some were sealed in what became known as "the X envelope." Nixon and his lawyers also kept Haldeman's notes, which confirmed Nixon's guilt, hidden for decades.

The droves of circumstances prevent the conclusion that Nixon's intervention cost the United States the opportunity to terminate the war in the fall of 1968, sparing tens of thousands of American and Vietnamese lives and four years of agonizing domestic political conflict. The intransigence demonstrated by both North and South Vietnam in subsequent negotiations, and historical examination of the internal political machinations and external factors at work in Saigon and Hanoi, limit such a quick judgment. "Probably no great chance was lost," concluded Democratic national security specialist William Bundy in a book-length analysis of Nixon's foreign policies.

But Bundy wrote with hindsight. What may also be claimed is that Thieu's sluggishness was aided by Nixon's signals, which closed a window that Johnson and his advisers felt had been opened with the assistance of the Soviet Union. For them, a moment of actual optimism—perhaps unlikely, but hope nonetheless—was taken. Given the lives and human misery at risk, and the internal strife that was tearing the United States apart, it is difficult not to conclude that this was the most heinous of Richard Nixon's actions during his political career.

By hook or crook, Nixon escaped Johnson's machinations. Humphrey closed the gap quickly after the bombing halt gave the Democrats something positive to say about the war. Blue-collar workers in Michigan and Pennsylvania, and peaceniks in college towns, affluent suburbs, and silk-stocking regions, all returned to the Democratic Party. Nixon's advisers expected "a November 1 crest—then a few days of statesmanship and rest." Instead, October went to Humphrey.

Nixon dodged by capitalizing on the public's well-founded distrust of LBJ. "I am told that this spurt of activity is a cynical last-minute attempt by President Johnson to salvage Mr. Humphrey's candidacy," stated Nixon, channeling Uriah Heep. "This I do not believe."

The guest was "the familiar Nixon of old...managing with artful rhetoric to convey a vicious and false accusation without taking responsibility for his words," O'Brien explained. Bundy commented that the "old Nixon" made a cameo, combining "maximum innuendo" with "pious dissociation." Johnson complained to Dirksen over the phone that "Dick's statement was ugly...that he had been told that I was a thief and the son of a bitch...but he knew my mother and she really wasn't a bitch."

But Johnson's credibility was questioned. The revelation of Thieu's stubbornness, combined with Nixon's insistence that the peace push was nothing more than a political gimmick, fueled voters' already-existing suspicion of the Johnson-Humphrey alliance. And as Wallace receded, the conservative vote in the "peripheral South" shifted toward Nixon. And Humphrey's tide fell just short of victory.

DICK AND HIS FAMILY reserved separate suites at the Waldorf Astoria in New York on election night. He opted to be alone, to go through the emotional ups and downs without Pat and the daughters at his side. On the way east that day, he cautioned them that the election would be close and that they could lose. The bombing halt had caused significant pain.

Only Haldeman was permitted to carry reports with him, which Nixon experimented with on a legal pad. The early returns confirmed that Nixon had seized large chunks of Wallace's vote on the South's border—giving him states such as Tennessee, the Carolinas, Florida, and Virginia—but that blue-collar voters in New York, Pennsylvania, and Michigan were returning to the Democratic party. By midnight, Humphrey had a small lead in the popular vote. As in 1960, California, Ohio, Texas, and Illinois would be the final four. Pat threw up in her bathroom at 6 a.m., when the newscasters reported that Mayor Daley was withholding ballots in Chicago.

But it was not 1960. Humphrey won New York, Pennsylvania, and Texas, but Nixon won Ohio, the majority of the Midwest, the border South, and nearly the whole West. And this time, Nixon's campaign had taken efforts to protect the vote, particularly in Illinois. Outside Chicago, Republican election judges withheld their findings as the Nixon campaign teased Daley, daring him to reveal his precincts. Finally, he did it. It was not enough. Nixon had secured Illinois and the White House.

The Nixons returned home to discover a largely empty refrigerator and the president-elect's valet, Manolo Sanchez, gone for the afternoon. The family celebrated with canned soup and scrambled eggs. Dick went into his study, placed Victory at Sea on the stereo, and turned it so loud that "everybody on Fifth Avenue…could hear it," five storeys down. The bombing glow had faded just in time. "If the election had been one day earlier, we would have lost," Price told me. Nixon would enter office with only 43% of the vote in the three-way contest. It was a Goldilocks triumph. On November 5, he won by a narrow margin.

Johnson suppressed his disappointment and gave the Nixons a presidential plane to transport them to Florida for a brief holiday. Pat and Dick boarded and, away from the prying eyes of the journalists, "they turned to each other," Julie recounted. "Simultaneously, they embraced, and my father swung Mother around in a pirouette."

Chapter 13: Nixon's War

Johnson flew to Manila on election night in 1966 to promote the prospects for peace. Now, following a post-convention briefing at the LBJ Ranch in which Johnson informed Nixon there was reason to be optimistic, "I knew what was coming," Nixon remembered. Big events, such as a breakthrough in Southeast Asia, may "change people," he feared. "Events could cut down a lead as big as ours."

The key to a settlement was the Communists' unwavering insistence for an increasing share of power in South Vietnam. Doves like Kennedy and McCarthy were willing to consider forming a coalition government with the Viet Cong. However, getting President Thieu to participate would be difficult—if not impossible—given Nixon's insistence on his refusal.

Nixon used Anna Chennault and South Vietnamese ambassador Bui Diem as go-betweens to convince Thieu that if he helped elect a Republican president, Saigon would benefit more. Anna was the Chinese-born widow of Claire Chennault, the American commander who organized the Flying Tigers, a squadron of American pilots that fought the Japanese in China during WWII. She was a well-known hostess, a Nixon fundraiser, and a Chinese lobby grandee with friends in Asian palaces. Some nicknamed her the Dragon Lady, others the Little Flower. Thieu was easily persuaded. He delayed his feet, the press reported on his intransigence, and Johnson's idea quickly became an election-year Hail Mary.

"We could stop the killing out there," Johnson told his friend Everett Dirksen, the Republican leader in the Senate. "They've implemented a new formula: wait for Nixon. And they slaughter four or five hundred people every day while waiting for Nixon."

Thieu's opposition stifled the bombing halt's political appeal. Haldeman's notebooks from the 1968 campaign show Nixon personally directing the shady backstage negotiations with a foreign country in violation of US law.

"Keep Anna Chennault working on SVN," Nixon told Haldeman at the height of the plot.

In the backdrop of their midnight phone calls, Haldeman could hear Nixon playing the "Victory at Sea album—loud." Nixon handed him

Chennault's most recent report on how the Thieu government and the US commander in Saigon, General Creighton Abrams, had reacted to the prospect of a bombing halt: "D. Lady says Abrams screamed like a stuck pig." According to Haldeman's notes, Nixon also asked, "Is there any way to monkey wrench it? Anything RN can do," as well as Nixon's recommendation that Rose Woods call Louis Kung, another nationalist Chinese figure, and get him going "on the SVN—tell him to hold tough."

A New York businessman who discovered the idea alerted the White House about Nixon's plans. The United States government eavesdropping on conversations between the South Vietnamese embassy in Washington and Thieu's office in Saigon. Johnson had "The Dragon Lady" under watch. The FBI tracked the phone calls made by Agnew's campaign workers.

Rostow encouraged Johnson to "blow the whistle" and "destroy" Nixon. To expose the Republican campaign's deception on the day of the November 5 election, Johnson would have to reveal the surveillance of both a military ally and the domestic political opposition. The scandal would tarnish the next presidency and, possibly, cause a disastrous breach with South Vietnam. Neither Johnson nor Humphrey were willing to pay the price. Johnson did not have proof of Nixon's direct involvement. A skeletal version of the Chennault affair leaked immediately, but the records and White House tapes that proved the story were kept locked away at the Johnson presidential archives. Some were sealed in what became known as "the X envelope." Nixon and his lawyers also kept Haldeman's notes, which confirmed Nixon's guilt, hidden for decades.

The droves of circumstances prevent the conclusion that Nixon's intervention cost the United States the opportunity to terminate the war in the fall of 1968, sparing tens of thousands of American and Vietnamese lives and four years of agonizing domestic political conflict. The intransigence demonstrated by both North and South Vietnam in subsequent negotiations, and historical examination of the internal political machinations and external factors at work in Saigon and Hanoi, limit such a quick judgment. "Probably no great chance was lost," concluded Democratic national security specialist William Bundy in a book-length analysis of Nixon's foreign policies.

But Bundy wrote with hindsight. What may also be claimed is that Thieu's sluggishness was aided by Nixon's signals, which closed a window that Johnson and his advisers felt had been opened with the assistance of the Soviet Union. For them, a moment of actual optimism—perhaps unlikely, but hope nonetheless—was taken. Given the lives and human misery at risk, and the internal strife that was tearing the United States apart, it is difficult not to conclude that this was the most heinous of Richard Nixon's actions during his political career.

By hook or crook, Nixon escaped Johnson's machinations. Humphrey closed the gap quickly after the bombing halt gave the Democrats something positive to say about the war. Blue-collar workers in Michigan and Pennsylvania, and peaceniks in college towns, affluent suburbs, and silk-stocking regions, all returned to the Democratic Party. Nixon's advisers expected "a November 1 crest—then a few days of statesmanship and rest." Instead, October went to Humphrey.

Nixon dodged by capitalizing on the public's well-founded distrust of LBJ. "I am told that this spurt of activity is a cynical last-minute attempt by President Johnson to salvage Mr. Humphrey's candidacy," stated Nixon, channeling Uriah Heep. "This I do not believe."

The guest was "the familiar Nixon of old…managing with artful rhetoric to convey a vicious and false accusation without taking responsibility for his words," O'Brien explained. Bundy commented that the "old Nixon" made a cameo, combining "maximum innuendo" with "pious dissociation." Johnson complained to Dirksen over the phone that "Dick's statement was ugly…that he had been told that I was a thief and the son of a bitch…but he knew my mother and she really wasn't a bitch."

But Johnson's credibility was questioned. The revelation of Thieu's stubbornness, combined with Nixon's insistence that the peace push was nothing more than a political gimmick, fueled voters' already-existing suspicion of the Johnson-Humphrey alliance. And as Wallace receded, the conservative vote in the "peripheral South" shifted toward Nixon. And Humphrey's tide fell just short of victory.

dick and his family reserved separate suites at the Waldorf Astoria in New York on election night. He opted to be alone, to go through the emotional ups and downs without Pat and the daughters at his side. On the way east that day, he cautioned them that the election would be close and that they could lose. The bombing halt had caused significant pain.

Only Haldeman was permitted to carry reports with him, which Nixon experimented with on a legal pad. The early returns confirmed that Nixon had seized large chunks of Wallace's vote on the South's border—giving him states such as Tennessee, the Carolinas, Florida, and Virginia—but that blue-collar voters in New York, Pennsylvania, and Michigan were returning to the Democratic party. By midnight, Humphrey had a small lead in the popular vote. As in 1960, California, Ohio, Texas, and Illinois would be the final four. Pat threw up in her bathroom at 6 a.m., when the newscasters reported that Mayor Daley was withholding ballots in Chicago.

But it was not 1960. Humphrey won New York, Pennsylvania, and Texas, but Nixon won Ohio, the majority of the Midwest, the border South, and nearly the whole West. And this time, Nixon's campaign had taken efforts to protect the vote, particularly in Illinois. Outside Chicago, Republican election judges withheld their findings as the Nixon campaign teased Daley, daring him to reveal his precincts. Finally, he did it. It was not enough. Nixon had secured Illinois and the White House.

The Nixons returned home to discover a largely empty refrigerator and the president-elect's valet, Manolo Sanchez, gone for the afternoon. The family celebrated with canned soup and scrambled eggs. Dick went into his study, placed Victory at Sea on the stereo, and turned it so loud that "everybody on Fifth Avenue…could hear it," five storeys down. The bombing glow had faded just in time. "If the election had been one day earlier, we would have lost," Price told me. Nixon would enter office with only 43% of the vote in the three-way contest. It was a Goldilocks triumph. On November 5, he won by a narrow margin.

Johnson suppressed his disappointment and gave the Nixons a presidential plane to transport them to Florida for a brief holiday. Pat and Dick boarded and, away from the prying eyes of the journalists, "they turned to each other," Julie recounted. "Simultaneously, they embraced, and my father swung Mother around in a pirouette."

Nixon was a skilled liar, but this was an outright whopper. He puttered incessantly with the trappings of the presidency, immersing himself in detail as a balm for his soul, teaching Haldeman and the others about art, music, pageantry, and gastronomy.

"Any individual can only focus on the weightiest matters for certain lengths of time....You need a diversion," Haldeman told me. "For some people it's exercise; for some people it's sex; for some people it's reading Western novels" whereas for Nixon, "it was sitting talking about things that don't matter very much."

Pat was in charge of social events, decorations, and furniture. She worked well with the White House curators to acquire historic objects for the home. She also received memos. Five days after the inauguration, "The President" sent a memorandum to "Mrs. Nixon" saying, "With regard to RN's room, what would be most desirable is an end table like the one on the right side of the bed, which will accommodate two dictaphones as well as a telephone." RN must utilize one dictaphone for current things and another for memos from the file that he does not want transcribed at this moment. Furthermore, he requires a larger table on which to work at night. Needless to say, Pat had her own bedroom.

Nixon issued a presidential edict prohibiting soup courses at state meals. The stated purpose was to shorten the nights, but word quickly circulated that he had bungled a spoon and spilled soup over his white shirt. The steaks served on the yacht Sequoia were excessively thick, he concluded. The canned music in the resident dining area should be substituted with songs from the Nixon record collection. The chairs in the Cabinet Room were overly firm. LBJ's shower was remodeled. An ice machine was discarded because the president liked ice cubes without holes. "When the oval room is re-done I would like to have the coffee table in front of the fireplace replaced by one that does not block the view of the fireplace from the desk," he wrote to Haldeman. The image of George Washington needs to be raised, and a better clock purchased. According to Nixon, donors were "rich, fat, drunk, and dumb," hence television cameras should be banned from fund-raising events. "You want to get on TV with the real people, not these sodden looking bastards."

The Nixon campaign bumper stickers required improvement. "The President wants his phone redesigned," Haldeman informed the crew, who then did an inventory of the presidential golf bags. There was little golf, but when there was, it was never at country clubs that allowed cameras on the links. He was never going to have a caddie; he found the relationship unpleasant. The tinkering with details did not stop at the water's edge. "I want a check made with regard to the incredibly atrocious modern art that has been scattered around the embassies around the world," Nixon texted. "This Administration is going to turn away from…offbeat art, music and literature."

Nixon's Idiosyncrasies were mostly innocuous. But one of the president's eccentricities proved disastrous. As the stresses and responsibilities of the office increased, he sought relaxation by giving frightening directives to his assistants, leaving them to decide which ones to heed and which to ignore. During the transition period leading up to the inauguration, he signed off on the procedure in writing. "There may be times when you or others may determine that the action I have requested should not be taken," Haldeman wrote in response to Nixon. "I will accept such decisions but I must know about them."

Most of the decrees were innocuous—banning a press reporter from Air Force One or threatening to cut off government funds to an errant university—but some, such as bombing Damascus following a Middle East skyjacking, could have serious consequences. "He had certain hot buttons and if you inadvertently tripped that wire, it was going to set off an explosive reaction," Tom Huston, his assistant, remembered. "He had a darker side and…"He wanted everybody around him to notice his foolish ideas and allow them to fester until he could rethink them.

"Oh hell, Bill—you know me better than that," Nixon told Rogers, after the secretary of state waited a time before double-checking with Nixon on a presidential order to terminate all department officials in Laos. Damascus was not bombed. But of all the unusual aspects of Nixon's presidency, this was the most hazardous. It may have allowed him to exorcise his problems and feel powerful by inflicting harm on an enemy—to soothe "his fevers," as Garment put it—but eventually a sycophant would have to take the president seriously.

Haldeman and Ehrlichman had years of experience defending the "mad monk," as they called Nixon, from himself. Kissinger and Laird learnt to do so swiftly. But Colson "vigorously stirred up the demons," Garment claimed. John Mitchell was no softie, but "that fucking

Colson is going to kill us all," he exclaimed loudly. When Ray Price questioned who Colson's constituency was, Mitchell responded, "The president's worst instincts."

Nixon's cardinal challenge was straightforward: bring the Vietnam War to a satisfactory finish. "Don't ever—no matter what facet of the Nixon presidency you consider—don't ever lose sight of Vietnam as the overriding factor in the first Nixon term," Haldeman was about to say. "It overshadowed everything, all the time, in every discussion, in every decision, in every opportunity and every problem."

Nixon never claimed to have a secret plan to end the war, but he did. The covert plan was to win. Not win in the sense that he saw the North Vietnamese surrendering on the deck of an American battleship, as the Japanese had done. His goal was to wound and stay in Hanoi long enough for Saigon to establish institutions—an army, a government—and endure for at least a while on its own. In the meanwhile, he would appease the American people by abolishing the draft, decreasing losses, and withdrawing soldiers. During the campaign, he described it as "ending the war and winning the peace."

Nixon conveyed his concerns at a meeting with his foreign policy team five days after taking office. "We have difficult conversations in private but maintain a peaceful public stance to gain time...He told the NSC that he was providing the South Vietnamese an opportunity to strengthen the regime while punishing the Viet Cong. "Within three or four months bring home a few troops unilaterally...as a ploy for more time domestically, while we continue to press at the negotiation table for a military settlement."

Nixon and Kissinger categorically rejected a different option: a quick withdrawal of US forces under terms that would cause the unification of Vietnam under Communist rule. This course has some attractions. He could blame his predecessors for losing the war, as the French had done in Indochina in 1954 and de Gaulle did after the French left Algeria in 1962.

America's allies in South Vietnam could have been evacuated, reducing carnage. Cambodia, in particular, may have avoided the horrific suffering that was ahead. American prestige might recover, perhaps enhance. "There is more respect to be won in the opinion of this world by a resolute and courageous liquidation of unsound positions than by the most stubborn pursuit of extravagant or unpromising objectives," George Kennan told Congress in 1966.

Nixon lacked the necessary courage. He lacked originality and could not break out from the Cold War canon. And if he wasn't willing to quit, neither was the rest of the country. In a statewide referendum held in November 1970 in the liberal stronghold of Massachusetts, two-thirds of voters rejected a plan for immediate withdrawal. Nixon felt sympathy for those in South Vietnam who had placed their trust in the United States. He and his countrymen also believed they owed an obligation to the families of Americans slain or injured in conflict. And "credibility" dominated his thoughts. "What is on the line is more than South Vietnam," Nixon stated at a Cabinet and NSC meeting. "If we fail to end the war in a way that will not be an American defeat, and in a way that will deny the aggressor his goal, the hawks in Communist nations will push for even more and broader aggression."

The other Southeast Asian governments, such as Thailand, Malaysia, and Indonesia, had made significant progress in developing free-market economies. They required time and breathing room. And "what concerns me more than anything else is what happens in the United States." If a great power fails to achieve its objectives, it ceases to be a great power. When a great force looks inward and fails to live up to its promises, its grandeur diminishes," he added. Nixon was not a man of faded brilliance.

When the Cabinet and his aides cheered his remarks, he apologized, saying, "I really didn't mean to make a speech."

Nixon's Model was Eisenhower had put an end to the combat in Korea. During his tenure as vice president, he got a courtside seat to witness the great commander at work. Now, attempting to resolve another conflict on Asia's border, he drew on his experience and used Ike's techniques.

Soon after his election in 1952, Eisenhower informed Moscow and Beijing that the United States would employ any means necessary to resolve the Korean stalemate. The Communists couldn't be certain that the unsparing hero who had sent his army to Omaha Beach and oversaw the air assault on Germany was lying, and the rubble of two Japanese cities testified to America's willingness to use the bomb. So the Korean War ended.

There were carrots to be dangled alongside the madman's stick, as Nixon tried to enlist the Soviet Union in his hunt for an escape from Vietnam. It was another important aspect of the "secret" plan.

The Soviets were content to watch Washington struggle with its tar baby, and they provided the ammunition that allowed Hanoi to continue fighting. But Southeast Asia was only part of the world. The Soviet Union had various domestic and international goals that Nixon could assist them achieve. Kissinger met Soviet ambassador Anatoly Dobrynin in secret, with Nixon's agreement. The two met in the Map Room, on the East Wing's first level. Progress in trade negotiations or talks to reduce the cost of the arms race would be contingent on the Soviet Union's readiness to put pressure on Hanoi. It was to be called "linkage."

Kissinger persuaded Dobrynin that American pride did not require South Vietnam to be free indefinitely—only long enough for the US to withdraw with its banners waving. If the North eventually succeeded and South Vietnam went Communist after "a fairly reasonable interval," Kissinger believed it would be fine. When Dobrynin appeared unmoved, Kissinger used threats. Finally, Nixon joined them, lending the ambassador a yellow legal pad and urging him, "You'd better take some notes."

"The humiliation of defeat is absolutely unacceptable," Nixon told Dobrynin. "We will not hold still for being diddled to death in Vietnam."

The president used the China card, assuring the Soviets that America's willingness to deal with the Chinese would not be used against them, yet confirming that it was.

However, it was always a hard, paradoxical, and possibly doomed business to advocate peace at home while thumping one's chest abroad.

To demonstrate his commitment, the maniac ordered a military assault, which eventually became the basis for an article of impeachment.

Ten weeks into his administration, Nixon, on the advice and support of his military commanders, ordered the air force to begin bombing Communist camps and supply lines in Cambodia, a neutral country that shared a border with Vietnam. The enemy planned, refitted, and organized offensives from beneath the jungle canopy. Hundreds of Americans died each week. Nearly half of all Nixon administration casualties occurred in the first six months of 1969.

Since 1965, the Air Force has been utilizing high-altitude B-52 Stratofortresses in Southeast Asia. The swept-wing BUFFs were originally designed as nuclear weapon delivery vehicles, but with modified bomb bays and redesigned wing racks, they could carry 27 tons of high explosive. A cell of three bombers could use 500- and 750-pound bombs to cover a mile long and half-mile wide area. Humans, animals, machinery, and structures were pounded mercilessly inside that box, with no warning. When American troops entered the bomb zone following the attacks, they found no-man's land with moonlike craters, splintered and uprooted trees, and enemy soldiers wandering in a trance, covered in blood, with shattered eardrums and internal hemorrhaging. The B-52s were powerful weapons when deployed against concentrations of Communist forces and appreciated for breaking enemy morale, but they were expensive and inaccurate instruments for jungle warfare. The bombs fell from 30,000 feet. The threat to citizens was clear.

On May 9, the New York Times published a front-page report about the Menu bombing raids. Kissinger erupted in rage, and he and Nixon summoned J. Edgar Hoover, whose agents planted wiretaps on the phones of four news reporters and thirteen administration officials suspected of leaking, including Nixon allies such as John Sears and William Safire. When Hoover balked about bugging columnist Joseph Kraft, the White House hired a private investigator to finish the job.

By extending the bombardment into Cambodia, Nixon delivered a message to Hanoi. However, the message was mixed. The maniac had shown his willingness to escalate—but by doing it covertly, he had verified that the public's thirst for war was not limitless.

That July, to buy time and calm the people, Nixon openly supported Defense Secretary Laird's plan to replace front-line US fighting forces with South Vietnamese troops. It became known as Vietnamization. At a meeting on Guam, Nixon set the terms with President Thieu, laying out what became known as the "Nixon doctrine." The United States will no longer fight for those who refused to protect themselves, he told the reporters. The US military was not misled by Vietnamization and what it represented. Nixon's commanders knew that without American combat forces, South Vietnam's survival was "highly uncertain," according to Kissinger. It had been determined that "victory was impossible."

In the fall of 1969, Dobrynin wrote to Moscow that Nixon was becoming increasingly hostile, caustic, paranoid, and agitated by the Vietnam problem.To all indications, he is becoming increasingly concerned about the fate of his predecessor, Lyndon Johnson. Apparently, this is becoming so emotional that Nixon is losing control."

The madman's conduct helped shape Dobrynin's description. However, Nixon understood that his expectations of finishing the war in months were unrealistic. "I underestimated the willingness of the North Vietnamese to hang on," he'd tell me.

Johnson's negotiations with the North Vietnamese in Paris remained stalemate until the summer of 1969, when Hanoi consented to parallel secret talks between the two countries. Nixon's requirements were untenable: he insisted that the North leave the Saigon government intact. However, the North Vietnamese attended the talks with only one goal in mind: to engineer the South's capitulation. The losses incurred during the Tet campaign did not derail the Politburo's commitment. They, like George Washington's army, did not have to win—they only had to avoid defeat and exhaust an empire's will.

"Any incentive for the enemy to negotiate is destroyed if he is told in advance that if he just waits for 18 months, we will be out anyway," Nixon told the nation during a September press conference. He was arguing against a defined timeline, as members of Congress suggested—but he could just as well have been discussing his own approach. If the Americans were going, the Communist officials in Hanoi reasoned, why make concessions?

On the home front, Nixon faced a stark contrast between the World War II generation and their children, who had not experienced the difficulties of war and despair that had shaped their parents.

Eisenhower and Nixon debated the morality of war, notably the Allied strategic bombing missions, during a long trip across Virginia in 1954.

Eisenhower conceded that slaughtering civilians was wrong but justified by the enemy's depravity. The brutality of Nanking, the Blitz, and Treblinka justified the destruction of Dresden and Nagasaki.

Neither Kennedy nor Johnson had challenged the canon, nor would Nixon. Before Congress cut off funding for the bombing in the summer of 1973, the US dropped over 7.5 million tons of bombs on Laos, Cambodia, and Vietnam—the equivalent of one hundred A-bombs and more than three times the 2.1 million tons of explosives sown by American bombers throughout World War II.

"Just remember you're doing the right thing," Nixon would remind his staff. It was how he always consoled himself, "when I killed some innocent children in Hanoi."

The Air Force alone flew almost five million sorties. There were parts of Southeast Asia—such as the Cambodian border or Quang Tri province in South Vietnam—where the statistical pinpoints indicating a bombing strike were too numerous to detect and blended into lengthy, vast swathes of color on the maps.

Midway through Nixon's first term, a reporter stood up at a presidential press conference to question the morality of such a conflict. Nixon handled the encounter calmly, but in the Oval Office, he erupted and shouted.

With Vietnamization, Nixon could reduce American forces. However, the draft boards continued to summon a record number of young men. And as fall arrived and institutions welcomed students back, the peace movement accelerated. "Our job is to call down justice like rolling waters," the Reverend William Sloane Coffin, Yale's chaplain, told Kissinger. The antiwar groups scheduled a monthly series of demonstrations, including vigils, teach-ins, and other nonviolent actions, to begin on October 15. The first Moratorium went extremely well, with national media coverage and two million demonstrators across the country. "The young white middle-class crowds were sweet-tempered and considerate: at times even radiant," Moynihan wrote to the President. Some Washington protesters were descendants of Nixon advisers. The next event, the Mobilization on November 15, planned for a candlelit march past the White House and the reading aloud of the names of the deceased.

Nixon, like LBJ before him, was about to confront the most powerful peace movement in American history. His concerned aides distributed a column by journalist David Broder. "It is becoming more obvious with every passing day that the men and the movement that broke Lyndon B. Johnson's authority in 1968 are out to break Richard M. Nixon in 1969," according to Broder. "The likelihood is great that they will succeed again, for breaking a President is, like most feats, easier to accomplish the second time around."

Moynihan told his colleagues to prepare because Nixon "is going to be the first president to lose a war," according to Haldeman. Because loss was unavoidable, Moynihan argued, they should terminate the fighting now, while it was still "LBJ's war." Their window of opportunity was about to close. If they persisted much longer, Moynihan said, it would be "Nixon's war."

Nixon pledged additional withdrawals, but at his request, the Pentagon also prepared a comprehensive plan to punish North Vietnam. If Hanoi would not yield, it would face "measures of great consequence and force," he warned Ho Chi Minh that summer. Early versions of Operation Duck Hook called for bombing Hanoi, destroying dikes, mining harbors, and preparing tactical nuclear bombs to cut off crucial supply routes. To dissuade Soviet or Chinese intervention, America's nuclear forces around the world would be put on high alert.

Finally, Nixon blinked. Worried that escalation would tear the country apart, he rejected all Duck Hook possibilities to save the global alert. He needed to demonstrate in Hanoi that America supported him, and rioting and destroying college campuses would not suffice. Instead, he turned to the radio on November 3 to address his neglected Americans. He addressed "the great Silent Majority," asking for more time. Nixon described the actions he had taken to negotiate, Hanoi's ongoing resistance, and the risks of a hasty retreat. Noting that the Communists had slaughtered three thousand civilians in Hue during the Tet Offensive, he warned that "these atrocities in Hue would become the nightmare of the entire nation" if the US departed.

"The first defeat in our nation's history would result in a collapse of confidence in American leadership," according to him. "A nation cannot remain great if it betrays its allies and lets down its friends."

The "silent majority" speech was a magnificent piece of political communication—one of the few talks that, as Nixon famously stated, changed history. Telegrams poured Washington, reinforcing Nixon's leadership and confidence. His poll numbers skyrocketed. With the increased bombing and troop withdrawals he had ordered, the American casualty rate in Vietnam was decreasing, and in late November, Nixon signed legislation to replace the current draft system with a lottery: those who drew high numbers would no longer have a personal stake in the war debate.

He purchased time, but at what cost? Americans were shocked when journalist Seymour Hersh revealed that in 1968, US soldiers slaughtered hundreds of South Vietnamese people, including women, children, and newborns, at a hamlet called My Lai. The atrocity occurred before Nixon took office, but instead of seeking justice—as he promised the American people in a December 8 press conference—he directed his aides to use the necessary "dirty tricks" to discredit the army witnesses who had bravely refused to participate in a cover-up.

The "Forward Together" theme for the inauguration was dropped. Vice President Agnew was assigned to disparage antiwar activists as a "effete corps of impudent snobs who characterize themselves as intellectuals," as well as to chastise network commentators for criticizing the president's statements. Nixon would divide and rule.

The November mobilization reinforced the siege mentality. The candlelit march from Arlington past the White House to the Capitol continued through a stormy night and into a gloriously sunny but freezing windy day. Nixon's staff, trapped inside the White House, guarded by paratroopers and secluded from the demonstrators, was frightened, especially when the marchers paraded down Pennsylvania Avenue, flags waving like a Napoleonic army, and it became evident that over 500,000 people had come that weekend.

Kissinger chastised the North Vietnamese negotiators in Paris for attempting to polarize Americans over "Nixon's War." Now, the president has done exactly that.

Chapter 14: Not Fish nor Fowl

On January 20, 1970—the first day of his second year in office—Richard Nixon donned his overcoat and was on his way out of the Oval Office when he paused to open a silver cigarette box. Not for a smoke: it was a gift from an admirer that played "Hail to the Chief" when the lid was lifted. "Got that box just a year ago," he said to Bob Haldeman and Rose Woods, as the now-familiar notes filled the darkened room.

The first twelve months of Nixon's presidency had been remarkably consequential. Vietnam alone would have made them so. But in the Nixon era—in those days before Ronald Reagan would inaugurate his presidency with the declaration that "government is the problem" and Bill Clinton would proclaim that "the era of big government is over"—there was still the presumption that Americans wanted an activist government addressing the nation's ills. And Nixon had met that goal.

As he prepared to take office, Nixon had told Theodore White that he planned to focus on foreign affairs, for when it came to domestic policy, the cabinet and Congress could run the country. Even had he wanted to dismantle the popular achievements of the New Deal or the Great Society, there was no constituency on Capitol Hill, or in the federal bureaucracy, for such action. The Republicans had whittled down the Democratic majority in the two elections since Lyndon Johnson's 1964 landslide, but there were still 57 Democrats and 43 Republicans in the Senate, and 245 Democrats and 192 Republicans in the House. Nixon was the first first-term president since Zachary Taylor, in 1849, to take office with both houses of Congress in the hands of the opposition party.

In coping with the presidency's demands, Nixon often fell back on the lessons he had learned as Eisenhower's understudy. Ike was the leader with whom he had apprenticed. It was the presidency he had known up close. "He was a great admirer," aide James Schlesinger recalled. "He would frequently cite what Eisenhower felt about this or that."

Like Ike, Nixon sought to govern from the center, installed his campaign manager as attorney general, and chose a deliberate pace when dealing with civil rights. His initial plans to end the Vietnam War were based largely on how Ike wrapped up the Korean conflict. Like Eisenhower, Nixon made strong claims of executive privilege, employed the CIA to mount coups overseas, sought détente with the Soviet Union, and flirted with the notion of replacing the GOP with a new centrist majority party. They both considered dumping their vice president and running for reelection with a Texas Democrat on their ticket. Ike added the phrase "under God" to the Pledge of Allegiance—Nixon stuck a U.S. flag pin on his lapel, and for decades American politicians failed to do so at their peril.

LIKE EISENHOWER, NIXON entered office with expansive notions. Haldeman was told to cast a wide net, and newsman Mike Wallace, scholar Doris Kearns, Kennedy speechwriter Richard Goodwin, and other liberals were considered for positions on the White House staff. Civil rights leaders Roger Wilkins and Whitney Young were offered jobs in the Nixon administration, and Freedom Rider James Farmer took one. A Democrat—Scoop Jackson—was Nixon's first choice for secretary of defense. Jackson rejected Nixon, but Harvard professor Daniel Patrick Moynihan, a Kennedy Democrat, took a position as a presidential adviser on urban affairs. Kissinger sowed the National Security Council offices with bright Ivy Leaguers like Anthony Lake, Winston Lord, and Morton Halperin. The cabinet had its share of duds, but talents like George Shultz and Elliot Richardson bloomed as skilled, principled administrators. Men like Len Garment and Ray Price were "warm, decent, humanitarian liberals," Nixon told Haldeman. "We need such men on our staff because they give leaven to the hard-nosed people like Buchanan." Within the Nixon White House, there were learned debates, and dollops of wit. One Price memo on youthful unrest was as gentle, forgiving, and perceptive a statement about America's alienated children as any White House aide ever wrote about an administration's political foes.

The problem with the right-wingers, the president told Haldeman, is that "they have a totally hard-hearted attitude where human problems and any compassion is concerned."young Yalie—especially in those fleeting moments when the morning sun catches those long flowing locks illuminating, as if from some inner source, the subtle, raptured irregularity of prayer beads worn in quest of, yet somehow also in testament to, a fundamental unity with all things."

Moynihan's mischievousness was not without cost. A January 1970 memo he wrote, accentuating the quiet progress being made in black

America and ridiculing the attention being given by Manhattan liberals to radicals like the Black Panthers, suggested that the White House would be well advised to lower the temperature of the national debate on race and treat the plight of African Americans to some "benign neglect." The memo was leaked to the press and the phrase misconstrued by Nixon's foes, then and ever after, as evidence of bigotry.

The president endorsed Moynihan's policy innovations, and other liberal measures, not just because they were good politics but also "for personal psychological reasons," Burns concluded. Nixon "wanted to think of himself as a great innovator, a bold man, creative, a man of ideas. He needed that.

Nixon gagged at the potential effect on collegiate football and other big-time men's athletics, but he okayed the requirement that women athletes have access to equal funding when he signed a higher education act with the far-reaching Title IX, banning gender discrimination in education and giving millions of young women the opportunity to demonstrate dash and skill on the playing field. The Nixon administration ended the draft, created a volunteer military, and approved a drop in the voting age from twenty-one to eighteen. A "new federalism" policy proposed to return federal revenue to the states.

Nixon's "self-determination" policy—reversing decades of government coercion forcing Native Americans to assimilate—made him an honored figure on many Indian reservations. Indian country was not immune to the spirit of the sixties, but in a series of sometimes violent disputes with young militants—the 1969–1971 occupation of Alcatraz, the seizure of the Bureau of Indian Affairs in Washington in 1972, and the 1973 "siege" at Wounded Knee—Nixon's lieutenants helped bring the crises to a close with a minimal loss of life.

The White House staff showed intellectual spryness. Senator Edward Kennedy, a longtime advocate for a federal health insurance program, would come to rue his opposition to Nixon's health care plan, which was based on the private market, with mandated coverage, augmented by public subsidies. It would return, in somewhat altered form, as the Affordable Care Act, and be enacted by Democrats in the first term of Barack Obama.

Nixon stayed resoundingly square, but did not choose to exploit many of the divisive issues—like gun control, gay rights, and abortion—that would come to preoccupy cultural conservatives. In Nixon's first term, they "weren't even on the table," Huston recalled.

"On abortion—get the hell off it," the president told his aides. "Just say it's a state matter and get the hell off it." Over time, Nixon's Supreme Court appointees—particularly William Rehnquist—would leave a lasting legacy, turning the high court, and American jurisprudence, in a rightward direction. But it was a Nixon appointee—Harry Blackmun—who wrote the opinion in Roe v. Wade, establishing a woman's right to terminate a pregnancy.

Nixon would never admit to watching commercial television, but he sometimes chanced upon shows or scenes he'd tell his aides, while surfing the channels for a sporting event. Midway through his first term, he caught an episode of All in the Family—a comedy that lampooned both the silent majority and the woolly-headed left and, on this occasion, was making the case for tolerance for gay Americans.

Nixon's more libertarian leanings were generally subject to changes in the political breeze. When pollsters showed that the public was increasingly alarmed about the increase in drug use in the inner cities, among the troops in Vietnam, and on college and high school campuses at home, Nixon launched a national "War on Drugs." It was "the single greatest opportunity we have by a thousand-mile margin," he told his aides after studying the polls.

The drug war had some early success—the efforts to combat heroin abuse in the District of Columbia, using methadone treatments, were particularly noteworthy. But as implemented and augmented by opportunistic Congresses, governors like Nelson Rockefeller, and Nixon's successors—notably Ronald Reagan and Bill Clinton—the "war" on drugs and the battle for "law and order" would metastasize, yielding punitive measures like mandatory minimum sentences, no-knock raids, and other relaxations of defendants' rights. When Nixon launched his "war," American prisons held 200,000 inmates. In the decades to follow, a country founded on the principles of individual freedom achieved the disgraceful distinction of becoming the world's greatest prison state—with more than two million people incarcerated. By 2015, with less than 5 percent of the planet's population, America had 25 percent of the world's prisoners. The cost of jailing those men and women reached $80 billion a year and the effect on African American families and communities—where one out of three young black men could expect to be imprisoned at some point in his life—was appalling.

Eight days after Nixon's inauguration, a blowout on an offshore drilling platform dumped 100,000 barrels of oil into the Pacific Ocean off Santa Barbara, fouling the beaches and slaying birds and marine wildlife. The black goo spread along the California coastline as far south as Catalina. Shorefront residents were evacuated, lest they become sick from the fumes. It was the largest oil spill to that time in America and captured national attention just as the injured environment was emerging as a potent issue in American politics.

The president flew to California and surveyed the scene by helicopter. He told the traumatized Santa Barbarians that the disaster had touched the nation's conscience. The percentage of Americans who rated the environment as their number one concern in the White House polls soared from 1 to 25 percent in months. It was "a political hurricane," said aide John Whitaker, and two Democratic presidential hopefuls—Senators Scoop Jackson of Washington and Edmund Muskie of Maine—were angling for the movement's support.

Nixon was not averse to a Teddy Roosevelt sort of environmentalism, preserving natural resources for future generations. Russell Train, a well-known conservationist, had chaired Nixon's transition task force on the issue and been appointed undersecretary of the interior. Ehrlichman, a land-use lawyer from Seattle, was supportive of the cause, as was his deputy Whitaker, a native of British Columbia, and Moynihan—who (in 1969!) alerted Ehrlichman to the "apocalyptic" dangers of global warming. By May there was a new White House environmental council. In July Nixon gave a ringing endorsement, and a pledge of federal support, to population control. In September the administration announced its opposition to construction of a new South Florida airport close by the Everglades. And on New Year's Day, 1970, Nixon signed the National Environmental Policy Act—the far-reaching law requiring environmental impact statements for large-scale federal actions.

He was just getting started. Nixon appointed Train as chairman of the newly established Council on Environmental Quality. And, as the nation prepared to mark the first Earth Day that spring, the Nixon administration sent a wide-ranging environmental message to Congress, with thirty-seven proposals to heal the earth and preserve its gifts. "No president before—or since—has offered such an extensive, coordinated legislative agenda" to protect the environment, scholar J. Brooks Flippen wrote in 2000. The Environmental Protection Agency (EPA) was established by executive fiat and placed in the capable hands of William Ruckelshaus. When Ruckelshaus moved on, Train succeeded him. With a stroke of Nixon's pen, the National Oceanic and Atmospheric Administration (NOAA) was born. The smog-killing capstone of the environmental movement emerged from Congress as the Clean Air Act of 1970. Nixon signed it and his EPA followed up with tough automobile emission and air pollution standards. He harked back to his childhood and, recognizing the political wisdom of offering benefits to working-class voters, ordered federal agencies to shed surplus properties—which were transformed into parks, for families to enjoy.

These were banner years, with worthy achievements, yet Nixon had a pervasive feeling that his record was not yielding commensurate rewards. No matter how deftly he played the game, he could not match the Democrats at catering to the environmentalists. "Some of these people are nuts," he told Barry Goldwater. America's business community was a formidable counterweight, and Nixon's commitment to U.S. leadership in high technology led him to endorse projects like the environmentally dubious Super Sonic Transport (SST). "We shall continue to do environment [events] once a month for defensive reasons," Nixon would write in the summer of 1971. "But not at the cost of jobs."

Sensing a change in momentum, Whitaker made the argument that the president should stay the course.

Nixon relented, and maintained his bona fides with the movement by signing legislation to regulate pesticides, to police ocean dumping, to protect marine mammals, and to safeguard coastal zones and shorelines. But evidence of an approaching energy crisis prompted further recalibration of priorities. To the dismay of the environmentalists, he supported the proposed Alaska Pipeline and, in late 1972, vetoed the Clean Water Act, which he claimed was too costly. Congress disagreed and overrode the veto.

As a motivating issue for American voters, the fate of the environment had flashed from spark to conflagration in a matter of months; then settled into a steady flame. Nixon's interest in the issue followed the course of the public's passion and left an abiding legacy. In 2012, the leaders of major environmental organizations—the Sierra Club, Greenpeace USA, Friends of the Earth, and others—were asked in a poll to name the U.S. president who did most for the environment. Nixon trailed only Teddy Roosevelt in the results.

with a shape-shifter like Nixon, little was indelible. The campaign to clean up the environment was one of several causes for which he launched creative initiatives—then retreated as time passed, the country returned to its Tory predilections, and his reelection campaign beckoned. He found it most irritating when he did not receive the political mileage he was due, because rancorous liberals and unappeasable liberal-leaning commentators kept carping about his performance. "During those first few years of Nixon, there was some damn good government. But Nixon couldn't get any credit for it," Moynihan recalled. "The press and others just kept denying it, denying it, and he gave up. He gave up trying."

The president's warring priorities, and internal conflicts, showed themselves in an outburst before his aides, in the summer of 1971. "I am not a liberal," Nixon raged, "I am a conservative!"

SPENDING MONEY WAS easy work. Nixon's chief domestic challenge—the continued integration of America's schools, neighborhoods, and work sites—was not. Confronted with that duty, he trudged ahead, fixed in his commitment but mindful, ever, of the political cost. The Nixonian solution: to take actions that were "operationally progressive," as Leonard Garment put it, "but obscured by clouds of retrogressive rhetoric."

Garment claimed that in these politicized times, a chief executive cannot be expected to do more. Perhaps. Successful presidents must be effective political leaders who build and maintain support. However, the Nixon administration's concrete achievements—the implementation of affirmative action as a remedy for generations of mistreatment of women and minorities, as well as the historic gains made in desegregating southern schools—must be measured against the harm done to the cause of civil rights by the president's cynical romancing of voters who remained prejudiced.

Sallyanne Payton, an African American legal expert on Nixon's staff, described the political subtext as "nods and winks."

"The subliminal appeal to the anti-black voter was always in Nixon's statements and speeches on schools and housing," Ehrlichman told me. "He was not as outspoken as George Wallace or Lester Maddox, but he conveyed a clear message that was difficult to ignore..."[presenting] his beliefs in such a way that a citizen would avoid confessing to himself that he was drawn to a racial appeal."

Nixon returned to Eisenhower-era rhetoric, contrasting civil rights activists seeking "instant integration" with bigoted radicals preaching "segregation forever." They were all "extreme groups," according to the president. Over time, the president of the United States lent weight to millions' beliefs, fueled by Wallace and his ilk, that blacks were ingrates, criminals, and welfare chiselers given undeserved benefits by the Democrats at the expense of hardworking, law-abiding citizens.

According to Payton, during the Nixon administration, the civil rights movement lost a vital asset: "the moral presence of the presidency."

Since 1957, when President Eisenhower ordered the 101st Airborne to Little Rock, the South's segregationists had given ground reluctantly, compelled by teargas and bayonets. After 160 US marshals were wounded, 28 by gunshot, it took 20,000 troops to quell an armed insurgency opposing University of Mississippi integration in 1962. The following year, then-governor Wallace gained national attention by standing in front of the "schoolhouse door" at the University of Alabama.

During the Johnson administration, the civil rights movement concentrated its efforts on Capitol Hill and the passage of historic civil rights, voting rights, and open housing laws. Threatening to cut off federal funds to segregated school districts, officials at the United States Department of Health, Education, and Welfare made very minimal headway at integrating southern classrooms. The federal government approved delays and extended deadlines in response to the claim that the South required more time. When Nixon took office, sixteen years after the Brown v. Board of Education ruling, the vast majority of the region's black students continued to attend segregated schools.

During 1968 and 1969, the Supreme Court issued no-nonsense opinions ordering the South to change its ways. The new president was tasked with executing the rulings, notwithstanding Johnson's preference for a more cautious pace. On no domestic subject was President Nixon's behavior more revealing. His efforts to fulfill the nation's commitment to black Americans while also winning the votes of disaffected ethnic voters and white southerners provide a lens through which to observe convictions merge with calculating.

Nixon's opponents claimed he was carrying out his southern strategy, which involved sacrificing the future of black children for political gain in the South. Rowland Evans and Robert Novak, two well-known columnists, anticipated that Nixon would fight for "token integration" and take "the first serious backward step from racial integration by any national administration in a generation."

As was often the case, Nixon's backtracking on civil rights stemmed from a combination of personal bitterness and political opportunism. The young man who attended integrated clubs and parties and called Jackie Robinson and Martin Luther King Jr. friends had matured into an aggrieved and more calculating politician who, like Eisenhower, concluded that black Americans, who rely on Democratic social programs, would not vote for Republican candidates.

Nixon felt misled by the cuff he received from blacks during his campaign against John Kennedy. In his private list of perceived foes, African Americans were never ranked as high as liberal Jews, but his rants against race and ethnicity sparked beliefs of black inferiority. "Most of them are basically just out of the trees," he informed Donald Rumsfeld, a young appointee.

During the 1968 campaign, Nixon told the South that he would oppose school busing to achieve racial integration. After the Supreme Court enabled cities and counties to utilize the practice to remove school district segregation in 1971, Nixon supported constitutional amendments prohibiting court-ordered busing and "forced" integration of housing in all-white communities. He repeatedly denied any overt political intent. "There is nothing that disturbs me more than to have to appear before the country as a racist," Nixon told his staff. "My feelings on race, as you know, are if anything ultra-liberal."

Busing was a virulent issue that drove a hole into the New Deal alliance, dividing liberals and minorities from blue-collar workers and suburbanites, prompting much hedging and hawing among Democrats.

THE WHITE SOUTH, of course, posed an enticing prospect for Nixon's and his party's strategists. Wallace had temporarily captured the hard-core racists of the deep South. But votes in Florida, Texas, Virginia, the Carolinas, and Tennessee, and expanding urban centers like Atlanta, were golden tickets to political prosperity that appeared to be up for grabs.

In the late 1960s, the civil rights movement became more violent, which alienated many white Americans. The photographs of nonviolent martyrs in Birmingham and Selma—being beaten by state troopers, bitten by police dogs, or tossed by fire hoses as they fought for their rights as citizens—had given way to images of "black power" advocates like Stokely Carmichael, defiant sports figures like Muhammad Ali, and the Black Panther Party's gun-toting revolutionaries.

The movement had also modified its agenda. With citizenship's essential rights now legally protected, civil rights leaders such as King pushed for economic advantages and tax-supported social programs, aggravating the white working and middle classes, who were becoming dissatisfied with growing income and property taxes. The year before his death, King joined the anti-Vietnam War movement, which was another controversial subject.

Blue-collar white voters in the North's cities and working-class suburbs had grown tired of liberal philosophizing and black militancy, just like their southern counterparts, especially as the courts' assault on de jure integration expanded to include de facto segregation north of the Mason-Dixon Line. Political leaders such as Anthony Imperiale in Newark, Frank Rizzo in Philadelphia, Sam Yorty in Los Angeles, and Louise Day Hicks in Boston tapped into powerful conservative currents outside the South.

In what became known as the Rust Belt, the prospect of a well-paying union job at the local factory was fading, adding to Wallace's anxieties about social disorder, race, and violence. As complacent American business executives and union leaders watched, Europe, Japan, Korea, and other Asian countries pushed their way into the global economy, establishing factories and staffing assembly plants with low-wage labor and cutting-edge gear. The 1970s saw a sharp reduction in the United States steel industry, and equally troubling declines in automobile, electronics, and other commodities production.

Lyndon Johnson's massive majorities in the aftermath of his 1964 landslide eroded: Democrats lost fifty-two House seats in the 1966 and 1968 legislative elections, and eight Senate seats.

The two most popular political books of the time—The Real Majority by Richard Scammon and Ben Wattenberg and The Emerging Republican Majority by the young Nixon admirer Kevin Phillips—predicted electoral realignment based on what was delicately referred to as "the social issue." Nixon's opinions were stated clearly in both volumes. "Have you read the Scammon book?" he would ask his aides.

The temptation was too much for NIXON and his assistants to resist. The "great Silent Majority" might be convinced not only on law and order, Vietnam, and patriotism, but also on the most powerful issue, race. Colson's administration used symbolic messages to polarize whites and blacks. They would portray Democrats as "the party in favor of sacrificing the majority of Americans…to appease a racial minority."

Michael Balzano, a Colson colleague, suggested in a 1971 memo to Nixon that the president send the following message to unhappy white voters: "Today, racial minorities are declaring that you can't make it in America. They genuinely mean that they won't start from the bottom of the ladder as you did. They want to exceed you and have it handed to them. You performed menial tasks to get where you are; let them do the same.

A RUSH OF retirements on the United States Supreme Court provided Nixon with an early opportunity to repay his debt to the South. However, in November 1969, the Democrat-controlled Senate rejected Nixon's nomination of federal judge Clement Haynsworth of South Carolina to the Court. Both the following nominee, Judge G.

Harrold Carswell of Georgia, and his confirmation procedure were equally bad. Democrats and liberal Republicans spent the spring of 1970 exposing Carswell's racist history and overall mediocrity, forcing Senator Roman Hruska, a Republican from Nebraska, to defend him in nearly legendary fashion.

"There are plenty of mediocre judges, individuals, and lawyers. "They are entitled to some representation, aren't they?" Hruska asked. "We can't have all Brandeises, Frankfurters and Cardozos." Perhaps so, but the Senate concluded that perfection was not such a bad thing, and it might be preferable if the next Supreme Court justice was not a segregationist. Carswell was rejected on April 8.

Nixon utilized the failures of his two southern nominees to establish a single identity among Dixie voters. He may have recovered more support than if both men had been endorsed. "As long as the Senate is constituted the way it is today, I will not nominate another southerner and let him be subjected to the kind of malicious character assassination accorded both Judges Haynsworth and Carswell," the president, who appeared angry, informed the nation. "I understand the bitter feelings of millions of Americans who live in the South about the act of regional discrimination that took place."

The politics were dangerous, "through which he had to weave his way," Garment added. But "his gut was on the right side." He wanted to see something accomplished. He was aware that this was a measure of his administration.

When they joined forces in the civil rights movement in the 1950s, King expressed concern that Nixon's prodigious abilities would make him "the most dangerous man in America." Nixon was now proving himself, if not dangerous, then certainly devious. He was an improviser, with no strong links to his era's liberal system and no desire to overthrow it. The question of race, like other domestic issues, was an impediment to negotiating; it had to be confronted in its various forms, with replies ready and contingent on the moment, while he pursued his dreams of History and Peace. When the Supreme Court called for immediate action on integration, Nixon the idealist reacted, as did the youngster who played by the rules, and the conniver who, realizing inevitability, tried to squeeze whatever benefit he could. He would obey the courts. However, he would do it via a rhetorical veil, telling the South that their mutual opponents compelled him to act. "What Nixon brought to Thurmond, and to the South generally, was an empathy," Huston observed. He informed the southerners that "the whole thing is very disquieting." It's disruptive. We're talking about destabilizing an entire culture and its norms. That was half of the message, as heard by the press, the left, and civil rights groups. The second portion of the message, which was either not heard or heard but rejected, was "I'm going to get it done."

"We will carry out the law," he said during a press conference on December 8, 1969. This was a promise he honored.

Nixon's Fundamental Declaration on Civil Rights, a white paper issued in March 1970 in response to federal court rulings on school desegregation, was emphatic in its denunciation of race-based exclusion. "Deliberate racial segregation of pupils by official action is unlawful wherever it exists," according to Nixon. "In the words of the Supreme Court, it must be eliminated, 'root and branch'—and it must be eliminated at once."

There was more than just principle at stake. Nixon didn't want another Little Rock, or a barrage of gunfire like the one that greeted James Meredith's enrollment at Ole Miss. Nixon and his political strategists intended to attract a small number of black votes in both the South and the North for his reelection campaign, and they understood that they needed to maintain their image as problem-solving moderates in order to appeal to the general public. There was a need to avoid "racist taint," Dent stated, and to provide "leadership to desegregate without bullets, blood, and bitterness."

The solution, Nixon determined, was to locate decent southerners, both white and black, who would band together to carry out the now-inevitable integration of their public schools. To meet the Supreme Court's directives, George Shultz, with the assistance of Garment and Moynihan, among others, established local advisory committees in seven southern states and, without fanfare, invited black and white citizens to sit together and devise methods for their children to share classes. As the start of the 1970 school year approached, Nixon personally joined the effort, meeting with state committees in the White House, playing on southern pride, and maintaining the weaponry they knew he possessed—the ability to cut off federal funds for their school systems or go to court for judicial orders—oiled but holstered.

Nixon's allotment of his time, and the often unpleasant task of personally appealing, demonstrated his dedication to the cause and the importance he placed on it. His performance with the Louisianans, the eighth delegation to receive the treatment, was possibly the most outstanding. After six successful performances in Washington, Shultz took the play on the road and discovered that, without the grandeur of the White House to inspire them, the black and white leaders assembled in a New Orleans hotel conference room were more resistive. When the president arrived, Shultz admitted to him, "Always before, it was all teed up, but you've got to tee it up yourself this time because we're not quite there."

Agnew warned Nixon that something like this may happen. "When the schools open, there will be blood running through the streets of the South, and if you go, this will be blood on your hands," Shultz recalls the vice president stating. "It's not your problem. This is the difficulty for liberals who have advocated for desegregation. Stay away. Southern Republican leaders had offered words of warning. "It will become Nixon's integration," a concerned North Carolina resident warned the White House.

However, even though Nixon was angered by the unanticipated shift in the scenario and the difficulty of "teeing it up," he did not allow it impact his performance. "He came in…and turned it around," Shultz recounted. persuasion, with remarkable effect." In his biography of the Nixon years, speechwriter William Safire summarized the policy as "make-it-happen, but don't make it seem like Appomattox."

"It worked," wrote Dean Kotlowski, a scholar from the time. "A confluence of presidential leadership, federal persuasion, Supreme Court rulings, Justice Department lawsuits, and the threat of NEW denying holdout districts federal aid broke white southern resistance."

Prior to 1969, just 186,000 African American pupils attended desegregated schools in the South, despite a total school population of 3 million. During autumn 1969, after the Nixon administration began to desegregate schools through litigation, 600,000 southern blacks entered desegregated schools," and by the end of 1970, "two million more African Americans were attending desegregated schools,"

Kotlowski said. "In this sense, Nixon was the greatest school desegregation in American history."

The budget office was notified and congressional appropriators cooperated. During Nixon's first term, the monies available for civil rights enforcement, including incentives for school district integration, increased from $75 million to $2.6 billion. Mitchell had previously met with a group of civil rights activists during the Nixon administration. "You will be better advised," he responded, "to watch what we do instead of what we say."

As a result, Nixon's race record is textured. "The standard indictment," noted academic Hugh Graham in 1987, "cannot account for the counterfactuals."

"Mr. Nixon was elected on a tide of reaction," said Payton, one of his few female and African American staffers. "There was a lot of space to his political right that he could have occupied, but he didn't." There was also a lot of symbolic political action aimed at appealing to discontented whites. But Mr. Nixon was hardly a counterrevolutionary. Neither was Mr. Ehrlichman or Mr. Shultz. "There is no villain in this piece," Payton explained. "Indeed, some conservatives have never forgiven Mr. Nixon for being so sensible."

The Nixon administration's success in ending de jure segregation was insufficient for civil rights activists, liberal members of Congress, and editorial writers who sought to eliminate de facto segregation in the North and South by busing school children across district lines or using court orders to integrate segregated neighborhoods. As a result, Nixon gained little credit for the educational revolution he initiated in the South. He generally rants about media unfairness, but in this case, he was willing to be a quiet hero.

the white house took additional unexpected moves toward racial equality. When southern hardliners attempted to avoid integration by enrolling children in segregated private academies, Nixon ignored Thurmond's and others' demands and rejected the proposal that all-white private schools be tax-exempt. "Federal aid to schools deliberately segregated on racial grounds is wrong constitutionally, and morally," advised Harlow. "The South will respect him for it, angered though it will temporarily be."

In 1970, Harlow was asked to investigate the likelihood of Virginia Senator Harry Byrd, a known segregationist, joining the state's Republican Party. After talking with Republican governor Linwood Holton, Harlow stated, "Senator Byrd would bring in the rednecks if he joined the party now, and this would undermine what we have been doing extremely effectively in Virginia. The current Republican Party in Virginia has no intention to fill its ranks with white supremacists."

If the South came to regard him as "the goddamned integrationist there is," Nixon told his advisers, then be it. In early 1969, he established the Office of Minority Business Enterprise to promote black, Latino, and American Indian entrepreneurs by allocating federal contracts to minorities. When Shultz and his African American deputy, Arthur Fletcher, presented the president with the first broad affirmative action plan, the Philadelphia Plan, which aimed to integrate construction firms and other federal contractors, Nixon supported it and defended it in Congress and courts.

Nixon did not invent affirmative action. Nixon's proposal, like everything else he did on civil rights, had a political component. Ehrlichman recalled how the Philadelphia Plan divided two Democratic constituencies: minorities and labor. Regardless of his motivations, Nixon was instrumental in establishing affirmative action, and two of his Supreme Court selections were important in its preservation. "In order to go beyond racism, we must first address race. "There is no other way," said Blackmun, concurring with Powell's 1978 decision in the case of University of California v. Bakke. "In order to treat people equally, we must treat them differently."

NIXON understood how artistically he handled race. At the 1970 Gridiron Dinner, he confessed with a wink while giving one of Washington's renowned performances to club members and visitors. The white-tied swells were surprised when two pianos appeared on the Gridiron stage, allowing Nixon and Agnew to perform as a duo, and everyone laughed when, no matter what song Nixon played—"Home on the Range," "Missouri Waltz," or "The Eyes of Texas Are Upon You"—Agnew drowned him out with "Dixie."

But one of the finest events in the Nixon White House—the one at which the president appeared to enjoy himself the most—was the

April 29, 1969, celebration of Duke Ellington's seventieth birthday, a party packed with black jazz musicians, at which Nixon exchanged hugs and kisses with Ellington, awarded him the Medal of Freedom, and sat down at the piano to serenade the great bandleader and composer with a presidential rendition of "Happy Birthday."

It was a particularly memorable experience for Ellington, who was born in Washington and whose father had worked as a butler in the palace at least once.

Chapter 15: The Week That Changed the World

HAVE PAVED Nixon traveled to China. His discomfort in the Ellsberg disaster was exacerbated by the tension of waiting for the outcome of his diplomatic efforts.

Europe was coming together, China was stirring, and Nixon saw a resurgent Japan on the horizon. The Russians appeared calmer, but this was due to strength and confidence: in the nuclear armaments race, the Soviet Union had caught up with the United States. In all this, Nixon sought opportunities. For a brave enough statesman, the grail of a stable international order with a variety of counterbalancing powers was within grasp.

"Everything is linked," Nixon told Kissinger and ambassador Kenneth Rush. "It's…part of a grand scheme." It would determine "where our kids are going to be, 25 years from now."

On July 6, Nixon talked aloud at an editors' conference in Kansas City on the momentous upheavals of the postwar era and how the end of American preeminence was "not a bad thing." He envisioned a pentagonal multipolar world "within our time" ruled by five big "superpowers": the United States, the Soviet Union, Japan, Western Europe, and China.

There was no Saul-like moment of revelation that led Richard Nixon to China. In the 1960s, a number of American politicians, including Lyndon Johnson, Nelson Rockefeller, and Hubert Humphrey, toyed with the idea of a diplomatic breakthrough. However, the right's entrenched ideology was to treat "Red China" as a pariah, a strategy strengthened by the powerful China Lobby and supported by periodic stories of Communist Chinese purges and massacres. As a result, American diplomats and Asian leaders were astonished when Nixon visited them during his "wilderness years," and he pressed them on rapprochement with the Communist juggernaut.

In 1967, Nixon spent two nights in Indonesia with Ambassador Marshall Green. After a diplomatic dinner party, Nixon took out a tape recorder and the two men talked late into the night. As Nixon was departing for the airport, Green asked him what he planned to do with his tapes and notes. Nixon said he would have his secretary transcribe them so he could have the material in his files.

Nixon and Ray Price collaborated on the essay "Asia After Vietnam," which was published in the journal Foreign Affairs in October 1967. It alerted Americans to significant changes taking place on the other side of the globe.

Nixon stated that the classic isms—communism, totalitarianism, colonialism, and even anticolonialism—were giving way to "the age of computers and cybernetics," in which autonomous Asian countries aspire to liberate and thrive from their populations' creativity rather than subordinate them. "The 'people,' in the broadest sense, have become an entity to be served rather than used," he stated." "In much of Asia, this change represents a revolution of no less magnitude than the revolution that created the industrial West."

China cast its shadow over these significant changes. It was time for the West to intervene. "We simply cannot afford to leave China forever outside the family of nations, there to nurture its fantasies, cherish its hates and threaten its neighbors," Nixon wrote. "There is no place on this small planet for a billion potentially capable people to live in angry isolation..."The world will not be safe until China reforms. Thus, to the extent that we have the ability to affect events, our goal should be to bring about change."

Mao read the piece and passed it on to Zhou.

Nixon wasted little time after taking office. In his second week as president, he wrote to Kissinger, who had delivered a bleak assessment on the state of low-level negotiations between American and Chinese diplomats in Warsaw. Nixon wanted to restart the negotiations. "I believe we should encourage the administration's attitude of 'exploring rapprochement with the Chinese.'" "Of course, this should be done privately and under no circumstances should it be published," Nixon told Kissinger. "However, in contact with your friends and particularly in any ways you might have to get to this Polish source, I would continue to plant the idea."

Kissinger, as Rockefeller's foreign policy adviser, advocated that the United States construct "a subtle triangle" with China and the Soviet Union. However, with Vietnam and the Russians on Nixon's plate, the prospect of establishing diplomatic relations with the Chinese appeared unrealistic. "Our leader has taken leave of reality," Kissinger informed his adviser, Alexander Haig.

Though not widely acknowledged at the time, the Soviet Union's 1968 invasion of Czechoslovakia was a Cold War watershed moment—not because it harmed Europe, but because it alarmed Mao and his colleagues in Beijing. The Soviets had declared the right to control ideological deviancy in Communist countries and employed the Red Army to repress the Czechs. The Americans might be jackals, but California was 5,000 miles away. Mao and the Soviets shared borders. An uneasy border. In 1969, Soviet and Chinese frontier guards engaged in running gun fights along the Amur and Ussuri rivers. Soldiers from both sides were killed as the combat developed into mortar and artillery duels and amphibious assaults. There was a tremendous military buildup, with more Soviet armor facing south and east than west. The Chinese tested H-bombs in the wastelands along the border. A Soviet envoy contacted an American counterpart, asking if the United States would cooperate in a preemptive attack on China's nuclear weapons program.

Mao had appointed four Chinese marshals—trusted revolutionaries—to examine China's defense. According to their study, the Soviet "revisionists" posed "a more serious threat to our security than the US imperialists." Moscow was preparing "an anti-China ring of encirclement." They told their old commander that an approach to the United States had to be handled cautiously, otherwise the U.S. would end up "sitting on top of the mountain [watching] a fight between two tigers." However, a "tactical" accommodation with the Americans "may result in strategic outcomes." Nixon "hopes to win over China," according to one of the marshals. "It is necessary for us to utilize the contradiction between the United States and the Soviet Union in a strategic sense, and pursue a breakthrough in Sino-American relations." It was crucial enough to push Taiwan's disputed status and the fate of Chiang Kai-shek's island republic to the back burner.

The breakthrough occurred in the spring of 1971, when the United States table tennis team, competing against the expert Chinese and others at the world championships in Japan, boldly offered themselves to China. Mao loved the idea. On April 12, the American athletes arrived in Beijing, where they were greeted cordially. Then, late in the afternoon of April 27, Kissinger received word that the Pakistani envoy wanted to see him. Ambassador Hilay submitted a two-page handwritten summary of a communication Zhou had sent to Pakistani leader Yahya Khan. "The Chinese Govt reaffirms its willingness to receive publicly in Peking a special envoy of the President of the US (for instance, Mr. Kissinger) or the US Secy of State or even the President of the US himself for a direct meeting and discussions," according to the statement.

The Americans responded with approval, and confirmation received via Pakistan on June 2. "Chairman Mao Tse Tung has indicated that he welcomes President Nixon's visit and looks forward to that occasion when he may have direct conversations with His Excellency the President," according to Zhou. China would welcome Kissinger as a secret envoy to prepare the historic visit. "This is the most important communication that has come to an American President since the end of World War II," the national security adviser told his superior.

Kissinger's group remembered the amusing touches, but also how moved they were. Soaring over the snow capped Himalayas that near-perfect morning, high above ancient trade routes, a cheerful handful dispatched to cheat grim-visaged conflict. Kissinger felt a rekindled sense of surprise and discovery, "the quality that in one's youth made time seem to stand still; that gave every event the mystery of novelty; that enabled each experience to be relished because of its singularity." Polo was their trip code name.

The Americans arrived shortly after noon on Friday and were led to the Diaoyutai, a compound of lakes and trees that had previously functioned as the imperial fishing hole but was now a guarded retreat for important foreign visitors. Zhou arrived about 4:30 p.m. that day and stayed for the majority of the first night and the next two. "His gaunt expressive face was dominated by piercing eyes, conveying a mixture of intensity and repose," Kissinger later recounted. He dominated the room "not by his physical dominance" like de Gaulle, but by an attitude of "controlled tension, steely discipline, and self-control, as if he were a coiled spring." Given the status of the world in the early 1970s, Kissinger concluded that a rapprochement between China and the United States was unavoidable. Nonetheless, "that it should occur so rapidly and develop so naturally owes no little to the luminous personality and extraordinary perception of the Chinese premier."

Kissinger wrote a 27-page report on his trip for Nixon, describing the

Chinese as "tough, idealistic, and fanatical" but possessing the "inward security" required to negotiate. Unlike the Russians, who made small compromises over time, the Chinese cut straight to an acceptable bottom line: "They concentrated on essentials; they eschewed invective and haggling." The future would necessitate "reliability, precision, and finesse," Kissinger concluded. Nonetheless, "if we can master this process, we will have made a revolution."

On July 13, Nixon drove his golf cart to the San Clemente helipad and greeted Kissinger in the morning sunshine. They crowded in his study above the shore, evaluating the revolution. They agreed that the opening to China contained many possibilities, but the immediate payoff was psychological: American pride and confidence would be restored, while the North Vietnamese would be equally unhappy. They had gained more time to win the war and the freedom to use more ruthless tactics without fear of Chinese intervention.

Then the exuberant president broke his personal protocol and took staff—Kissinger, Haldeman, Ehrlichman, and others—to Perino's Restaurant on Wilshire Boulevard, a now-fading hotspot whose plush peach-colored booths and red velvet bar stools had, for decades, cuddled the fannies of California politicians and Hollywood movie stars. Nixon "reveled in an unchallengeable triumph," Kissinger said, accepting the well wishes of fellow diners and lingering in the foyer after a magnificent wine (Château Lafite-Rothschild 1961), beef, and crab, unable to let the evening stop.

Americans were surprised by the announcement of the openness to China. Millions were happy. The Taiwanese weren't.

Nixon had told his adviser to be tough with Zhou and Mao before Kissinger went for his trip. He instructed his adviser to instill "fear" among the Chinese by presenting Nixon as a madman who may collaborate with China's rivals—the Russians, Japanese, and Taiwanese—in horrific atrocities. However, in his very first discussion in Beijing, Kissinger accepted China's precondition for a Nixon-Mao summit: he renounced the Taiwanese independence movement and a "two China" policy, and promised Zhou that the US would "not stand in the way" of a "political evolution" that would gratify the Communists at the expense of Taiwan's freedom.

Taiwan became collateral damage. On June 30, Nixon issued

instructions to Walter McConaughy, the US ambassador, who was preparing to leave to brief the Kuomintang.

"They must be prepared for the fact that there will continue to be a step-by-step, a more normal relationship with…the Chinese mainland," Nixon told reporters. "Not because we love [the Communists], but because they exist and the international situation has significantly changed…Failure to act would jeopardize our interests in other pressing matters.

Taiwan would endure and thrive. However, the immediate result of the shift in US policy was a minor diplomatic disaster: the United Nations voted to exclude Taiwan and accept the mainland government as China's representation.

The Japanese were a bit less distressed. Japan had put plans for its own rapprochement with China on hold in deference to the United States, and Nixon's surprise statement led Prime Minister Eisaku Sato to lose face. The Japanese had hardly recovered their composure when the United States responded with another "Nixon Shock"—a monetary coup that shook not only Japan, but the entire international economy.

It had taken Nixon months to locate the right ancillaries, but in Federal Reserve Chairman Arthur Burns and the new Treasury Secretary, former Texas Governor John Connally, he had finally found partners at the economic policy table. On Sunday night, August 15, the president commanded prime-time television (preempting Bonanza) with the summer's second stunning announcement: he would treat the ailing American economy with a dose of measures that included wage and price controls, an import tax, and the suspension of the Bretton Woods Agreement, which had governed global trade for more than 25 years. Nixon announced that the United States would abandon the gold standard for an unspecified alternative. The golden postwar era was formally buried.

Nixon was responding to two economic crises, one at home and the other abroad. The primary culprit on the domestic front, as with so many other difficulties, was the cost of the Vietnam War. Nixon, like Lyndon Johnson, collaborated with the Democratic Congress to pay for the war using borrowed monies, refusing to make real sacrifices to popular domestic programs and running up budget deficits. The Fed attempted to control the accompanying inflation by gradually tightening the money supply. Gradual or not, it contributed to a recession and Republican losses in the 1970 election.

Several of Nixon's advisers, including George Shultz and economist Milton Friedman, assured him that gradualism was working and that a solid rebound lay ahead. They persuaded him to continue the course. But Burns wasn't so sure. Economists were confronted with a new phenomena known as stagflation, which was a combination of unemployment and inflation that did not respond to the typical business cycle.

Burns, concerned about inflation but determined to help Nixon win reelection, saw a wage-price freeze as the only way out. It defied conservative philosophy, but they were able to stimulate the economy while maintaining control over the expense of living. With amazing ease, Nixon and Connally abandoned their past hostility to government regulations and planned a major announcement when Congress reconvened in September.

The other quandary was gold-colored. Since 1944, when Western nations met at a resort in Bretton Woods, New Hampshire, to devise a system of fixed exchange rates, the gold-backed US dollar has served as the foundation upon which bankers have constructed the church. It remained so while Western Europe and Japan rebuilt factories after World War II, and rising nations opened up new markets, encouraging American investors, consumers, and corporations to spend money abroad. Offshore vaults quickly filled up with "Eurodollars," and the list of foreign-made products that endangered US industries—automobiles, cameras, televisions, textiles, shoes, and pianos—grew longer with each passing year. America was about to run its first trade deficit. Everyone winked, but the money in foreign banks greatly outweighed the gold in the United States' Fort Knox storage.

The world did not cooperate. A reckoning came in August, when a gold rush drew Connally back to Washington from his Texas vacation. Connally and Nixon, who were predisposed to the bolder course of action, assembled their senior advisers and flew to Camp David for secret rites: they would marry the end of the gold standard with the establishment of wage and price controls.

Various tax and budget cuts rounded out the package, the most significant of which was a new 10% import tax. The border tax, along with a weakened dollar, would raise import costs, create domestic jobs, and appease a worried electorate. With the success he was making in global affairs, Nixon concluded that the lunch-bucket issue was all the Democrats had left, and he intended to strip them of it. This is "a political matter...our primary goal must be a continued upward surge in the domestic economy," according to Nixon. "We must not, in order to stabilize the international situation, cut our guts out."

Burns and Safire went for a nocturnal walk and discussed their chief's performance. "He's a President now," Burns stated. "He has a noble motive in foreign affairs to reshape the world—or at least his motive is to earn the fame that comes from nobly reshaping the world."

Nixon's speech was triumphant. The stock rose 32 points, its highest one-day rise to date. He surpassed Senator Edmund Muskie, the Democratic front-runner, in the polls. Variety's title read, "Prez Changes Economic Game Plan." new score: dow 32, nixon 72. Returning after a negotiation conference with the North Vietnamese in Paris, Kissinger found the president "elated," bordering on "euphoria."

There was one negative note. The president felt compelled to push his fellow Americans to rise above a troubling atmosphere that had taken hold even in the heartland—a feeling Kissinger referred to as "malaise."

The peace of the fifties and the electric thrills of the sixties had been replaced by a dismal mood—appropriate for the impending decade of shortages, defeat, skepticism, and constraints. Vietnam could do that to a country. Nixon sensed it; no politician so in tune with the spirit of the people could not. Taking a leaf from Franklin Roosevelt, he attempted to motivate Americans by encouraging them to "snap out of their self-doubt." He would not be the United States' last president to do so.

What stands out in retrospect is that Nixon and Connally had no plans for what came next—no substitute for Bretton Woods, no long-term solution to stagflation. They were improvising, making it up as they went, and barely made it to November 1972. "Are we going to build a new world in sheer bluff and bombast?" Burns consulted his diary.

Memos circulated about the government. "As the shock effect of

August 15 wears off and other countries develop their negotiating strategy, defining where we want to go becomes increasingly essential," Kissinger told President Nixon on September 20. "What exactly do we want others to do?"

At home, the pay and price freeze proved to be a popular and effective temporary measure. College students enjoyed ninety-eight-cent six-packs. Homemakers bought steaks. By Election Day 1972, inflation was limited to 3% and the jobless rate had fallen to 5.5 percent.

But the freeze only pushed the can down the road as the Federal Reserve, Congress, and Nixon's budget experts injected money into the economy. Not everything was a one-time stimulus: some of the spending measures, such as the Social Security cost-of-living increases enacted in 1972, had enormous long-term implications. Steam was accumulating in the boiler. It must eventually detonate. Milton Friedman's August 30 piece for Newsweek predicted that attempts to freeze prices and wages would fail, leading to the appearance of repressed inflation.

Nixon erred by choosing short-term political gain over the long-term consequences. The time would come to "answer for Santino"—to use a line from The Godfather—and it would come when he least expected it. Nixon's economic machinations, like CREEP's questionable political tactics, helped him win reelection. However, once wage and price restrictions were abolished, the cost of living for American households increased by about 10% in 1973 and more than 12% in 1974—the worst peacetime inflation in the country's history.

The Arabs, enraged by Nixon's support for Israel, used their oil position to their advantage. The price jumped from $1.77 to $10 a barrel. Unemployment began to rise as America entered a recession that lasted until 1975. Gross national output fell over 2% per capita. And Wall Street saw through Nixon's ruse. The stock market fell into a lengthy decline in December 1972, losing over half of its value during the next two years. During those critical months in 1973 and 1974, as the Watergate scandal erupted and the Democrats sought to reverse the results of the 1972 election, economic turmoil eroded Nixon's public support. The kick was great, but the hangover was terrible.

Kissinger's alarm over Connally's trade war was not the only reason

Nixon, having reaped the domestic political gains of the monetary issue, sought peace with Europe as fall moved to winter. His trip to China was on the horizon, and he intended to prepare for it with a series of headline-grabbing conferences with the presidents of France, the United Kingdom, and West Germany—rather than getting mired down in mind-numbing exchange rate negotiations.

The wellspring of tragedy was the typical neglect of an imperial force defeated by nationalists, returning home and leaving ancient grievances, arbitrary borders, and Cold War intrigue to exacerbate the catastrophe. In this case, it was Great Britain in Southwest Asia, not France in Indochina.

India gained independence from the British in 1947, but during the bloody partition that followed, the Muslims of West Pakistan were separated by a thousand miles of Hindu India from the Muslims of East Pakistan. To make matters worse, the two Muslim groups came from vastly different ethnic backgrounds (primarily Bengalis in the East and Punjabis and others in the West) and shared little other than their faith. Pakistan had been a small actor in the postwar era until its commander, Yahya Khan, proved to be a valuable conduit between Nixon and Mao.

Nixon liked Yahya, but he came with baggage. Despite its smaller territory, East Pakistan had a larger population than its more sophisticated western equivalent and felt ignored and exploited by the powers in Islamabad. The leaders of the East formed a political movement, fought for autonomy, and—enraged by the government's slow response to a hurricane that devastated their homeland in 1970—astonished the world by winning enough seats to take control of Pakistan's parliament.

Could Nixon have prevented the carnage? No. At least not in those initial, terrifying nights and days. As the world discovered in Biafra in 1969, and later in Rwanda and Bosnia, historic ethnic and tribal hatreds are among the most resistant to official intervention. A "bloodbath" loomed, warned In a meeting hosted by Kissinger three weeks before the crackdown, Under Secretary of State Alexis Johnson, an experienced diplomat, admitted that "we have no control over the events which will determine the outcome, and very little influence." Another experienced State Department official,

Christopher Van Hollen, warned that if the US put too much pressure, it risked losing its influence: "West Pakistan is very suspicious that we are supporting a separate East Pakistan state." If we tell Yahya to stop using force, this suspicion will only grow."

The United States had few carrots; it had abandoned the arms trade with Pakistan and India during the 1965 war, and a few million dollars in spare parts were its only hooks in the Pakistani military. Yahya and his generals are unlikely to have bowed, given their track record in the months after. Pakistanis saw themselves in an existential dilemma and sent one of their most brutal generals to East Pakistan to orchestrate the massacre. They were not concerned that the United States, embroiled in Vietnam, might engage militarily. Even in the face of war with their enormous and powerful neighbor, Pakistan's leaders refused to budge—not even to negotiate with imprisoned separatist leader Mujibur Rahman. If they were to lose East Pakistan, they would do so in a battle. Under such conditions, "I can't imagine that they give a damn what we think," Kissinger told his colleagues. The CIA and State Department representatives agreed.

Should Nixon have done more, even if it was just a gesture? Yes. Kissinger later admitted that there was "some merit" to "the charge of moral insensitivity" under the Nixon administration. As the situation progressed and the atrocities escalated into a brutal civil war, it is possible that the United Nations' strong protest, universal condemnation, and the potential of an international peacekeeping mission slowed Yahya down and saved lives. "No single Western country has much influence on the situation," according to the CIA; "but general Western disapproval may make the government in Islamabad less certain of the wisdom of present policies and more amenable to pressures for change."The American response was quiet. When India, which was dealing with millions of refugees suffering from cholera and other plagues, threatened Yahya, Nixon famously directed US policy to "tilt toward Pakistan." American ambassadors who voiced humanitarian concerns and issued a strong letter of opposition to Washington were humiliated and penalized.

There were reasons for Nixon's cool-bloodedness. China provided an exonerative explanation.

It's not like nothing was done. Under Nixon's leadership, the US sanctioned more aid for Bengali refugees than all other countries combined, averting a famine that, as CIA director Richard Helms put it, would "make Biafra look like a cocktail party." The US administration attempted to shut off military supplies to Pakistan, with varied degrees of success. American planes assisted in an emergency transport of refugees. The United States also pushed Pakistan's officials to deal with the separatists. But Nixon's reaction to Yahya was "not exactly strong," Kissinger admitted. On the bottom of Kissinger's April 28 memo providing policy possibilities, the president wrote: "To all hands." "Do not squeeze Yahya at this time." He underlined "don't" three times.

Typically, Richard Nixon's own resentments influenced the subsequent Indo-Pakistani war. Kissinger informed Keating that, while developing foreign policy based on personal ties was a recipe for disaster, Nixon had a "special feeling" for Yahya and a natural hate for Indians. "One cannot make policy on that basis…but it is a fact of life," he replied.

Nixon's affection for Pakistan extended back to his vice-presidential tours, followed by his wanderings in the wilderness years, when the Pakistanis greeted him with honors and admiration. He liked how open and honest they were. The Indians were a different story. The Nehru dynasty—Jawaharlal Nehru and his daughter, the current Prime Minister, Indira Gandhi—were arrogant and treated Nixon like a grocer's son. From their rung below the great powers, the Brahmins had adopted the attitude of moral scold, blasting Cold War adversaries for their militancy while claiming leadership of the "non-aligned" world, thereby cinching power by denouncing it. False piety was a Nixon technique, and he disliked having it used against him. "Nixon and Mrs. Indira Gandhi,Kissinger wrote, "were not meant to be personally congenial. She perceived moral superiority heightened Nixon's fears.

Meanwhile, back home, Nixon's critics sided with India, including the State Department and its Ivy League diplomats, Ted Kennedy and other Senate Democrats, and the liberal press. Kennedy, who chaired a Senate subcommittee on refugee affairs, toured the deplorable camps of Bengal in August—when the number of refugees was more than halfway to its eventual peak of 10 million—followed by a swarm of television cameras and reporters, ratcheting up American public opinion against Pakistan and infuriating the president.

Though India was clearly struggling to deal with the influx of migrants, Nixon suspected—not without reason—that Gandhi was using the humanitarian crisis as a cover for aggression. Her goal "was to destroy Pakistan," he informed Kissinger. India armed the East Pakistan resistance, trained Bengali insurgents, and backed up their operations with artillery across the border. There would be no peaceful settlement unless the Indians "stop screwing around in East Pakistan," CIA chief Helms advised.

On November 4, Gandhi traveled to Washington and met Nixon for a final round of talks. Given their mutual contempt, the outcome was predictable. Nixon didn't want to give India a reason to go to war with Pakistan, so his toast at the state dinner was polite, and his discourse was free of overt attacks. Instead, "We worked her around...""I dropped stilettos all over her," Nixon brags to Haldeman. However, as Gandhi went, the president was confident that India would find its own cause for action. She launched columns of tanks and troops into East Pakistan, provoking Yahya to strike India from the west on December 3.

Nixon initially kept a low profile. The United States pushed the issue to the United Nations, where it won a lopsided vote in the General Assembly to censure India. However, despite having forecast it for months, the reality of an Indian victory began to weigh on Nixon and Kissinger. As Indian forces closed in on Dacca and Indian bombers set fire to Karachi's oil tanks, Nixon became increasingly upset. The CIA sent him a report from a source in Gandhi's government: the prime minister had vowed to keep her armies moving until East Pakistan and parts of Kashmir were liberated and the "Pakistani armored and air force strength are destroyed so that Pakistan will never again be in a position to plan another invasion of India."

American prestige was at risk. Mao would never believe us, and the Chinese game would be lost. This was Suez. It was Czechoslovakia. It was Nixon's Rhineland. The Soviets humiliated the United States.

They could fail. Lose the Moscow summit. Perhaps both summits. Kissinger said that there was a "high possibility of disaster," but "at least we're coming off like men."

The crisis peaked on December 12, with apocalyptic rumblings from the Oval Office. Nixon and Kissinger met that morning to prepare a message to Brezhnev via the crisis hotline to bring his Indian customers under control or face "frightening consequences."

A sign had arrived from Beijing. Kissinger anticipated that "they're going to move" against India.

If the Chinese clashed with the Indians, Nixon said, the Russians would feel obligated to strike China. The US would side with China. And that could spark World War III.

The prospect of nuclear war drew both sides back from the edge. According to the CIA, Gandhi and Brezhnev shared Nixon's concern that a runaway crisis would pull the world's great powers into combat, just as the world had done in 1914 when World War I began. The Russians pressed the Indians to accept a UN cease-fire resolution as soon as Bangladesh—the newly formed nation from East Pakistan—was released, and Brezhnev assured Nixon that India would not dismember West Pakistan. Gandhi triumphed over a more militant faction in her government who sought to control parts of Kashmir, and the fighting ended in mid-December. Nixon's readiness to risk conflict with the Soviet Union was "a heroic act," the obedient Kissinger told his superior. Yahya's refusal to recognize the results of Pakistan's 1970 election, the homicidal crackdown in East Pakistan, the 10 million unhappy refugees imposed on India, and the fact that Pakistan initiated the war were all ignored or forgotten. Nixon and Kissinger imagined themselves confronting Hitlers.

Nixon was faced with a choice: purge the armed services leadership or accept the insult to keep the military's cooperation on Vietnam, SALT, and other issues. They had caught a skunk, Ehrlichman informed the president, and they needed to handle it cautiously.

Air Force One departed Washington on February 17, 1972. It made stops in Hawaii, Guam, and Shanghai (to take on a Chinese navigator) before landing in Beijing at exactly 11:30 a.m. local time on February 21—10:30 p.m. on the East Coast of the United States, ideal for Sunday-night prime-time television broadcast. As planned, Nixon and the First Lady walked down the stairs alone, and Nixon extended his hand to Zhou. It was a symbolic act to show the Chinese and the rest of the world that Nixon was not John Foster Dulles, who memorably snubbed Zhou at the 1954 Vietnam peace conference. Zhou shook the president's hand, and after a brief ceremony, the Nixons arrived at their guesthouse via vehicle, passing through cleared streets and vacant sidewalks. Pat stood out among the men in their dark clothes, wearing a bright red coat.

The first riddle Nixon faced was almost instantly solved. There had been nods of assurance, but no explicit pledge that Mao would meet with the president. The Chinese leader was supposed to be in ill health; perhaps he was hedging. However, Nixon had just arrived at his villa and was about to take a shower when he received word that Mao would be waiting for them.

Before departing Washington, Nixon and Kissinger met with André Malraux, a French man of letters who knew and spent time with Mao. They would be dealing with a very unusual man, Malraux explained— a visionary who had seen the tomb and intended to spend his remaining time to preserve his masterpiece after he died.

The conversation between Mao and Nixon lasted an hour and set the tone for the visit. Nothing significant was agreed, but their in-person meeting was exceptional, bordering on weird. Photographs of the two archenemies beaming and shaking hands circulated throughout the world, conveying signals from Tokyo to Hanoi to Moscow, and to voters in the United States, in ways that no dispatch or communiqué could. By embracing realism in that first session, Mao had virtually guaranteed that the summit would be a success, with no ideological or geopolitical posturing. Except for a trick—the Chinese were crafty, Kissinger kept warning his boss—Nixon had secured his diplomatic victory. There was toast after toast, usually with mao-tai, a flaming brandy. The Chinese pushed the Americans in the final talks of the summit communiqué, but not in an unfriendly manner. When the State Department retaliated for the White House's imperviousness— Secretary Rogers and Assistant Secretary Green discovered a mistake in the communiqué that necessitated an 11th-hour renegotiation with the Chinese—Zhou handled it with dignity.

There were few reminders of the twenty years of hostility since the People's Army and MacArthur's soldiers slaughtered each other in Korea, though the Nixons did watch The Red Detachment of Women, a revolutionary ballet chosen by Mao's hard-liner wife Jiang Qing, in which the dancers twirled rifles with fixed bayonets. At Zhou's proposal, the Shanghai Communiqué featured a clear declaration of ongoing disagreements, releasing both parties from accusations of betraying their values.

CHINA HAD ACHIEVED THEIR FIRST, SECOND, AND THIRD PRIORITIES: Mao had used "the American card" as a counterweight to the Soviets, obtaining U.S. intelligence reports and other assistance in his struggles with the Soviet Union; the United States changed its policy toward Taiwan (though fifty years later, Taiwan was still independent, free, and prosperous); and America remained involved in Asia, with enough presence to restrain China's rivals in India, the Soviet Union, and Japan without endangering China.

Nixon had mixed results when it came to America's priorities, which he had written down on a yellow pad during the flight aboard Air Force One. He had taken a significant stride toward incorporating China into a new international order in which a collection of big nations would bring balance and stability to global affairs. Taiwan, Malaysia, Indonesia, South Korea, and other free countries would thrive in an environment free of Chinese military threats and insurgencies. And Nixon had effectively used "the China card" with Moscow. Alarmed by the threat of being cornered between the hostile Far East and the resolute West, the Soviets expressed increased interest in a nuclear arms deal and otherwise restrained their actions.

However, Nixon's plan to utilize great power diplomacy to terminate the Vietnam War—his top priority on that legal pad—had only met with limited success. The Chinese and Soviets were contending for leadership in the Communist world, and both feared being chastised by the other for abandoning their comrades in Hanoi. They would counsel the North Vietnamese to be patient, to allow the Americans to withdraw, and to let history hand them Saigon in due course—but neither would stop the flow of weaponry, ammunition, and other supplies that supported the North's offensives. In the end, Nixon got the bare minimum of what he desired: the two Red titans would fuss and offer pro forma objections, but would not intervene as he increased military pressure on Hanoi and fought his way out of Vietnam.

Nixon's China project was simultaneously outrageously visionary and deeply practical. One of its lesser-known advantages was that it demonstrated to Americans and watchers abroad that the United States had not lost all of its inventiveness and passion in the paddies and mountains of Vietnam. The opening to China, like Nixon's other historic voyage to a mysterious, forbidding terrain, the Apollo moon landing, demonstrated that, for all its flaws, American democracy could still produce men and women with vision, drive, and ability among the sons of farmers, tinkers, and grocers. If the man in this situation was a depressed, self-tortured sourpuss, so be it. "It was not one of the least ironies of the period that it was a flawed man, so ungenerous in some of his human impulses, who took the initiative," claimed Kissinger. At a closing reception in Shanghai on February 27, Nixon praised "the week that changed the world," flying on mao-tai and the happiness of fulfilled ambitions.

It was, if anything, an understatement.

Chapter 16: Cancer on the Presidency

While Nixon crushed McGovern, pounded Hanoi, and issued decrees from his Catoctin hilltop, the Watergate thieves faced imminent imprisonment. The Cubans were stoic. Gordon Liddy seems to welcome it. Howard Hunt and James McCord were the group's weak links. A qualified defense attorney could have alerted the president about the dangers they posed to his presidency. The attitude in the Oval Office and throughout the Nixon White House was to hope it all went away.

Hunt sought money. The father of four children was ready to face a lengthy prison sentence. He and his wife had helped coordinate the hush money scam using scenarios from a third-rate espionage thriller, including anonymous phone conversations and secret code names, bundles of cash in airport lockers, and such hugger-muggery. Tony Ulasewicz, the bagman, spent so much time at pay phones that he began wearing a change machine on his belt.

Herbert Kalmbach, Nixon's lawyer, became increasingly concerned and, after being told by Ulasewicz that they had gone beyond the "kosher," announced his resignation from the team. In September, he burnt the cryptic record of his payments in an ashtray before John Dean and Fred LaRue. This drew Bob Haldeman even deeper into the conspiracy, since he now had to approve the use of the White House campaign slush fund for cash. By the end, in the spring of 1973, the hush money payments had totaled $429,500. The Cubans received relatively little of it, with the majority going to the Hunts and lawyers.

It wasn't enough for Howard Hunt, who believed that the White House had a commitment to sustain his family's middle-class lifestyle, and that Nixon and his men should behave like Marines, never abandoning a soldier on the battlefield. He begged Chuck Colson for more money and a pardon, becoming increasingly direct in his demands.

McCord was another thorny wicket. As he approached his prison cell, the wireman began to stumble, conjuring up apocalyptic visions about Nixon and Watergate threatening his beloved CIA. "Every tree in the forest will fall," he told Jack Caulfield, the White House private detective. "It will be a scorched desert," if the White House attempted to blame the scandal on the agency. Caulfield was appointed to argue with him. McCord, too, was given a vague hope of clemency. However, Nixon and his advisers neglected to take the threat seriously, assuring one another that McCord's knowledge was mere hearsay—he only knew what Liddy told him. They deceived themselves yet again. Hearsay may be prohibited in court, but it was perfectly legal for congressional investigators and their media allies.

Jeb Magruder was a step up the ladder, having lied under oath at the Watergate burglars' trial in January. After reading the Washington Post account that fall, US District Court Judge John Sirica was keen to learn the whole story. He badgered prosecutors, quizzed witnesses from the bench, and declared that he would use his sentencing authority to get the prisoners to name culpable higher-ups; else, they may languish in prison. The judge made a lasting effect on Hunt and McCord. They were agitated, as was Magruder, who knew he was the perfect fall guy and was constantly turning to the White House for reassurance.

Then there was John Dean, who was having to deal with the disturbing news that the CIA had handed the Justice Department copies of the photographs Hunt had taken on his trip with Liddy to Ellsberg's psychiatrist, Dr. Lewis Fielding's, office. Dean felt that it would only be a matter of time until the FBI realized what was going on and revealed the Fielding burglary as a White House plot. Dean's worries escalated to tremors as Pat Gray, the FBI director, explained how Dean had hampered the bureau's probe during his confirmation hearings. John Dean was suddenly where he didn't want to be: out of the shadows, on the front pages, and under congressional investigation.

On March 21, an overworked Dean mustered the courage to inform Nixon about the current situation. The cover-up was disintegrating, according to the counsel. "We have a cancer that is spreading within and near the presidency. It grows on a daily basis. "It's compounding and growing geometrically now," Dean informed him. "We're being blackmailed...people will start perjuring themselves very quickly who haven't had to protect others." "And there is no assurance."

"That it won't bust," Nixon added, completing the concept.

They needed to find a method "that this can be carved away from you, so that it does not damage you or the presidency," Dean added. "Some people are going to have to go to jail....I could, for one."

However, Nixon dodged the thought of a public burning. It would take years, if ever, for a president to recover from such an event. And he was more involved than Dean realized. Nixon learned almost nothing new from Dean's "cancer on the presidency" speech. It didn't matter that Nixon hadn't directly directed Liddy's team to investigate Watergate: he had collaborated with Haldeman, Ehrlichman, and Colson about wiretaps, dirty tricks, break-ins, hush money, and clemency. Could he rely on a dozen scared men—from the Cubans to Haldeman—to defend him? With a hung judge and zealous prosecutors dangling offers? No.

They needed to buy time, Nixon told Dean. Hunt's immediate requests must be fulfilled. "You can acquire a million dollars in cash." "I know where it can be obtained," the president informed his lawyer. After Dean left the Oval Office, Nixon inquired with Rose Woods about the condition of his own private slush funds, which totaled approximately $200,000.

On March 23, Sirica read aloud a letter from McCord in court while Nixon and his advisors were still flailing about.

McCord left the courthouse and headed straight to Capitol Hill. In February, the Senate voted 77 to 0 to establish the Select Committee on Presidential Campaign Activities to examine the Watergate crisis, which would be chaired by Senator Sam Ervin, a North Carolina Democrat. Sirica surprised McCord, who repeated his testimony to committee staff and subsequently to senators in private. He knew little more than what Liddy had said, but that was enough. Within days, rumors of the Gemstone plan were leaked to the media, publicly linking Dean, Magruder, and Mitchell to the Watergate break-in. The excitement was on. "Watergate was a bloodbath in the water. "And every other newspaper became a shark," the Washington Post managing editor, Howard Simons, recalls. "They would take a bite and swallow it without chewing."

After hearing the dean propose that they all confess and rescue the president, Haldeman and Ehrlichman consulted and devised a better solution: they would blame it on a fall guy. Dean could be a nice "hors d'oeuvre," but only a "big fish" would satisfy their adversaries: they would give Mitchell. Despite their strong language, they avoided approaching their former comrade.

Nixon's cat-calling was normal. Instead of chastising his old friend, Nixon rambled on about the fund scandal and Ike's desertion of Sherman Adams, the White House chief of staff who received a vicuna coat and other inappropriate gifts from an industrialist under investigation by the government.

Nixon attempted to isolate himself from the headlines, anxieties, and sleepless nights by traveling between the White House, Key Biscayne, San Clemente, and Camp David. He and his men planned one more ruse: they would claim that the president personally solved the case, blaming Magruder and Mitchell for the break-in and Dean for the cover-up. But before they could do so, Dean and Magruder appeared at the U.S. attorney's office, offering to testify in exchange for favorable treatment. Right behind them, LaRue led a group of people.

The White House learned of Magruder's alleged betrayal Friday, April 13. The next night, while Nixon and his staff pretended to be friendly with the baying hounds at the White House correspondents' dinner, the U.S. Attorney Earl Silbert informed Henry Petersen, the chief of the Justice Department's criminal section, that Magruder and Dean had begun to sing.

On April 17, Nixon made a public declaration that his personal "investigation" had resulted in "major developments" and "real progress...in finding the truth." He was attempting to distance himself from Haldeman and Ehrlichman—but slowly, given their knowledge. He needed to feel as comfortable as possible. The "separability," as he put it, took two weeks.

Nixon requested Secretary of State Bill Rogers to terminate the two men, but he refused. Haldeman and Ehrlichman had earned an in-person dismissal. On Sunday, April 29, the two aides were summoned to Camp David, flown to the presidential retreat by helicopter, and individually called in to see Nixon. He sobbed and told them that he had asked God to take his life so that he would not wake up that morning. Haldeman handled the situation better than Ehrlichman, who encouraged Nixon to resign. "Just explain everything to my kids, will you?" Ehrlichman stated. "I still feel I have done nothing that was without your implied or direct approval."

Haldeman attempted to console him. The switchboard has been instructed to screen his calls. The lines were undoubtedly packed.

"No, no, no." They know. They know. They know who to call, you know. "They know they can get through," the president stated.

His agony gushed out. "You are a strong man, goddammit. "And I love you," Nixon told his former chief of staff. "And, you know, I adore John and the rest, so by God, preserve the faith. Keep the faith. "You're going to win this, son of a bitch."

Shyly and pathetically, he urged Haldeman to make phone calls—"like the old style"—to evaluate public reaction to the speech. "Do you mind?""

Haldeman declined, and Nixon withdrew. "No, I agree," he replied. "Do not call a goddamn soul. "The hell with it."

"God bless you, boy." Nixon mumbled, "God bless you," as he said goodbye. He spoke softly, providing a picture of his troubled personality. "I love you," he added, "like my brother."

Richard Nixon had been forging the sword he delivered his opponents for two years. The demands of his job were unrelenting, and he'd added to the stress with his own bravado. It is hardly surprising that he cracked—or that the fissures spread along well-known faults.

In an interview with journalist Stewart Alsop, Kissinger marveled at what Nixon had done himself.

"All his life he's been assailed by the fear of the horrible disasters—now everything that can possibly happen to him has happened," Mr. Kissinger added. "In an attempt to stave off the worst, it's all been brought on."

Such discussions occurred throughout Washington. In a private lunch at the Federal Reserve, Moynihan and Burns turned to Freudian philosophy for an explanation. "Repressed homosexuality; sense of deprivation—a castration sense," they whispered.

But there was plenty to help Nixon get into the tumbrel.

The president "was sardonic about all kinds of government agencies," according to CIA Director Richard Helms. "His attitude was that the only bright, really intelligent fellow in town was himself....He was constantly disparaging everybody else about their abilities."

Nixon was more than merely insulting. He intended to reorganize the government, threatening institutions such as the FBI and the CIA, whose archives contained information that could humiliate and implicate the president and his advisers. He attempted to make the bureau more obedient by replacing Hoover with a toady. In May, Nixon wrote to Haldeman: "One department that really requires house-cleaning is the CIA. The problem in the CIA is muscle-bound bureaucracy, which has completely paralyzed the brain, and the fact that its personnel, like that of the State Department, is predominantly Ivy League and Georgetown set." He directed Haldeman to investigate "how many people in the CIA could be dismissed."

The judiciary was not exempt either. Nixon planned to terminate the lifetime tenure of federal judges.

Congress led the cavalcade. Its members were proud, independent operators who had built their own professions. They had always bridled when Colson, Haldeman, or Ehrlichman issued instructions from the White House, as if legislators were nothing more than shills for the president. "I detested them," remarked Representative Gerald Ford of Michigan, the House Republican leader at the time. "I resented the way they treated Congress."

After Kleindienst resigned as attorney general, the Judiciary Committee demanded that his replacement, Elliot Richardson, appoint a special prosecutor. Richardson was from Massachusetts and a Harvard graduate. He recruited Archibald Cox from Harvard Law School to head the Watergate Special Prosecution Force. Cox had served as John Kennedy's solicitor general. Both Edward Kennedy and Robert Kennedy's widow, Ethel attended the swearing-in ceremony. The WSPF, the Ervin committee staff, and the House Judiciary Committee staff would be dominated by leftist Ivy Leaguers, many of whom had served in the Kennedy administration or on campaigns. The most notable example is that eight of the twelve senior attorneys on the WSPF previously worked for RFK as attorney general. Pat described the Ervin committee to her friend Helene Drown as "a snake about to devour people."

The Watergate committee began its hearings in mid-month, setting the groundwork with McCord, Ulasewicz, Caulfield, and other captivatingly Runyonesque witnesses. It was an excellent public theater. Other Senate committees held closed-door hearings, providing the first proof of Nixon's complicity in the cover-up.

Vernon Walters wrote a series of memcons to his files in June 1972, documenting Haldeman, Ehrlichman, and Dean's attempts to utilize the CIA to thwart the FBI's investigation into the Watergate break-in. Walters was a Nixon supporter. He had been with Nixon in Caracas. He had taken part in the covert Paris peace talks with Kissinger, aided in the opening with China, and was rewarded with the position of CIA deputy director, where the White House regarded him as its man in Langley. But Walters' expertise and experience—with Nixon and the ways of Washington—had prompted him to compose the self-protective memoranda when the White House instructed him to obstruct the FBI probe.

The Watergate committee welcomed John Dean in June, after the proceedings were temporarily halted when Soviet Premier Brezhnev met with Nixon in Washington and San Clemente. The public was enthralled for five days as he dispassionately revealed the White House atrocities and Nixon's attempts to conceal them, clothed and coiffed like a straitlaced junior partner and with his blond wife sitting primly behind him. "He was going further than we had gone," Bob Woodward remarked. "What Dean said was that Nixon was at the center and involved."

However, the conversations described in the Walters memcons were hearsay. And, while Dean provided first hand testimony, it was his word against Nixon's. As the hearings unfolded that summer, Haldeman, Ehrlichman, and Mitchell took turns confessing their misdeeds while defending and protecting the president. By autumn, the act was stale; the audience was tired of the hot antics. According to a Republican pollster, the current political climate appears to have reached its apex, barring any fresh shocking revelations. "We've survived it," Nixon assured Kissinger.

However, it appeared Dean's testimony could be verified. The Watergate committee discovered the secret in July. Nixon had been recording himself. The cassettes would convey the story.

Chapter 17: The Final Days

The Watergate scandal had been reduced to its essence: a ferocious tug-of-war between Archibald Cox and Richard Nixon over the White House tapes.

The White House had a long history of keeping electronic records. It monitored the decision-making process for historical accuracy, bureaucratic accountability, and political indemnity. Franklin Roosevelt had a microphone in the Oval Office, and aides in the basement transcribed what was said. Ike used tape recorders, and his personal secretary, Ann Whitman, listened in and took notes throughout his meetings and phone calls. During times of stress, John Kennedy kept cassettes rolling. And Johnson, who enjoyed technology, filmed hundreds of talks and carried them with him when he departed for Texas.

Nixon directed Haldeman to remove Johnson's tape equipment. So Kissinger had secretaries listen in and transcribe phone calls, while Haldeman, Ehrlichman, and other aides took copious notes on their conversations with the president. Ultimately, it appeared easier to return the machinery. Nixon's predecessors utilized a manual switch to record only the conversations they chose. The efficient Haldeman (knowing Nixon was a bit of a stumblebum) set the system to record everything, including the scratch of pens, the rattling of silverware, and the tinkling of ice cubes.

"It never occurred to me that anyone in his right mind would install anything so Orwellian as a system that never shut off, that preserved every word, every joke, every curse, every tantrum, every flight of presidential paranoia, every bit of flattery and bad advice and tattling by his advisers," Haig would have observed. The secret was meticulously guarded—not even Kissinger and Ehrlichman were aware they were being recorded. Even though Nixon and Haldeman were aware that the machines were working, they generally relaxed their guard. It would be intellectually tiring, blatantly manufactured, and of questionable utility to attempt to influence every interaction. Besides, they felt, no one would ever hear the tapes except Nixon.

The president had a window to destroy the tapes when White House official Alexander Butterfield, a system custodian, informed the

Senate of their existence in July. Nixon was being treated for pneumonia at the Bethesda Naval Medical Center and could hear competing arguments from his hospital bed. His Watergate attorney, Fred Buzhardt, advised him to destroy the recordings. They hadn't yet been subpoenaed. Even though Nixon faced a biased Congress, no Senate would convict a president of destroying his personal documents. Impeachment was a political action. The only president—Andrew Johnson's trial by Radical Republicans in a Reconstruction Congress in 1868—had so soiled the process that the country swore it off for a century. Impeaching a Cold War president for selling his personal tape collection? Not likely. Len Garment, who is now functioning as general counsel at the White House, took the opposing position. Although the tapes had not yet been subpoenaed, case law indicated that their deletion would still be considered an act of obstructing justice. And for the public, burning the tapes would appear to be an admission of guilt.

Nixon inclined towards Garment. Nixon, having seen Truman and Eisenhower make and sustain audacious claims of executive privilege, assumed the courts would respect his presidential authority and rule in his favor. Keeping the taped record may prevent Dean, Haldeman, Ehrlichman, and other desperate aides seeking prosecutorial favor from making false accusations against him. Furthermore, the tapes served as a record—or certification, for himself and others—of his accomplishments. Nixon valued his difficult and, he believed, honorable decisions on Vietnam, China, and the Soviet Union—and intended to polish his image for history in his memoirs by selectively using taped discussions.

THE AUTUMN OF 1973 then unfolded like an overheated screenplay, with violence, controversy, bloodshed, and intrigue culminating in a third-act conflagration.

Nixon was not concerned about impeachment while Spiro Agnew was his successor. To the Democrats in Congress and their media allies, the vice president had most of Nixon's shortcomings but none of the president's talent for foreign affairs, which, even they had to concede, was making the world a better place. However, Nixon's luck was now only going one way. A federal corruption investigation in Baltimore uncovered allegations that Agnew, as governor of Maryland, accepted bribes from consulting businesses doing business with the state. Elliot Richardson and Henry Petersen had reviewed the case in late summer and confirmed its veracity. Indeed, while serving as vice president, Agnew continued to take cash envelopes, with at least one $10,000 payout sent to his office at the White House. Agnew's offenses became public in August. For two months, he flopped around like a gaffed fish. He resigned on October 10, after pleading no contest to a federal indictment. The deal kept him out of prison.

Nixon was required by the Twenty-fifth Amendment to the Constitution, which was established in response to Ike's sicknesses and Kennedy's murder, to nominate a new vice president who would be confirmed by Congress. John Connally topped his list, which included Nelson Rockefeller, Ronald Reagan, and others. However, the president no longer wielded enough power to select his own successor. Ray Price cautioned Nixon, "We simply cannot afford another imbroglio, ending in defeat." "The selection of John Connally might spell calamity. It would be brutally divisive among Republicans and an open invitation for Democrats on Capitol Hill to engage in the crassest of politics, crippling if not destabilizing the presidency.

"They'd comb every inch of his past and I can't believe that in 20 or whatever years of acquiring millions while in Texas as a protégé of Lyndon Johnson, there isn't something that could be unearthed," quoted Price as saying. "In the course of the confirmation hearings every dead cat in the Southwest would be dragged across the hearing-room floor."

The price was right. The Democrats promised to reject Connally and persuaded the president to appoint Gerald Ford, the House minority leader, instead. Ford was a respected member of the House and a beloved cloakroom attendant. He did not offer Nixon any "impeachment insurance." But, as a friend of Nixon's for over two decades, a colleague in the Chowder & Marching Club, and a good and decent guy, he had his own plea to a president who was beginning to consider clemency for himself.

A gang of House liberals asked Speaker Albert to postpone Ford's confirmation until they could impeach Nixon and appoint Albert, Majority Leader O'Neill, or another Democrat, such as Ted Kennedy, as president. "Get off your goddamn ass, and we can take this presidency," Representative Bella Abzug of New York ordered the small Speaker, pushing him on the chest. Ted Sorensen, a senior Kennedy aide, submitted the Speaker a twenty-page "contingency plan" for a Democratic takeover, including options for an inaugural address. Neither Albert nor O'Neill wanted to be remembered as the leaders of an antinomian coup, so Ford was confirmed. If Washington needed more tension, the Russians were happy to oblige, and Nixon's peace partners could take advantage of his weakened state. On October 6, a Jewish holy day, Egyptian and Syrian forces launched surprise strikes, forcing Israeli forces to retreat from the Suez Canal and the Golan Heights in what became known as the Yom Kippur War. The Soviet Union saw an opportunity to expand its influence in the oil-rich Middle East and provided the attackers with military advisers, anti-aircraft missiles, guns, and other equipment.

"The Israelis must not be allowed to lose," Nixon instructed his staff. He directed them to deploy tanks, fighter jets, and ammunition to the besieged Jewish state. The American airlift delivered a thousand tons daily. When diplomatic red tape stalled the procedure, the president exploded. "Do it now!" he instructed Kissinger. The US was defending Israel, and no amount of diplomacy would appease Arab rage. "We are going to get blamed just as much for three planes as for three hundred," Nixon informed the crowd.

It was one of those moments, Nixon told Kissinger, that demonstrated "what we are here for." The catastrophe was incredibly freeing. Watergate "gave him the composure of a man who had seen the worst and to whom there were no further terrors," Kissinger recounted. "He probably welcomed staking his future on defending the interests of free peoples...rather than on the outcome of a sordid litigation over events that had clearly gotten away from him."

AMID ALL OF THIS—as Agnew left office in ignominy and shame, Ford was appointed vice president, and Israel and the Arabs launched war—Nixon decided to remove Cox.

Nixon had first endorsed Richardson's appointment of a special prosecutor, believing that the bow-tied former solicitor general would not participate in a plan against him. When Cox went to court to collect tapes, including the "cancer on the presidency" recording, Nixon had second thoughts, and his wrath erupted when Cox's staff began investigating topics unrelated to the Watergate break-in. "He is purposefully delving into unrelated areas. "He can't get away with this," Nixon warned Alexander Haig, the incoming White House chief of staff, that summer. "As Special Prosecutor he is derelict in his duties in trying to conduct a partisan political vendetta."

Cox's squad indicted former White House assistant Egil Krogh for perjury in the Ellsberg scandal and investigated Nixon's income taxes, real estate transactions, and financial ties with Bebe Rebozo. The special prosecutor disregarded a federal appeals court's advice and declined White House proposals to compromise on the tapes, including one plan supported by Senator Sam Ervin. Even Cox publicly questioned whether he had become "too big for my britches—that what I see as principle could be vanity." But he continued marching. Nixon instructed Haig to prepare: they would force Cox to cease his demands, and if he refused, he would be fired.

After several frustrating days of negotiations, plagued by allegations of bad faith on both sides, Nixon brought Richardson to the Oval Office, where the attorney general resigned after refusing to fire the special prosecutor. Richardson saw it as a moral act and shared the following quote from the Iliad with Cox: Now, if the numberless destiny of death faces us, which no mortal can escape or avoid, let us march ahead together, and either we will honor one another, or another will honor us. It was that type of weekend. Richardson's deputy, William Ruckelshaus, fell on his sword in the same noble manner. This allowed Solicitor General Robert Bork to fire Cox.

It was October 20, a Saturday night. The White House said the special prosecutor's office "has been abolished." As reporters and Cox's enraged staff watched, federal authorities took custody of the prosecutor's files. "Firestorm" was the common and apt description of what followed. "The country tonight is in the midst of what may be the most serious constitutional crisis in its history," newsman John Chancellor informed NBC viewers, breaking from the typical prime-time lineup with a special broadcast. The Saturday Night Massacre became a historical event. "You will be returning to an environment of major national crisis," Haig informed Kissinger, who was on his way home from negotiations on a Middle East cease-fire. "The situation is in a state of white heat.... An impeachment stampede could well develop."

Nixon was forced to yield after being "taken by surprise by the ferocious intensity" he had sparked. "For the first time I recognized the depth of the impact Watergate had been having on America," he told the story. "I suddenly realized how deeply its acid had eaten." He said he will release requested records.

On the Tuesday following the Massacre, Tip O'Neill urged Congress to "examine its constitutional responsibilities." The House moved toward impeachment. Julie scrawled on her calendar, "Fight. Fight. Fight." Nixon may be heard playing the piano alone at night. He performed "Rustle of Spring," his mother's favorite. The tone in the capital changed—away from the exhilaration of the pursuit and the wonderful jolts of new revelation that had characterized the spring and summer. A horrible depression struck in. "You felt empty because you weren't with us." "These things don't happen in America," White House reporter Helen Thomas recalled. "It was darkness at noon…as inexorable as a Greek tragedy," and she added the president was "like a dead man walking."

Nixon took a direct role in the war's early stages, directing Kissinger and Defense Secretary James Schlesinger to keep Israel resupplied regardless of the political or geopolitical implications. In response, the Arabs used their oil as a weapon, raising American gasoline, industrial, and home heating costs, stoking inflation and harming the US economy.

On the night of October 24, Nixon was missing, preoccupied with Watergate—"down, very down," according to Haig—and bunkered in the White House living quarters. Kissinger had already complained to aides about Nixon's lack of focus and excessive drinking during the crisis. Soon after 7 p.m., the president contacted Kissinger. He was "as agitated and emotional as I had ever heard him," the secretary of state said. "We were heading into what could have become the gravest foreign policy crisis…with a president overwhelmed by his persecution."

Nixon rants about his opponents. "They are doing it because they want to kill the president," he informed Kissinger. "And they may succeed. "I may physically die."

Nixon was not present in the White House Situation Room that night, when Kissinger and others issued a readiness alert, the aircraft carriers John F. Kennedy and Franklin Delano Roosevelt were dispatched to the eastern Mediterranean, and the Eighty-second Airborne troopers were told to prepare for war. Haig had shuttled to the upstairs living quarters, telling the others that he had notified Nixon of what was going on.

"We have to go to the mat on this one," Kissinger warned Haig shortly before 10 p.m. "Should I wake up the president?"

"No," Haig replied.

The next morning, October 25, Americans learned that the United States' nuclear weapons forces had been moved to DEFCON III, a state of high alert, to prevent the Russians from intervening.

The Soviets stepped back. "Nixon is too nervous," Brezhnev informed his colleagues. "Let's cool him down."

The Soviet Union supported the concept of a UN peacekeeping force, and Kissinger lobbied Jerusalem until Cairo, Damascus, and the surrounding Egyptian army were safe. Sadat's combat ended badly, but he claimed a significant psychological win by thrashing Israel in the first round, restoring Arab pride, and establishing an equal footing for discussions that finally led to peace.

In the following days, Nixon boasted that the standoff was the deadliest since the Cuban missile crisis. "Even in this week, when many thought the president was shell-shocked, unable to act, the president acted decisively," he told the news media. "The tougher it gets, the cooler I get."

His aides let Nixon have his way, but they didn't hesitate to express their reservations when they reflected years later. Bill Rogers had left office in September, and Kissinger was now both national security adviser and secretary of state. "Nixon no longer had the time or nervous energy to give consistent leadership," he told me. "He was too distracted to shape the decisions before they reached him."

Congress detected vulnerability. It eroded presidential authority via the War Powers Resolution, which was approved over Nixon's veto on November 7, limiting his and future presidents' ability to lead the country into undeclared wars.

Fed chairman Arthur Burns subsequently stated that when he and Kissinger met, "Kissinger became very forceful in saying Nixon should go."

"What happened to President Nixon is a human tragedy," Kissinger exclaimed in a later interview with a journalist. "A tragedy does not necessarily imply that it was undeserved..." "It was like one of those Greek things where a man is told his fate but fulfills it anyway, knowing exactly what will happen to him."

When it was revealed that two of the disputed audio recordings were missing and one had an eighteen-and-a-half-minute gap, Nixon suffered yet another humiliating defeat. Haig proposed that an unknown "sinister" force was responsible. A panel of experts told Judge Sirica that the missing piece had been erased repeatedly. Nixon denied doing anything, and Rose Mary Woods walked forward, contorting like a gymnast, to show how she could have accidentally destroyed the video. The New York Times, the Denver Post, and Time magazine, Nixon's former cheerleader, led a chorus of news outlets asking for Nixon's resignation. To add spice to his wounds, Sweden announced that Kissinger and North Vietnamese negotiator Le Duc Tho had received the Nobel Peace Prize for ending the Vietnam War.

Collateral concerns also harmed Nixon. The press and Congress questioned the need for $100,000 in taxpayer-funded upgrades to San Clemente and Key Biscayne. The ITT scam, and the administration's manipulation of milk subsidies, were investigated again. Newspapers in Baltimore and Providence reported that Nixon reduced his federal income tax payments with elaborate deductions, including a $576,000 write-off for donating his vice-presidential files to the National Archives. (It did not help Nixon when an aide was discovered to have backdated the deed.) The president paid only $792 to the IRS in 1970 and $878 in 1971, and the legislative Joint Committee on Internal Revenue Taxation found that he owed $476,000 in past taxes and interest. At a meeting with the nation's editors in Disney World in mid-November, Nixon felt compelled to reassure them: "People have the right to know whether or not their president is a crook. "Well, I'm not a crook."

On January 5, Nixon welcomed the new year with a note to himself. "Above all, dignity, command, faith, head held high, no fear, cultivate a new spirit, drive, act like a President, act like a winner. Opponents are ferocious destroyers and haters. It's time to employ the President's entire power to combat the enormous forces arrayed against us."

He had very little to quit. But Nixon's family saw his arrogance. "Something Daddy said makes me feel absolutely hopeless about the outcome," Tricia wrote in her diary. "He has repeatedly stated that the tapes can be interpreted either way." He has warned us that there is nothing harmful on the tapes and that he may be impeached due to their contents. Because he said the latter, and knowing Daddy, it is how he truly feels."

Politically, things looked bleak. "We are dying by inches," Buchanan informed Nixon. "Our margin for error has disappeared; our reservoir of credibility with the American people dried up."

ARTHUR BREMER, who shot George Wallace in May 1972, had followed Nixon to a ceremony in Ottawa, Canada, in April of that year, but changed his attention to Wallace after deciding that the president's security was too tight. "You can't kill Nixie boy unless you're close to him," Bremer wrote in his diary. He titled his journal "My diary of my personal plot to kill by pistol either Richard Nixon or George Wallace."

On the morning of February 22, 1974, Samuel Byck, an unemployed salesman, arrived at Baltimore Washington International Airport with a stolen firearm and a crude improvised firebomb in his briefcase. He had spent much of his time in recent days, including the travel from his home in Pennsylvania, talking into a tape recorder. In a calm voice, he described intentions to hijack an airliner and seize control as it flew over the nation's capital, guiding the jet into the White House, where the Nixons had just returned from a holiday to Florida. It was better to live "one day as a lion," according to Byck, than to continue in failure. "My death will be linked to Watergate," he mumbled. He claimed that the administration was led by "cheats" and "thieves," and that "I will cleanse it by fire."

Byck was known to the Secret Service because he had been mailing threatening letters and parading around the White House with protest placards, and wearing a Santa Claus suit on Christmas Eve. But the authorities deemed him harmless. Far from it. He breezed into the terminal with his small arsenal and approached Gate C, where a Delta

Airlines DC-9 was about to take off for Atlanta. Byck shot and killed a guard before storming down the ramp to the cockpit and ordering the crew to "fly this plane out of here!". When they halted, he shot the copilot, then turned to face the pilot and stated, "The next one will be in the head." When the pilot attempted to argue with him, Byck shot him too. He then instructed a terrified female passenger to pilot the jet. "Emergency. The wounded pilot radioed, "Emergency." "We're all shot."

Byck's attempt was foiled when a moonlighting local cop working airport security fired at him through an airplane window. After being wounded twice, Byck ended the situation by raising his rifle to his temple and firing. The airport shooting was widely covered in the media, except that the US government failed to reveal that Nixon was Buck's target. It would not do so until 1987, for fear of inciting more hijackers.

Spring has arrived. In April, Nixon made one more, unsuccessful attempt to turn things around. In a televised address, he said he would make over 1,300 transcribed pages from 46 cassettes available to Congress and the public. With a stack of volumes beside him, he resembled an encyclopedia salesman. The transcripts captivated the public, with two paperback editions selling three million copies in a single week. As with each release of Nixon audio, journalists concentrated on the scandalous and sensational. The president would have been better served if he had kept the swear words intact—the frequent use of "expletive deleted" left too much to the imagination. And the White House's editing of the recordings was poor, allowing the House Judiciary Committee, which leaked its own transcripts while considering impeachment, to demonstrate how Nixon made self-serving omissions.

Haldeman had cautioned Nixon three years earlier that publishing the Pentagon Papers would erode Americans' trust in government. The My Lai prosecutions and Watergate hearings had exacerbated the corrosive effects. But the harsh, caustic interactions revealed in the transcripts were unlike anything the silent majority had ever heard. "This thing is hemorrhaging terribly," Buchanan informed Haig. The Watergate tapes, with their crudity and cruelty, shattered Nixon's image as an upright, virtuous son of the heartland. "Sheer, flesh-crawling repulsion. Columnist Joseph Alsop described it as "the backroom of a second-rate advertising agency in a hellish suburb." "A shabby, disgusting, immoral performance," declared Senate Minority Leader Hugh Scott.

Pat has quit reading the newspapers. "If there is hell on earth," Rose Woods told Julie, "we are living through it right now." Julie began campaigning for her father, accepting speaking engagements across the country, with the assistance of her mother. When Nixon advised that she be less involved, she said, "But, Daddy, we have to fight." Mel Laird and Bryce Harlow, two longtime comrades and former aides who had joined the White House staff to help right the ship, discreetly quit the administration, furious that Nixon had misled them. Vice President Ford felt betrayed.

The Judiciary Committee subpoenaed further tapes, including those from the June 23, 1972 talks. The White House objected, and the matter went to the United States Supreme Court. As the Judiciary Committee prepared for impeachment proceedings, word spread that Jaworski's grand jury had designated Nixon as a "unindicted co-conspirator." The Nixon administration floated aimlessly toward the rocks.

Nixon sought relief in foreign affairs. On June 10, he departed for Europe and the Middle East. The images from Cairo of hundreds of thousands of Egyptians celebrating Nixon and Sadat nearly rivaled the big greetings from Saudi Arabia, Israel, Syria, and Jordan. Nixon's leg pain was diagnosed as phlebitis, a serious vascular disease that requires sufferers to rest and elevate the affected limb. Nixon insisted on extending the trip, despite the lengthy hours he was spending standing and sitting in the Middle East. "The purpose of this trip is more important than my life," he informed his doctor, Walter Tkach. He presented a similar justification to the Secret Service, which was shocked by the prospect of Nixon visiting Egypt in an open automobile with Sadat.

The president and his entourage returned to the United States briefly to repack before departing for the Soviet Union for his third summit meeting with Brezhnev. Nixon brought a car, as he had done in their previous two encounters, when he presented the Soviet leader with a Cadillac and later a Lincoln Continental. This time, it was a Chevrolet

Monte Carlo. The nicest thing to say about the conference is that, despite his zeal to play peacemaker for the people back home, Nixon made no detrimental concessions.

Nixon's family continued to support him. When John Rhodes, the House minority leader, intimated to a reporter that Nixon could wish to quit, Pat gave him a cold greeting when they met at a reception.

"Oh, yes," she replied as they posed for a shot. "Let's smile as if we like each other."

Mrs. Nixon. "It's not the way you heard it," Rhodes informed her.

"Yeah. Pat replied, "That's what they all say."

—

THE JUDICIARY COMMITTEE hearings were primarily drama to maintain an existing consensus: Tricky Dick needed to go. When the political elite reaches a conclusion—as happened in Washington in the weeks following the Saturday Night Massacre—it requires a powerful opposing force to overturn the consensus. In Nixon's case, the following months produced only supporting evidence.

"Teddy Roosevelt used to talk about standing at Armageddon, doing battle for the Lord,' " a disgruntled White House adviser, Ken Khachigian cautioned Haig. "We are standing at Armageddon, but not fighting..."Now is the moment to establish political lines.We cannot allow the articles of impeachment to be treated with respectability and legality. "They are producing a bastardized product of dubious parentage, conceived in clandestine back room trysts."

There were enough conservative Democrats and Republicans to oppose two impeachment articles: bombing Cambodia and alleged tax cheating. However, the counts of obstruction of justice and abuse of authority approved by large, bipartisan percentages. A piece criticizing Nixon for refusing to follow congressional subpoenas received a smaller vote. "I was getting dressed" after a dip in the Pacific, Nixon would say. "That was how I learned that I was the first President in 106 years to be recommended for impeachment: standing in the beach trailer, barefoot, wearing old trousers, a Banlon shirt and a blue windbreaker emblazoned with the Presidential Seal."

Nixon wrote in his diary that night about Pat: "God, how she could have gone through what she does, I simply don't know."

The Supreme Court's July 24 ruling was unanimous. The court accepted the notion of presidential privilege but ruled that it did not apply in Nixon's case, which involved criminal action. The president would have to reveal additional tapes.

Haig called Robert Bork and told him that the president was considering defying the court. "That is instant impeachment," Bork warned him. There was no wiggle room. The result was unanimous, with three Nixon appointees voting against him and Chief Justice Warren Burger writing the opinion. Nixon was correct the entire time. He was alone. "If you're a nice guy and make a mistake, they'll forgive you," claimed his former treasury secretary, William Simon. "But if you are a prick, they're going to step on you and not let up."

After hearing the decision, one of Nixon's first calls was to Buzhardt. "There may be some problems with the June 23 tape, Fred," he told me.

On Tuesday, August 6, Washingtonians awakened to discover, in the top article of that day's Post, a Woodward and Bernstein report that began: "President Nixon personally ordered a pervasive cover-up of the facts of Watergate within six days after the illegal entry into the Democrats' national headquarters." The transcript of the June 23 tape, the smoking gun, was made public.

Haig had already begun to plan Nixon's resignation, surreptitiously showing the transcript of the June 23 recording to congressional leaders, Nixon's closest aides, and cabinet members. Some were furious to learn that Nixon had listened to the recording that spring without informing them of its contents. Kissinger and Ford were informed, and Haig asked the vice president if he was prepared to be president.

Haig was concerned that Nixon may harm himself. "You fellows, in your business, you have a way of handling problems like this," Nixon had told him before. "Somebody leaves a pistol in the drawer." On Capitol Hill, congressional leaders were concerned about his mental state. Schlesinger's fears at the Pentagon were identical. To prevent a military coup, a nuclear Götterdämmerung, or another frenzied act, the secretary of defense informed the Joint Chiefs that any last-minute orders from the White House must be verified through the chain of command.

On Wednesday afternoon, Republican leaders Barry Goldwater, Hugh Scott, and John Rhodes arrived at the White House and met with the president in the Executive Office Building. They told Nixon he did not have a prayer. Not in the house. Not in the senate. He would undoubtedly be impeached and convicted. Nixon received the news quietly, said goodbye, and departed the Oval Office for his home, where his family had gathered in the Solarium.

"We're going back to California," he said. They ate dinner off trays before posing for presidential photographer Ollie Atkins, smiling through tears. Pat despised the photo. "Our hearts were breaking and there we are smiling," she informed us. As the party dispersed, Atkins captured a final photo of Julie and her father in each other's arms.

The final hours had more than a few Shakespearean scenes. Nixon rushed out of the room after telling old friends from Congress, "I hope you won't feel I have let you down"...House and Senate leaders left Nixon and heard "God Bless America" being sung outside the White House gates.Nixon requested Kissinger to join him on his knees in prayer in the Lincoln bedroom.To avoid further agony, the president resigned in a televised address.Pat worked through the night preparing their belongings for the trip to California.

"There are worse things than jail," Nixon warned Garment during one of the dozens of late-night phone calls he made following his Thursday night speech. "There is no phone there." There is, however, tranquility. A difficult table to write on. The best political work in this century has been done in jail."

But no scene in a career of breathtaking spectacle, not Checkers, not Caracas, not the first debate with Kennedy or the last press conference in 1962—or even the predawn visit to the Lincoln Memorial—was as unforgettable as Nixon's farewell speech to the White House staff on Friday morning. The performer seized the situation. It may have been the most visceral, heartbreaking, and memorable speech in American political history.

"Do not trip over the wires. Stand on the nameplate. Reach for Mama's hand. Hold it. Applause. Daddy is speaking. People are shedding tears.

Must not look. Tricia wrote in her diary, "I can't think about it right now." "The real Nixon was being unveiled in the only way he could reveal himself. Speaking from the heart, people may finally get to know Daddy. "It was not too late."

Nixon began by criticizing the press. Then he told the familiar story about Frank selling the lemon ranch before oil was discovered on the property. He tried again to tell them who he was. How lonely. How alone. "Nobody will ever write a book, probably, about my mother," he told me. "I suppose all of you would say this about your mother. My mom was a saint. And I think of mom, two boys dying of tuberculosis, nursing four more so she could care for my older brother in Arizona for three years, and witnessing each of them die, as if they were her own. Yes, she will not have any books written about her. "But she was a saint."

His nervousness moved over the stage. "I had a little quote in the speech last night from T.R.," he told the audience. "As you know, I enjoy reading books. I'm not educated, but I do read literature."

Then came confirmation of his incredible tenacity. "We think that when someone dear to us dies, we think that when we lose an election, we think that when we suffer a defeat, that all has ended," according to him. "That's not true. Always remember that this is just the beginning.It must be known by both the young and the old. It must always support us, since greatness comes and you are truly tested when you endure some blows, disappointments, and pain, because only if you have been in the deepest valley can you ever understand how glorious it is to be on the highest mountain."

Kissinger said the individual had "a faded doom" about him. Many people in the audience wept. In the end, Richard Nixon delivered words as insightful as any ever spoken in the great old house. Rich in self-knowledge, but at a cost: "Always remember, others may hate you—but those who hate you don't win unless you hate them, and then you destroy yourself."

dick and Pat strolled out to the South Lawn, down a long red carpet, shook hands with a funereal vice president, and climbed the steps of Army One, the presidential chopper. Finally, Nixon turned and grimaced, giving one sweeping, protective gesture, as if to ward off endless grief. Then he flung his arms upward, flashing the customary

Vs for victory, turned, and boarded the aircraft.

Army One ascended off the grass, rising over the steamy capital. The National Mall darkened in a summer morning haze. Below, L'Enfant's magnificent boulevards and Brumidi's halls and corridors were alive with visionaries, parvenus, and hustlers; dreams and scheming; avarice, ambition, rivalry, and purpose. The helicopter flew above statues of heroes and monuments to great leaders, whose ranks the awkward grocer's lad had dared to join with such American boldness, only to fall. "It's so sad," Pat told no one in particular.

They spent the entire voyage to California alone, each in their own compartment in Air Force One. The president drank a cocktail. The resignation became effective at noon, while they were somewhere above Missouri.

Printed in Great Britain
by Amazon